Artist Development in the Music Business

++

Artist Development in the Music Business

Copyright © 2014 Some Rights Reserved
Latimer Publishing, LLC
Box 94040, Cleveland, Ohio, 44101 USA

Artist Development in the Music Business

About the Author - John Latimer

As a songwriter, entrepreneur and music business professional, John Latimer has over 30 years experience in various aspects of the entertainment and music business. He has been a talent buyer, booking agent, event and concert promoter, artist developer, record label owner, manager, video director, record producer, publicist, publisher and consultant.

Latimer began his career in the entertainment business as a talent buyer and booker, promoting events and concerts. After graduating from The Ohio State University, Latimer's first real gig in the entertainment business was booking and promoting performances and events for the Pirates Cove Nightclub located in the Flats Entertainment District of Cleveland, Ohio. After a few years, Latimer became an agent with Energy Talent Agency to book local and regional talent. Later, Latimer turned his attention back to talent buying and promoting concerts for the Limelight Entertainment Complex. Latimer then formed Bullseye Booking Agency, where he booked and promoted acts throughout the Eastern U.S.

As a producer, Latimer's works with audio as well as video. Latimer formed Play Records which released 13 albums. Latimer also co-produced and co-directed, two television shows: "Good Rockin' Tonight" and "Alternate Beat." In 2011, Latimer co-hosted a weekly podcast, "The Music Biz Workshop," to explore the business side of music. Latimer also produces the Undercurrents Radio Show.

Undercurrents, Inc. is one of Latimer's companies and began as an annual music business conference and showcase. It has since evolved into a niche marketing and promotion company. Latimer regularly consults with artists and entertainment professionals about their specific projects.

In addition to providing consulting services to musicians, songwriters, bands and independent labels, Latimer teaches music business courses and regularly participates as a speaker and panelist at entertainment conferences, seminars and workshops.

Latimer's books, "Event and Concert Promotion," "Forget the Majors, Launch Your Own Record Label," "Music Industry Tips and Tats," "Record Label Marketing in the Digital Age," "Business Plan for Artists," and "Artist Development in the Music Business" are available through Latimer Publishing.

For more information about John Latimer, visit his website http://JohnLatimer.us

++++++++++++++++++++++++++++++

Artist Development in the Music Business
Copyright © 2014 by John Latimer

Printed and bound in the United States of America. Some Rights Reserved. No part of this book may be reproduced in any form or by any electronic or mechanical means including information storage and retrieval systems without permission in writing from publisher, except by a reviewer, who may quote brief passages in a review.

Published by:
Latimer Publishing, LLC
Box 94040
Cleveland, Ohio 44101
(440) 331-0700
http://www.LatimerPublishing.com

First Edition

ISBN: 978-0-9814934-8-0
0-9814934-8-3

Printed in the U.S.A.

To my children Kathryn and Patrick

Artist Development in the Music Business
Table of Contents

INTRODUCTION

CHAPTER 1 (page 1)
Artist Development Overview
Content Creation
Content Protection
Lessons & Coaching
Management
Ego, Attitude, Passion & Grit
Business Set-Up & Establishment
Image & Branding
Legal & Agreements
Finance & Funding
Trademark
Publishing
Performing Rights Organizations
Gear, Instruments & Equipment
Teams & Collaborators
Preparing for Product Development
Project Management
Pre-Promotion Preparation

CHAPTER 2 (page 11)
Product Development Overview
Pre-Promotion Preparation
Producing Recordings
Recording Audio / Video
Mastering Recordings
Record Labels
Discography/Content Management
Film and Video Production
Design
Packaging
Manufacturing
Distribution
Promotion
Publicity
Branding
Sales
Live Performances
Merchandising
Web
Working the Product
Production Development Tips

CHAPTER 3 (page 19)
Expectations
Self Evaluation
Expectations of Oneself
Expectations of Collaborators
Expectations of Co-Writers
Expectations of Musicians
Expectations of Managers
Expectations of Booking Agents
Expectations of Publishers
Expectations of Record Labels
Expectations of Promoters
Artist Development Expectations
Product Development Expectations

CHAPTER 4 (page 31)
Content Creation & Interpretation
Content Users
Content Creators
Songwriters
Co-Writers
Arrangers
Record Producers
Recording Engineers
Musicians
Technicians
Video Directors
Content Acquisition
Public Domain

Derivative Works
Creative Commons
Finding Copyright Registrations
Publishers
"Cover" Songs
Content Creation
Music Genres
Songwriting Basics
Song Structure
Song Review
Content Catalog
Building a Songwriting Career
Content Creation Tips

CHAPTER 5 - (page 47)
Content Protection
Proprietary Rights
Intellectual Property
Copyright
Content Protection
Copyright Infringement
Copyright Protection
Work for Hire
Copyright Myths
How to get a Copyright
Length of Copyright
Fair Use
Copyright Symbols & Notice
Creative Commons Copyright
Copyright Tips

CHAPTER 6 – (page 59)
Lessons & Coaching
Learning Music Notes Fast
Technique vs. Groove
Education and Experience
Preparing for Success
Alexander Technique
Music Schools
Music Business Conferences

CHAPTER 7 – (page 67)
Management
Self-Management
Manager Collaborators
Types of Managers

Management Duties
Building the Team
Finding Management
Friend Managers
Management Contracts
Compensation
Experience
Myths of Artist Management
Tips About Talent Managers

CHAPTER 8 – (page 81)
Ego, Attitude, Passion & Grit
Ego
Attitude
Positive & Negative Attitudes
Law of Attraction
Success
Passion
Motivation
Confidence
Grit

CHAPTER 9 – (page 101)
Business Set-Up
Artist Business Plan
Business Names
Business Types

CHAPTER 10 (page 115)
Image & Branding
Niches
Image & Brand Management
Logos & Slogos
Tips for Brand Building
Living Up to the Brand
Branding the Artist
First Impressions
Image & Branding Tips

CHAPTER 11 (page 129)
Legal Issues
Agreements Overview
Proposal or Offer
Promises
Consideration
Contract Establishment

Voidable Contracts
Agent and Principals
Licenses
Contract Clauses
Agreements Types
Songwriter Agreements
Product Development Agreements
Performance Agreements
Record Label Contracts
360 Deals
Entertainment Attorneys
Legal Tips

CHAPTER 12 (page 149)
Finance & Funding
Setting Up a Payment System
Income Reality
Active vs. Passive Income
Band Fund
Income Sources
Endorsements
Royalties
Controlled Compositions
Harry Fox Agency
Income – Content Licensing
Finance Plan
Start-Up Summary
Spending Strategy
Budgets
Project Finance
Project Funding Requests
Paper Trail
Investors
Artist Funding Tips

CHAPTER 13 (page 171)
Trademarks
What is a Trademark?
Trademark Types
Trademark Symbols
Reasons to Trademark
Advantages of Trademarks
Trademark Categories & Classes
How to Trademark a Logo
Logo Designs

CHAPTER 14 (page 181)
Publishing Preparation
A Music Publishers Job
Working with a Publisher
Publishing Royalties
Mechanical Royalties
Performance Royalties
Synchronization Royalties
Print Royalties
Grand Rights Royalties
Foreign Royalties
Sound Exchange
About Licensing
Pitching to Music Publishers
Publishing Tips

CHAPTER 15 (page 191)
Performing Rights Organizations
Types of Licensees
ASCAP
BMI
SESAC
SoundExchange

CHAPTER 16 (page 197)
Gear, Equipment & Instruments
Equipment List
Endorsements
Funds for Instruments
Types of Musical Instruments
Care of Musical Instruments

Chapter 17 (page 203)
Team & Collaborators
The Creative Team
The Music Business Team
Building a Positive Team
Collaborators & Partners
Potential Music Business Collaborators
Team Building
Attracting Collaborators
Finding Quality Team Members
Firing a Collaborator

CHAPTER 18 (page219)
Preparing for Product Development

Overview
Promotion Preparation
Image and Brand Promotion
Visuals
Product Development Tips
Promoting Your Image & Brand
Branding & Company Promotions
Promo Kit

CHAPTER 19 (page 229)
Project Management
50 Checkpoints
Gantt Charts
Project Plan
Project Control
Project Managers
Stages of Project Management
Project Management Processes
Project Initiation
Defining the Project
Executing the Project Plan
Monitoring the Project
Closing the Project

CHAPTER 20 (page 239)
Preparing to License
Music Supervision
Music Clearance
A Note on Score
Summary & Strategy

CHAPTER 21 (page 249)
Preparing for Performances

CHAPTER 22 (page 253)
Preparing to Record

CHAPTER 23 (page 257)
Quick Tips

CHAPTER 24 (page 259)
Glossary of Terms

CHAPTER 25 (page 279)
Forms & Sample Agreements

Artist Development in the Music Business
Introduction

++

The story to the success of any artist in the music business includes the proper preparation and implementation of a plan of attack. Well, not everything. Quality is quality. The room at the top is still there for art but the number of those on the musical and artistic ladder has increased dramatically. In today's world, the low cost of entry into the music business makes it possible to write, compose, arrange, record, mix, master, distribute, sell downloads and make money… ALL IN ONE DAY!

The music business has changed a lot, that's true. With the advent of digital downloads, the Internet, and the plethora of other "attention getters," the job of a struggling musician just got harder. In addition, since the barrier to entry into this over-hyped, glamour business is almost non-existent, smart artists looking for longevity not only can focus on their art, but also on their knowledge of developing their craft.

Preparation is key. Quality is imperative. Good is not good enough. Only quality art sustains. Artists should always think quality. They should always think GREAT. Every show, every song, every recording, every piece of merchandise, must exude quality.

In my efforts to write this book, I utilized ideas generated from owning my own record label, running my own booking agency, dealing with major and independent artists, producing audio and video recordings, promoting concerts and events, as well as debates in specialized classroom situations.

Questions and inquiries from students and clients generated handouts and prompted discussions. This book is an accumulation of those handouts as well as many written results of those discussions. "Artist Development in the Music Business" is an organized and detailed approach to helping the artist move forward in their career. As opportunities become available for artists, being prepared is crucial. Having an Artist Development Plan helps an artist focus and move forward in their chosen career. Many opportunities for artists may be lost if the artist has to stop their momentum and go back to fix or acquire a needed aspect of their potential opportunity. This is already a hard business. It makes no sense to make it harder.

Upon completion of this book, and the following of its instructions, artists will only have to look back when they are updating their Artist Development Plan. The entertainment business is full of projects. Planning, managing and prioritizing those projects are identified in the Artist Development Plan. In many instances, checklists, tips, and warnings within the book will assist artists with their journey to success.

> **Music business professionals expect artists to have all aspects of their Artist Development Plan completed before launching into Product Development.**

When a music business professional such as a record label executive or concert promoter signs a new artist or band, they presume the act has sufficient musical, songwriting, and performance talent, and are ready for the next big step in their career. This means that music business professionals expect artists to have all aspects of their Artist Development Plan completed before launching into Product Development.

Cases of commitment to Artist Development are apparent when looking at the careers of artist/bands like Radiohead, Justin Timberlake, The Barenaked Ladies, Taylor Swift, or the Dave Matthews Band. Artist Development is also behind the success of today's teen acts that dominate the pop music charts. If a thirteen or sixteen year old boy or girl has the looks, personality, and musical talent at a young age, and a record label can sign a long term contract with them, it leaves many years for their investment to pay off. Music business executives may collect revenues from dozens of new releases over the (potentially) long careers of these kids as some of them make the transition into adult superstars.

For the most part, in today's competitive music business, the responsibility for Artist and Product Development has changed hands. Independent labels and entrepreneurial managers have inherited the responsibility of nurturing new talent by fine-tuning their artistic and business development and then slowly growing their careers over several album releases and constant performances.

This book is not only useful for artists but also for managers and other music business professionals as well.

++++++++++++++++++++++++++++++

Artist Development in the Music Business
Chapter 1 – Artist Development Overview

Artist Development and Product Development go hand-in-hand. They should work in combination and coordination with each other. When a balanced approach to developing music and business affairs are respected equally, a more realistic opportunity for achieving success for an artist is created. Art is no less important than commerce for today's developing musician.

Artist Development is pre-everything for an artist in the music business. There is no income derived from any of the parts of Artist Development. In fact, there are only expenses: not many, but expenses none the less. Artist Development comes before performing. It comes before recording and it comes before licensing content (songs). Artists cannot be performers if they cannot sing or play an instrument. Artists cannot record if they don't know any songs. Artist-songwriters cannot license their content if they have no songs to license.

Artist Development is pre-release. It's the creating, planning and preparing of the artist before launching into Product Development. Successful artists are prepared. They understand the need for quality as well as perseverance. They know that in addition to their art, they need to focus their attention on the business side of their career.

Artist Development comes before Product Development

- Content Creation
- Content Protection
- Lessons & Coaching
- Management
- Attitude & Ego, Passion & Grit
- Business Set-Up & Establishment
- Image & Branding
- Legal & Agreements
- Finance & Funding
- Trademark
- Publishing
- Performing Rights Organizations
- Gear, Instruments & Equipment
- Teams & Collaborators
- Preparing Product Development
- Project Management
- Pre-Promotion Preparation

Artist Development involves: content creation, content protection, lessons & coaching, management, attitude & ego, passion & grit, business set-up & establishment, image and branding, legal and agreements, finance & funding, trademark, publishing set-up, performing rights organizations, gear, teams, preparing product development, project management and pre-promotion preparation.

1. Content Creation

Before an artist starts performing, recording or licensing songs, they must put into place a few essential elements. The first step is creating, or selecting the songs to perform or record. Everything in the music business starts with content. This usually means a song or a combination of songs, lyrics and music. Without great songs, there is no music business. Songwriting is not just an artistic expression; it is the axis upon which the music business spins.

Good songs are not good enough. When preparing to market music, the content has to be of the highest quality: the song, the recording of the song, and the musician-artist interpreting and performing the song. People only respond to what they feel are great songs. The songs must have some commercial appeal, if only to a certain musical niche. (Folk, Hip Hop, Alternative Rock, New Age, Jazz, Blues, etc.) Finding that musical niche and managing its growth is essential to developing a successful artist. The quality of the songs and the way they are performed or recorded by an artist must be of a very high caliber. The delivery of the songs, either vocally or instrumentally, comes with practice and experimentation. So, not only do the songs have to be great, but the artist's interpretation and delivery of the song must also be great.

Creating a buzz about the artist's music will attract the attention of fans which, in turn, will attract music business professionals. These professionals may eventually want to collaborate with the artist. Collaboration exists with promoters, talent buyers, booking agents, publishers, record label executives, etc.

2. Content Protection

The second part of an Artist Development Plan is really aimed at the songwriter-artist and the producer-artist. It is the protection of the artist's content: their songs and their recordings. Part one of the Artist Development Plan is also about the songs of the songwriter-artist's content but it is also about the songs of the songwriter whom a musician-artist may perform, such as "cover" songs.

Artist Development is about protecting the great songs created by the songwriter-artist by registering them with the U.S. copyright office. Copyrights that are registered offers protection of the art. It also protects the songs, the lyrics, the music and the recordings of the songs. It acts as an incentive for artists to keep creating. In addition, copyrights can be licensed and are a valuable income source for the owner-creators.

> "Positive anything is better than negative nothing."
> - Elbert Hubbard

3. Lessons & Coaching
Many developing artists begin learning music at a very young age. Many start taking music lessons in elementary school, while others begin as teenagers. It's never too late to start. Part three of the Artist Development Plan is about lessons and coaching. A songwriter-artist does not need to know how to play an instrument. However, a musician-artist and a performer-artist does.

As careers develop, artists may wish to improve on some creative talents by investigating further, voice or instrument lessons, or master classes from more experienced musicians. Workshops, clinics and seminars can assist artists with helpful tips about the music business. In addition to learning about music, many artists who get into the "business," learn about creating and maintaining their own music business company(ies), as well as music production, performing, recording, stage craft, and various other ways to earn income within the music business.

4. Management
Who is looking at the big picture? All successful artists have a great team and an artist's team usually begins with a qualified manager. At the very beginning, artists (or their parent(s)) are their own manager.

Managers need strong organizational skills. They need negotiating skills and should have an entrepreneurial spirit. A music business background doesn't hurt. New artists should manage their own career. This way they learn about Artist Development and Product Development and help build their own network. They work on their own Artist Business Plan. They learn the business by doing. Only after they can afford a manager, should they hire one, and when they do start working with a manager, they will know much about management duties because they've done part of it themselves.

Good managers plan. They look at the overall picture of the artist and make educated decisions about the current status as well as upcoming projects. They set goals and work in the best interest of the artist.

5. Ego, Attitude, Passion & Grit
The importance of ego and attitude must not be overlooked. Many talented songwriters and musicians stall their career because of ego. Many artists fail because of a negative attitude. Maintaining and strengthening attitude and ego, passion and grit is a big part of Artist Development.

Artist with a positive attitude are much more likely to succeed. The law of attraction works well in the music business. Ego may kill an artist.

Confidence is one thing but an explosive ego will do just that: explode.

Passion is what drives the artist. Without the passion, an artist will burn out and fail. If you don't like staying up late, travelling a lot, waiting for your turn to overdub, or starve for the first few months, get out. This business does not have room for you.

Grit is how well an artist sticks to it. It is an inbred trait and involves lots of patience.

There is more about this in Chapter 8.

6. Business Set-Up & Establishment

One of the functions of Artist Development is the action of setting up the business of the artist. Is the artist's business a sole proprietorship, a partnership, or a corporation? Many beginning artists ignore setting up their business. This is a big mistake. Registering a business with the state and federal government legitimizes an artist. In addition, when an artist owns a legitimate business, a whole new mindset is established. This is a necessity if artists want to have more control over their career. Remember, this is the MUSIC BUSINESS.

As other music business professionals start to collaborate with artists, they will want to know whom they are working with. If a concert promoter, for example, writes a check to a performer after the gig, is the check written to the order of the band or an individual member of the band.

7. Image & Branding

One of the most delicate issues involved with Artist Development is the matter of creating and consistently maintaining a clear and honest image. What people hear in the music must be seen in how the artist dresses for the stage. A succinct image can help or hurt an artist. When creating promotional materials and artwork for web promotion, compact discs, posters, flyers, etc., the opportunity window for fakes closes very fast. Artists should weave a thread of consistency with their chosen image throughout all areas of their marketing and branding efforts: with image comes the brand. All successful artists effectively manage their brands. Over-exposure or under-exposure can hurt an artist's brand. There is more about image in Chapter 10.

8. Legal & Agreements

The music business has a plethora of agreements. Due to the many potential team members of an artist, there are agreements for every situation. There are agreements as a part of Artist Development and there are agreements as a part of Product Development. Artist Development agreements include band member agreements, management agreements, co-writing agreements, etc. Product Development agreements include booking agreements, record contracts, producer agreements, publishing contracts, etc.

Artist Agreements should include writing up band agreements that defines the issues related to running the artist's career as a business, as well as how artists will work with the people in the band and on their team.

Lawyers play an essential role in the entertainment industry. Smart artists retain entertainment attorneys who have had experience within the music business. Attorneys may be needed to look over any band agreements, booking contracts, publishing deals, or any other number of legal matters. Part of Artist Development is ensuring all agreements with collaborators have been identified and settled. There is more about the artist's legal issues in Chapter 11.

9. Finance & Funding

How is the artist planning to fund their projects? Self-funding is a typical option for beginning and emerging artists. Perhaps the artist's family of friends will contribute to funding the artist. However, after that, fans and customers should be a growing income source for the artist and their patience will generate an income for the artist as well as fund the artist's projects. This will happen only if the artist has quality songs, quality recordings and/or quality performances.

In addition, music business professionals and potential collaborators such as record labels, promoters and/or publishers may contribute advance funds to an artist towards future sales. When this happens, the artist knows their collaborators believe in them and their art.

10. Trademark

The name and logo of an artist has to be protected. Other wanna-be artists with the same name, who may release inferior music, may affect the sales and success of the artist if their name and logo is not protected. This is another form of intellectual property in the music business (copyright is the other). To avoid problems, artists should file for a trademark to prevent others from using their chosen name. It is also part of the business organization of properly developing an artist's career. Artists should invest in registering their name or stage name, as well as their business name, by trade marking it. Many businesses in the entertainment industry will not collaborate with an artist if the artist does not have a registered trademark of their name and/or logo.

> "Life isn't about finding yourself. Life's about creating yourself."
> ~ George Bernard Shaw

11. Publishing

The pot of gold at the end of the music rainbow is the income received from the use of songs. This is passive income and may flow into a songwriter-artist's bank account year after year. The business of music publishing, which is really the business of finding uses for songs, is very important for the success of all songwriter-artists. Publishing should create a demand for the songs. If an artist is a songwriter, they should investigate the possibility of self-publishing or working with a quality music publisher. One great song promoted by one great music publisher may mean an entire life of income for the songwriter-artist.

Note: the beginning artist will probably not generate their first dollars from publishing. It's a long-term play. Most beginning artists earn income from performing.

12. Performing Rights Organizations

Songwriters and music publishing companies need to affiliate with a Performance Rights Organization (P.R.O.) For songwriters, it's free to join. In the United States, there are three (3): ASCAP, BMI, and SESAC. If and when the songs written by the songwriter-artist are played by the broadcasting industry, or in certain public places, they will receive proper payment for the use of those songs. Payments are collected and distributed by Performing Rights Organizations. If the artist-songwriter does not belong to a P.R.O., they may not be paid when their song is played.

If songwriters are interested in getting paid from performances of their music from such sources as broadcasting, online streaming, live gigs, and many other potential income sources, they need to belong to a P.R.O.

13. Gear, Instruments & Equipment

Artists should invest in the best equipment and musical instruments. No artists can perform their best work using mediocre equipment. Gear, instruments and equipment does not need to be expensive. It just needs to be quality.

In addition to having gear, instruments and equipment, artists will need to know how to properly take care of them.

14. Teams & Collaborators

Part of Artist Development is identifying the artist's team. An artist may need to build a team of potential collaborators including, band members, a manager, agent, co-writers, producer, publisher, and publicist as well as a record label to release their songs and recordings.

As an artist career develops, there may also be more collaborators who may be added to the artist's team. These might be individuals such as road managers, sound technicians, street-teamers, personal assistants, etc.

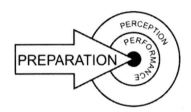

15. Preparing for Product Development
Once an Artist Development Plan has been completed, the artist's direction and goals begin to focus on recordings, performances, licensing, and above all, survival in the entertainment industry. The products and/or services that an artist releases are the reasons why individuals become artists. Yes, they love music but they want to play it for someone. They want to record and tour. They want it all. If they want it all, what comes first? Preparing for Product Development is where Artist Development becomes fun.

There are multiple income sources available to each artist such as: live performances, recording royalties, performing rights, mechanical royalties, merchandise sales, and publishing.

- **Preparing to License**

In the music business, there are a few licenses that artists may consider, especially if they are songwriter-artists. Licensing can be a very valuable asset and is one of few potential income sources. There are four main licenses related to the music business: song licensing, performance licensing, image licensing and the licensing or recordings. Song licensing is a valid income source for artist-songwriters. Performance licensing is when a musician receives royalty income from the sale of recordings. Image licensing is valuable for an artist when merchandising compact discs, t-shirts or hats, and the licensing of recordings for artists who own their own recordings and license the recordings for use in television, film or advertisements.

Preparing to license content involves many other aspects of Artist Development such as content creation (songwriting) and content protection (copyrights). Artists will need to compile their song catalog, prepare their musical chops and solidify their name, photo, image and logo.

- **Preparing to Perform**

Artist Development is also about preparing an artist for performing. Many musicians start performing their repertoire when they learn a new song. They may perform for a parent or a friend. That's great practice but performing for a paying audience is a whole different story. Beginning artists dream about future public performances. They know that their individual practice of their chosen instrument(s), (and yes, voice is an instrument), their confidence of their skill, their chosen songs, and their logistics of getting to and from the performance are all going to play a role in all performances.

- **Preparing to Record**

Many artists want to release recordings of their songs. In addition to writing, or selecting the songs, artists may need to consider arrangements, rehearsals, pre-production, etc. In addition, artists will need to consider any potential collaborators to assist them such as producers, engineers, and other technicians.

Recording is one thing. Preparing to record is equally important. Pre-production is 90% of the recording project. The more prepared an artist is prior to entering the recording studio, the faster and cheaper the recording will be.

- **Preparing to Merchandise**

Although, merchandising is a part of Product Development and is usually begun after an artist begins performing and recording, being prepared is half the battle. Artists will need to incorporate other parts of their Artist Development Plan, such as image, logos and trademarks, to make it much easier when it's time to create their merchandise. Merchandising is another important income source for artists. When prepared, the income for an artist will come faster.

16. Project Management

The music business is full of projects. Managing these projects is essential to the success of any artist. Projects in the music business may include such things as writing a new song, producing a new recording, preparing for a performance or even working out the logistics for a publicity campaign or world tour. The process of planning, organizing, staffing, directing and controlling the desired goal is a big part of Project Management. Understanding and implementing project management techniques keeps the artist on track and focused. When an artist begins working on multiple projects at the same time, their project management techniques become a crucial component to success. This is another big part of Artist Development.

Product Development

- Preparing Promotion
- Publishing
- Producing Recordings
- Film & Video
- Packaging
- Manufacturing
- Distribution
- Promotion
- Publicity
- Branding
- Sales
- Performances
- Merchandising
- Web

---

17. Pre-Promotion Preparation

As Product Development comes closer to reality and an artist begins to focus on performing or recording or releasing products for their merch table, they need to think about how their products or services will be promoted. I call the promotion materials that an artist accumulates "promo ammo." This is the ammunition that an artist, or their collaborator, will need to promote the artist effectively. Without promotion, there will be none, or little, sales.

To get attention from concert promoters, potential managers or others in the music business, an artist needs to put together a promo kit.

Part of the promotion that an artist will need preparing a promo kit includes a photograph, a biography, a logo, a website and a presence on many online social networks.

++++++++++++++++++++++++++++++

Wrap-Up

The hard work for artists begins after they start collaborating with others. This includes working with potential band members, managers, booking agents, record label executives, publishers, etc. If someone is going to put time and effort into an artist's brand, they will want to ensure that the artist is as motivated as they are. They will also want to ensure that most, if not all, of the Artist Development Plan has been completed.

Very few music business companies or individuals will take the time to work with emerging artists on their development. Many music business experts want the work to be already completed. Yes, like most people, they are inherently lazy. They want artists who have established fan bases. They want material that needs no additional work. They want it all to be easy. Artists need to recognize that nobody is going to do it for them. Artists need drive, ambition, tenacity and, yes, talent. Their collaborators will react only when there is something to be gained. Artists who have completed all the tasks of their Artist Development Plan have a much better chance at attracting music business professionals to their team. Quality artists with quality content who are ready for Product Development are in great demand within the hardest industry in the world: The Music Business.

Artist Development Tips

1. Be yourself. Fakes never make it
2. Always think quality
3. Always think positive
4. Always be prepared
5. Set realistic goals & objectives
6. Plan your work
7. Work your plan
8. Believe in yourself
9. Remove mental roadblocks
10. Remember failure spurs success
11. Enlist only a positive team
12. Develop networking skills
13. Consider all relationships
14. Take responsibility
15. There is no "good enough"
16. Remember gratefulness
17. Thank those who helped
18. Understand all income sources
19. Don't settle
20. Write down your plan
21. Chart goals and successes
22. Practice, practice, practice
23. Dream BIG
24. Have fun
25. Begin now

To Do

One of the hardest things to do, you've already done; getting started. It is assumed that if you are reading this, then you are about to enter the music business as an artist. In this business, artists are songwriters, musicians, performers, singers, arrangers, and/or producers. Discover what you're good at doing, and become great at doing it.

Notes:

Artist Development in the Music Business
Chapter 2 – Product Development Overview

Although the Artist Development Plan is fluid and a constantly changing document, the end goal of Artist Development is to be prepared for Product Development. Product Development focuses on all the business arrangements after the Artist Development details have been completed. Although this book is about putting together an Artist Development Plan, it's a good idea for artist to know where they're heading and what products (recordings) and services (performances) the artist may plan to release.

Products / Services of Artists

Licensing
Recordings
Performances
Publishing
Merchandising

Since the entertainment business is all about projects and these projects turn into products, the products and services that an artist releases are all using project management techniques. When an artist gets to this stage in their career, they should be well versed with their craft as well as their focus and their direction. Their Artist Development Plan should be complete. That doesn't mean that it is. Many eager artists want to start performing. That's okay and part of learning the craft. However, in order for the artist to begin performing, they must have many parts of the Artist Development completed anyway. Product Development is all about taking the resources that the artist completed in their Artist Development Plan and then steering it to start making some income. The making, manufacturing, marketing and sales are all part of Product Development.

Product Development for a musical artist is about performing, recording, licensing, marketing and selling products. Once the Artist Development Plan has been completed, the Product Development Plan is implemented. This includes the recording and performing of the songs as well as developing the stage and video persona of the artist.

1. Pre-Promotion Preparation
Before moving into Product Development, artists should mentally prepare for the promotion of the project. This preparation makes it easier when the time comes for the artist to release their product or service. While the

product is being developed, the promotional aspects can start coming alive. Artists need to envision how the music will be promoted and sold by the time the act enters the recording studio or by the time the act enters the stage.

2. Producing Recordings

The choices of what studio to record in and what producer or engineer to be hired to make the record are uppermost in the mind of an artist preparing to record. Smart artists are aware that if a certain sound, for a certain music genre isn't recorded properly, the chances of radio airplay and commercial success could be hampered. If so, there may be no significant sales of the recording. Once again, the word "Quality" creeps into the discussion.

So, the production choices, as a part of the Product Development equation, are very important when deciding how to present a new artist or band to fans and potential customers.

3. Recording Audio

One major part of Product Development for an artist is the production of recordings. This is especially true for songwriter-artists trying to make a demo. In addition, recording a master available for sale to the public is a major part of the music business.

Researching the right recording studio, right producer and engineer is a key issue in Product Development. Where will the record be recorded? Who will record it? Both of these questions must be considered quite seriously before making a final decision. This is true for recording a demo at a friend's house as well as recording a master product in a high-end recording studio.

Product Development

Pre-Promotion Preparation
Producing Recordings
Recording Audio
Mastering Recordings
Record Labels
Discography
Content Management
Film & Video Production
Design
Packaging
Manufacturing
Distribution
Promotion
Publicity
Branding
Sales
Live Performances
Merchandising
Web
Working the Product

4. Mastering Recordings
After recording and mixing, up next is mastering. Mastering is not something to be passed over lightly. The mastering engineer can enhance or hurt an artist's recording. Choose a mastering engineer who understands the genre of music.

5. Record Labels
Many artists release their own recordings on their own record label. This may be accomplished by uploading the recordings to the Internet or releasing the product as a compact disc or vinyl record.

If the artist decides to collaborate with a third-party record label (either major or independent), then it is important to know who owns and controls the copyright of the recording.

6. Discography/Content Management
Recording the project is just the beginning. A good content management system is needed to maximize the use of those recordings. Artists need to be prepared by having many different file formats of the recordings available such as WAV, Mp3, etc. This part of content management makes it easy when it comes time to license these master recordings.

7. Film & Video Production
Recently at a music business conference, one question was asked to a panel of Independent Record Label owners. "Name one main investment an artist should make for their career?" Every answer given from each panelist was to purchase a quality video camera. With the increasing use of the Internet, video is playing a more important promotional role than ever before.

In addition, songwriter-artists may reap the benefits of synchronization licenses with video directors for the use of their songs in connection with film or video.

8. Design
Who will design the artwork for the release? Album cover artwork, packaging material design, and printing issues are important. The design must match the image of the artists as well as the style of the music. Remember, artists are creating a product that will be competing for the attention of music fans that have an abundance of music releases to choose from. Is there something about the album cover that

might attract a customer to the recording?

9. Packaging
When planning the promotion of the product, the packaging plays an important role as it portrays and solidifies the image of the artist. This holds true whether the release is online or offline. The graphics used should be consistent with the product's image.

10. Manufacturing
Who will manufacture the recording? Yes, this is another part of Product Development as well. Finance and funding will most likely determine this, as they probably determined production decisions. Take the time to make a recording that sounds and looks like something you would want to buy yourself.

11. Distribution
Luckily for the independent record label, the Internet has made the distribution of music recordings much, much easier. Consignment at area stores is a difficult chore and collaborating with a regional distributor can be costly. The budget for offline distribution must take in account charge backs, defective products, promotion items and shipping.

12. Promotion
Preparing an artist's promo ammo was established in the pre-promotion section of the Product Development Plan. What has or has not been accomplished in the areas of Artist Development and Product Development will make or break the chances of success with the artist's music. The artist and the artist's record label will promote and publicize the music and artist to maximize the prospect of sales and ultimately, income. Promotion should involve offline as well as online exposure for the artist and the artist's music.

13. Publicity
Publicity is the deliberate attempt to manage the public's perception of a product. The subjects of publicity include performing artists, recording artists, recordings, tours and the general activities of an active artist.

> "When you get into a tight place and everything goes against you, never give up, for that is just the place and time that the tide will turn."
> ~ Harriet Beecher Stowe

14. Branding

A brand is a name, logo, slogan, and/or design scheme associated with the artist's product or service.

Branding is the process of creating a relationship or a connection between an artist's product and emotional perception of the customer for the purpose of generating segregation among competition and building loyalty among fans and customers.

Although establishing a brand is part of Artist Development, the process of branding an artist is an ongoing task of Product Development.

15. Sales

Once a record has been manufactured and is ready to be sold to the public, Product Development turns its attention to sales. In addition, once a musician-artist hones their chops, develops a quality set of songs to perform on stage and is ready to be sold to talent buyers / bookers, then Product Development again enters the picture. Many young labels and developing artists forget this in their rush to record their music. If the artist or record label is going to spend thousands of dollars recording the music, wouldn't it be a good idea to find a way to sell it beforehand? The same is true for an artist who just booked a gig. That's how professionals think. They make sure a system is in place to sell their audio recordings and performance tickets to their artist's fans. Many young artists and record labels make the mistake of trying to get some radio airplay for their recordings, or other media attention, before they've found a way for the public and their fans to buy it. Smart artists don't make such mistakes.

16. Live Performances

Another critical part of an artist's business model involves booking live performances. Artists may attempt to do this themselves or work with an agent to secure performances for them. There are advantages and disadvantages to either. Artists have a vested interest in how often and where they appear in public. It's a big part of their income.

17. Merchandising
In the broadest sense, merchandising is any practice which contributes to the sale of products to a retail consumer. At a retail in-store or club level, merchandising refers to the variety of products (t-shirts and compact discs) available for sale. In addition, merchandising involves the display of those products in such a way that it stimulates interest and entices fans and customers to make a purchase.

18. Web
The use of the World Wide Web in Product Development includes promotion and marketing as well as distribution and sales. A quality web presence for any artist is essential to the success of any product. In today's world, an artist's website is their front door to fans and customers.

In addition, online social networks are a great way for artists to stay in touch with their fans and to establish new fans.

19. Working the Product
The importance of knowing the various parts of Product Development will be reflected in the success of a release of a sound recording for public sales or the success of live performances through ticket sales. It may seem obvious, but all of the items that make up Product Development should be considered in a broad sense. For example, labels should consider distribution when planning the recording of songs. There is no sense in having product gather dust in the garage while the label scurries to find a way to get it into the marketplace.

Product Development Tips

1.) Focus on the active and passive income streams: publishing, live performances, recordings, merchandising, licensing and royalties
2.) Identify projects: gigs, recordings, tours, special events, etc.
3.) Assemble promo ammo for each project
4.) Plan your work and work your plan
5.) Utilize project management techniques for maximum productivity
6.) Communicate regularly with your team on short / long term objectives
7.) Keep accurate records to insure goals are being achieved
8.) Review, evaluate and learn from each project
9.) Set calendars and agendas for future recordings and performances
10.) Prepare for each gig – set list, announcements, logistics
11.) Remember the importance of pre-production before you enter the studio
12.) Determine and communicate goals prior to recording
13.) If your recording is not a demo, don't forget Mastering.
14.) Packaging includes how your song is visually represented online
15.) Determine the format for physical recordings – CD, vinyl
16.) Sales and licensing includes publishing, merchandise and live appearances
17.) Consider both online distribution as well as physical distribution
18.) Plan your publicity campaign in the early stages of a new project / product
19.) The front door to today's artist is their web presence
20.) Promote, promote, promote… and then promote some more

To Do

Notes:

Artist Development in the Music Business
Chapter 3 – Expectations

Before an artist can expect to be working with others in the music business, a true self-evaluation might be in order. Other musicians, for example, may not be eager to work with someone with no stage experience or recording experience. Many artists get frustrated with fellow band members and many times, other band members get frustrated with the artist. Either way, a true, honest evaluation of oneself is essential to discovering if the artist is really cut-out to be in this business in the first place. It certainly is not for the weak-of-heart. Beginning artists will be put-down more times than they can count. They hear the word "NO" a lot. There are plenty of hopeful wanna-bes everywhere. In the music business, everyone thinks they're a star. There used to be a band on every street corner, now there are two. In the author's opinion, these wanna-bes are just clogging up the pipelines for true artists. Confidence is great but delusion can be a catastrophe.

If you are interested in becoming a full-time artist, where you are making enough income to survive and to possibly support a family and/or children, ask yourself these questions:

1. What do I like best about my role or potential role in the music business? Least?
2. What critical abilities does my role require? To what extent do I fulfill them?
3. What do I expect to be doing five years from now?
4. What are my specific accomplishments in the past year that will aid me in being successful in the music business?
5. Which goals or objectives did I fall short of meeting?
6. How could I do a better job?
7. Is there anything that hinders my creativity or effectiveness?
8. What changes would improve my performance?
9. How could I become more productive?
10. Do I need more experience or training in any aspect of my musical goals?
11. Where could I get more training?
12. What new standards and goals or objectives should be established for the next evaluation period?
13. Which old goals need to be modified or deleted?
14. Was feedback provided from peers or fans on my work performance throughout the year?
15. Do I see myself performing on stage in 50 years?

Although many collaborators won't be working with beginning artists, it's a good idea for artists to know what to expect when they are ready to start working with collaborators. Somewhere along the way in an artist's musical life comes a moment when they think about what they want to do or who they want to be as a musician. The possibilities of various ways to participate in the music business are almost infinite and sometimes overwhelming. Some artists are interested in being a studio musician as a session player. Many artists are interested in touring. Perhaps some artists play acoustic guitar but feel there's an electric guitar beast inside of them. Maybe the artist plays drums in a jazz band but is secretly swept away by those progressive-rock musicians. The artist may sing, write, play guitar but may want to learn another instrument. Most people who enter the music business want to make a living out of it and pursue a career with their art.

There are so many choices. An artist can be a songwriter or a singer-songwriter, a rhythm guitar player, lead player, music producer, session player, instrument instructor, or street musician. They may play in a cover band performing at coffee houses, weddings, bars, small venues, etc. The list is endless. And then there are all those different music styles: blues, rock, jazz, hip-hop, easy listening, alternative, country, classical, etc. Isn't it great? Yeah but it doesn't make it any easier.

Although, this book is about Artist Development, many artists wear more than one "hat" at any one time. That's good and that's not so good. How can a songwriter continue working his or her craft if they constantly have to do other duties within the music business?

Artistic / Creative Jobs In the Music Business

- Accompanist
- Arranger
- Associate Producer
- Audio Engineer
- Backing Singer
- Band Member
- Composer
- Conductor
- Recording Engineer
- Graphic Designer
- Lighting Technician
- Make-up Artist
- Music Director
- Musician
- Producer
- Remixer
- Session Musician
- Singer
- Songwriter
- Videographer
- Vocalist
- Voice-Over Artist
- Writer

What is Expected?

There are many artists who are musicians as well as songwriters as well as arrangers as well as performers as well as entertainers as well as producers as well as bookers. The list goes on and on.

Hint: Do what you're good at and then become great at it.

Self-Evaluation Questions

Here are some questions to help you figure out your purpose as a musician / entertainer / artist / music business professional. You may think about the answers, but if you write them down, it will solidify in your sub-conscious faster. So, write down your answers and get to know yourself better.

1. What kind of music do you listen to most?

2. What styles of music gets you excited or makes you feel alive?

3. What things are you naturally good at?

4. What instrument are you playing and / or would you still like to learn?

5. What would you regret not having done before you turn 80 years old?

6. What musician, songwriter, performer inspires you most?
7. Describe what kind of person you are?
8. What's your favorite thing to do?

9. What kind of musician do you think you most likely are?

10. What would you teach if you had to?

11. Do you like to be the center of attention?

12. Are you a leader?

13. Would you like to play in a band, an orchestra or on your own?

14. Are you a social person?

15. Are you passionate, devoted, persistent or committed?

16. What values matter most to you?

17. What makes you happy?

18. What doesn't make you happy?

19. What does success mean to you?

20. What would you like to share to the world?

21. What makes you lose track of time?

22. How do you feel about living in a van while touring?

Expectations of Oneself

In the first two chapters, we discussed many important aspects of Artist Development. Now apply yourself to each:

1. **Content** – Are you a content provider? Are you a lyricist? Are you good at creating new melodies? Do you write songs? Are you good at arranging song structures? What are your content expectations?

2. **Protection** – Are you familiar with copyright issues? Are your songs or stories in tangible form? Have you identified all the creative content that you own or control? What are your content protection expectations?

3. **Lessons & Coaching** - How well do you know your instrument? How can you be a better singer? Is your stage presence as good as it can be? Where can you find a good coach? What are your learning expectations?

4. **Management** - Can you self-manage? Can you see the BIG picture? Are you good at getting work done? Do you have good organizational skills? Do you need help getting things done? If not, are you willing to pay someone to do this for you? What are your management expectations?

5. **Ego & Attitude, Passion & Grit** – Do you believe in the Law of Attraction? Are you generally a positive or negative person? Does your shit stink? How do you rate your passion for success? Got any grit? How long before you give up? What are your expectations?

6. **Image and Brand** – How do you perceive yourself? Do others see the same image of yourself that you do? Is your music reflected in your image? Does your sound project your image? What do you expect of your image or brand?

7. **Business** – What type of business are you or your band? Do you fully realize that this is the music BUSINESS? Are you able to separate the "hats" your wear: you as the artist and you as the business owner? What business expectations do you have?

8. **Legal** – If you are collaborating with anyone (no matter what the job), do you have an understanding of "what if?" Are you averse to putting all agreements in writing? Who is your legal counsel? Got any expectations?

9. **Finance** – How do you plan to fund your career and your business? How are your projects going to be financed? Do you have a business bank account? How do you expect your finances to be handled?

10. **Trademark** – Is your stage name that you're using for yourself or your band or your business available for world-wide use? Are you sure? Do you have a logo? Is it registered? What do you expect from your trademark?

11. **Publishing** – Do you plan to publish your content / song through your own publishing company? Are you prepared to wear another "hat?" Do you plan to collaborate with a quality music publisher? What do you expect from your publishing?

12. **Performing Rights Affiliation** – What Performing Rights Organization do you belong to? Who is your rep? Does your publishing company belong to the same P.R.O. as you do? What do you expect by joining a P.R.O.?

13. **Gear / Equipment / Instruments** - As you envision your career; do you have the necessary gear, equipment and instruments needed to fulfill your goals and objectives? What's missing? What are the plans to acquire the gear, equipment and instruments that you need? What instruments or gear do you expect to be purchasing soon?

14. **Team & Collaborators** – Who's on your team? Do you have other musicians who collaborate with you on a regular basis? Are they the best at what they do? Do they believe in you and your art? What do you expect from your team? From your collaborators?

15. **Preparing Product Development**
In your eagerness to be a part of the entertainment industry, is your Artist Development Plan completed? Have you reviewed your Business Plan and thought about your goals and objectives? What do you expect from completing your Product Development Plan?

16. **Project Management**
Now that your Artist Development Plan is complete, are you ready for performing and recording? Have you prioritized your projects? Is one project easier to accomplish than another? Do you expect all projects to run smoothly?

17. **Pre-Promotion Preparation** – Do you have a photo? A website? A biography? Are you a member of multiple online social networks? Have you prepared a promo kit? What promotion do you expect for your upcoming projects?

When you finish your Product Development Plan, come back and re-answer these questions again.

Expectations of Collaborators

Both mentally and physically, the hard work begins once an artist starts collaborating with others. This includes trying to work with musicians, band mates, managers, agents, producers, promoters, record labels, and publishers. This is in addition to co-writers, technicians, record promoters, stage managers, road managers, and song-pluggers. If someone is going to put time and effort into an artist's brand, they will want to ensure that the artist is as motivated as they are. They will want to believe in the artist. They will want to know that the artist is the real thing.

If you act like a professional, you will be treated as a professional.

If you strive for quality, you will emit quality.

If you expect success, you will be successful.

Let's face it, humans are inherently lazy. Most of us would love to be paid to work less. This is true for the entertainment industry as well. A booking agent would love to sign an act that every promoter wants to book with no sales pitch required. Publishers would love to license a song from a songwriter that every major artist wants to record. Managers would love to sign an artist that is already making a lot of money. Record labels would love to work with an artist that is already selling tens of thousands of recordings and downloads on their own. The bottom line is that if an artist is already successful, many potential collaborators will be available for that artist. If the artist is unknown and needs a lot of attention, then the amount of potential collaborators will be greatly diminished. The easier a quality artist can make it for potential collaborators, the more likely the collaborator will be available and responsive to the artist. (Read that sentence again.)

For an artist to become desirable to others in the entertainment industry, a good first step would be for the artist to understand the roles of these potential collaborators and what they expect. Artists need to have what potential collaborators want. Music business professionals will want to know how they may make money by working with an artist. Artists should expect this.

Keep in mind that an artist does not necessarily need to work with collaborators and may choose to be his or her own manager, agent, publisher, publicist, session player, road manager, record label, bongo player and cook. Most successful artists have a team of professionals, each of which takes a piece of the artist's pie. That's okay. The pie is much bigger.

Expectations of Co-Writers

If a songwriter-artist collaborates with another person to write song, that other person is the co-writer. One thing both writers will want when working together is a spirit or attitude of "no-ego." Songwriter-artists need to leave their ego at the door when they start collaborating. An important consideration is that there are no bad ideas when collaborating on a song. One bad idea from one writer, may lead to a genius idea from the other writer,

++++++++++++++++++++++++++++++++

Expectations of Musicians

Many musicians perform with other musicians because they are friends and they both share the love of music. In the early stages of an artist's career, this most often is the case. However, as a business, or as a career, why would other musicians want to work with an artist? Is the artist paying them? If so, perhaps that's the best arrangement for the both of them. If they don't deliver the creative and technical skills that the artist demands, the artist may fire them and hire another.

Perhaps other musicians are friends. They like the artist and believe in the artist's creativity and likelihood of success. They may be willing to contribute their talents to the artist's (and their own) success.

> **Question: How long is a friend-musician going to work with an artist for free?**

Are you creative? Perhaps you are a good singer or a superior songwriter. Maybe your stage presence is over-the-top. There must be a reason for other musicians to collaborate with you. Quality works every time.

++++++++++++++++++++++++++++++++

Expectations of Managers

There are two types of personal talent managers in the music business: artists who manage themselves (self-managers) and then there are managers who are hired by artists. Of the managers that are hired by artists, there are a few more categories: talent manager, business manager, and road manager. Management is actually a separate topic of Artist Development but because this is a chapter on Expectations, let's take a look at what managers might expect before or while working with an artist.

This may be easier if an artist looks at this from the manager's perspective. Why might a manager want to work with an artist? This is, in fact, a good question to ask about any potential collaborator. Does the artist have talent, drive and motivation needed to succeed? This is the most obvious question. However, other questions might be: Does this artist really have the tenacity, willpower and grit to be successful? And every prospective manager will ask them self: How much time will be put into this artist and how much financial return will be earned? Yes, it's all about time and money. The manager must believe in the artist. This is imperative.

Managers will expect from the artist:

(a) To be available and to comply with the manager's reasonable requests to undertake activities pertaining to the artist's career at the artist's discretion.

(b) Not to attempt to directly negotiate agreements with third parties relative to activities for which the manager is responsible and to refer all third parties to the manager.

(c) To refer all press or booking inquiries to the manager.

(d) To notify the manager of any changes in address or contact numbers.

++++++++++++++++++++++++++++++++

Expectations of Booking Agents

One of the most important functions of a booking agent is selecting the right performers for bookings. For an artist to become desirable to a booking agent, most artists must first have a track record of quality performances and a good chance that their fans will purchase a ticket to the artist's performance. Many artists may ask: How can I get bookings without an agent? Welcome to the career building game. Once an artist creates a buzz, booking agents will find them. That's part of their job.

Needless to say, a completely unknown performer will have less drawing power than a well-established act receiving major radio airplay. In addition, the performance fee of an unknown artist may be much lower, which means that the commission that a booking agent makes will be lower as well. The more established and popular the artist, then the more money the booking agent can request for performances. The more money an artist is paid for an appearance, the more money an agent will make. If an artist is paid $100 for a gig, the booking agent would make $10. This is not much incentive for an agent. How long will an agent continue to work with this scenario? If the artist is only performing gigs that pay $100, perhaps the artist doesn't need an agent.

In addition to knowing the types of songs or the number of musicians, the booking agent will want to know the types of fans that the artist attracts. They will want to know the kinds of venues where the artist would perform at their best. The booking agent will want promotional material of the artist to help them make the sale to talent buyers and promoters.

Just like there are artists at various stages of their career, there are booking agents at different levels too. The national booking agents who handle major artists are much harder to attract to a new and upcoming artist unless there is a good reason, such as an artist who just signed a contract with a major record company or a powerful manager. In addition to national agents, there are regional agents as well as local agents. There are booking agents that are good at booking tours and there are booking agents who specialize in placing artists on television shows. There are booking agents who book local shows and there are booking agents who book weddings and DJs. Booking agents can be a major influence on the success of an artist.

Artists should go back and look at their goals. Knowing the types of bookings they want will help them focus on the type of booking agent they may need. Artists should not try to collaborate with a national booking agent if they are booking local coffee shops. They'd be wasting their time as well as the national agent's time.

Booking agents are paid a commission based on a percentage of an artist's earnings. Typically, an agent will charge an artist ten percent (10%) of what an artist receives for services.

So… what does an agent expect when working with an artist? Believe it or not, the first question an agent will ask an artist is not "How many songs do you play?" or "How many musicians are in the band," but "Does the artist have reliable transportation to get to the gig?" Sometimes, that's half the battle. This is especially true for booking agents who schedule tours.

++++++++++++++++++++++++++++++

Expectations of Publishers

The job of a music publisher is to find a commercial use for a song. A publisher will license a song from a songwriter in order to have the right to pitch and contract the use of that song for commercial purposes. If and when the publisher is successful completing a licensing deal, the monies they collect are called royalties and they are split with the songwriter or songwriters. Sometimes, publishers split revenues with other publishers.

If the artist is a songwriter or a team of songwriters, then working with a qualified music publisher may be a great option for them. Many songwriter-artists are their own publisher and are good at it. Many songwriter-artists are their own publisher but do not put the time and effort into making their songs successful. A good quality music publisher has many contacts and knows the upcoming possibilities for the use of songs. These publishers know music supervisors, ad executives, record producers as well as recording artists and record label executives, all of whom are potential users of the publisher's song(s).

What expectations does a publisher have of a songwriter-artist? For artists, who wear the songwriter "hat," to be attractive to a publisher, their song(s) must be commercially viable. It all comes down to the quality of the song, not the looks of the lead singer, not how many fans a band has and definitely not how well an artist-musician plays an instrument. A publisher may offer a single-song publishing agreement to a songwriter if the publisher sees ways to make money from the song. A publisher may also be interested in an artist who writes their own material if the artist is about to release an album by a major record label.

Eventually, if the songwriter-artist is prolific and has some quality songs, the publisher may offer them a staff-writing position.

++++++++++++++++++++++++++++++

Expectations of Record Labels

Once again, although we're jumping into the idea of working with collaborators in the field of Product Development, smart artists know to plan their Artist Development with the idea that eventually, they will be working with professional collaborators, such as record label executives.

The number one, primary reason that a record label would be interested in signing an artist is that the label believes that the artist will make them money. That's all. If the record label believes that an artist might financially break-even, or worse, lose money, they will not spend their time and effort on that project. Record labels are in business to make a profit, not break-even, and certainly not to lose money.

As we all know, a record label company releases to the public for sale. Their products are either physical, such as compact discs, or non-physical such as downloads or ringtones. If an artist wants to attract the attention of a major record label or an independent record label, they must be prepared. Believe it or not, the hard work begins after an artist signs a record deal. If the artist thinks it's hard now, just wait!

Every record label, either major or independent, will expect that an artist has ALL of their Artist Development Plan completed. They will not sign an act that does not have a trademark on their name, for example. Imagine a record label signing a contract with an artist with a name that they already know is in use by another artist. They wouldn't. Might they want to sign a contract with a band or artist who does not have an agreement amongst the band members? Nope.

It is the artist's job to know these expectations in advance, so their goals and objectives can be focused on their desires.

Expectations of Promoters

There are various types of event and concert promoters that may be involved in an artist's career. There are coffeehouse promoters and there are arena promoters. There are promoters who own nightclubs and there are promoters who produce complete tours. There are also festival promoters and promoters who produce special events.

How does a concert promoter determine which artists to schedule for their event? In many cases, they take the word of a booking agent. Other times, they know of the artist through word of mouth or via the media. Sometimes a promoter may not book an unknown artist but may book an artist whom he or she personally knows. It's better to be known than unknown. Remember, this business is about relationships.

What does a promoter expect from an artist when they are preparing their next concert or event? First and foremost, the promoter expects the artist to be professional. Yes, that means showing up on time. They also expect the artist to be exactly as described when the booking agent sold the act to them. (If a member of the band booked the gig, that member wore the agent "hat.") If the promoter expects a dynamic show, the artist had better deliver a dynamic show. Promoters will also expect the artist to promote the show to the artist's fans, and most important, deliver a quality performance.

Artist Development Expectations

1. Be professional at all times and expect others to be professional
2. Be prepared mentally, physically, musically and creatively
3. Prepare and follow a plan and schedule
4. Identify your team
5. Regularly communicate with your team, band and fans
6. Create constant flow of new quality content
7. Accept and delegate responsibilities
8. Provide incentives for delegated and completed jobs
9. Hone chops, tighten songs as well as performance set lists
10. Practice – instrument, vocals, song parts and breaks
11. Respect others on the team and their time, contributions and commitment
12. Be prepared for rehearsals
13. Chart your goals and your success
14. Review, evaluate and set new improvement levels constantly
15. Demand quality from yourself and your team
16. Complete team agreements
17. Separate, if only mentally, you, the person; you, the artist; your partners and your companies, etc.
18. Register the artist's name and trademark it
19. Secure image and crossover
20. Treat every action as a career move

Hint: Do what you're good at and then become great at it.

Product Development Expectations

1. Focus on the active and passive income streams
2. Identify upcoming projects – gigs, recordings, tours, events, etc.
3. Consider possible promo ammo needs for each project
4. Plan your work and work your plan(s)
5. Utilize project management techniques for maximum productivity
6. Communicate with your team on short and long term objectives
7. Keep accurate records to insure goals are being achieved
8. Review, evaluate and learn from each project
9. Set agendas for future recordings and performances
10. Prepare for each gig – set list, announcements, logistics, etc.
11. Pre-production before the studio
12. Determine goals before recording
13. If your recording is not a demo, don't forget Mastering
14. Consider your product's packaging and include how you are visually represented online
15. Determine format for physical recordings – CD, vinyl
16. Focus on sales and licensing which may include publishing, merchandise and performances
17. Consider both online distribution as well as physical distribution
18. Plan your promotion and publicity campaigns in the early stages of each new projects / products
19. Remember, the front door for today's artist is their web presence
20. Promote, promote, promote… and then promote some more

++

Notes

_____

_____

_____

_____

_____

Artist Development in the Music Business
Chapter 4 – Content Creation & Interpretation

After a person has made up their mind to try their hand at succeeding in the music business, acknowledged their artistic potential and determined their true inner-desire and drive to play music, they then begin to look at the many aspects of Artist Development.

The first part of Artist Development is content creation. In the music business, everything begins with a song. Without great songs, there is no music business. In today's world, where everything is so "30 seconds ago," good songs are not good enough. And many, many times, great songs are not good enough either. This creation of content is not only done through songwriters, but also through the interpretation of those songs by musicians and singers in live performances and/or recordings.

The quality of the song has got to stand high and above everything for an artist. The quality of the content, I should say. Songs are a part of that content. So are the lyrics, as well as the melodies. Content, or potential content, is everywhere. That doesn't mean there's quality content everywhere. Quality content is a rarity.

Owning or controlling content is the money tree in the music business. That "content" is songs (Artist Development) as well as the performance of those songs or the recordings of those songs (Product Development).

The content for every successful artist has got to be of really high quality for people to pay attention to it and, hence, to want to listen to it; to play it over, and over and over. Artists would like fans to tell all their friends about the song, including such things as the emotion and feeling of the song, or the desperation in the voice delivering the song or even the groove of the beat of the song. Hopefully, the song becomes a fan's favorite song. Every artist would love to have a product available that is somebody's favorite, or better yet, everyone's favorite.

So, the first part is determining the content. Is the content an original piece of art, or a version of someone else's creative endeavor? In the music business, content is the song, the lyrics, the verse, and the catalog.

Artist Development is about the music itself. Remember, good songs are not good enough when preparing to market music. People only respond to what they feel are great songs. The songs must have some commercial appeal, if only to a certain musical niche. (folk, hip-hop, alternative rock, new age, jazz, blues, etc.) Finding that niche and managing its growth is essential to developing a successful artist. So, the content (the songs) must be of a very high quality.

So, if a songwriter-artist is writing for them self and nobody else, then they are the only one who may care. But if they're writing for anybody else, then they need to consider who the market is and where the commercial appeal is in order to write for that market. Yes, that's true even if the song is about a loved one. That loved one is the target market. If a songwriter-artist is writing only for them self, it can be as avant-garde as they want because nobody will ever hear it and nobody will ever care. And that's fine, if that's the goal. If a songwriter-artist wants someone to buy it (or license it) from them, or to be "moved" by the art, it has to have some appeal. It better be good. The more the appeal the song has to fans and customers, the bigger the paycheck for the songwriter and artist.

Songwriters and musicians sometimes talk about the 1 – 6 – 4 – 5 chord progression of a song or the 12-bar blues progression, or the 1 - 4 – 5 chord progressions. All of these are so standard that thousands and thousands of songs of been written using those chord progressions. Does that mean they're bad? No. But, if any one of us wrote a song using those chords, it would be immediately familiar to us in some way or fashion. Those progressions are very familiar to our ears because we've heard them so many times.

When songwriter-artists or performer-artists are preparing content creation, they have to consider their niche within the music business. They then have to be able to select content that fits that niche. If the artist's musical direction is blues oriented, the artist would be best served if the artist performed blues songs. If the artist has a classical style, the artist may not do as well performing Hip-Hop, for example. Artists must stay true to who they are. Artists who follow trends are not leaders.

Finding that musical niche and managing its growth is essential to developing a successful artist. So, when we talk about Artist Development, artists have to identify their niche, and then manage that niche to succeed.

I can't say this enough times....Think QUALITY, QUALITY, QUALITY. After self-evaluation and establishing expectations, the first part of Artist Development is CONTENT and the creation of content. Content is King. Quality content is crucial.

++++++++++++++++++++++++++++++

Content Users

All businesses in the music and entertainment business, no matter how large or small, are in need of one thing: Content. Not just any content: quality content. Some content is freely available and other content may be extremely rare in the music business. Content comes from writers and producers and comes in the form of songs and recorded productions. Content is delivered through singers, musicians, producers, engineers, and story tellers.

In addition, businesses use song and recording of song all the time. Restaurants, gas stations, and retail shops regularly use songs to enhance the shopping experience for their customers.

++++++++++++++++++++++++++++++

Content Creators

In the music business there are numerous content creators. As we discuss Artist Development, the focus on the songwriter is an important consideration. In addition, the musician who interprets the songwriter's song also comes into play.

After looking at the content creators within Artist Development, we look toward creators of content in Product Development. These creators are producers, engineers, videographers as well as the musician performing on stage.

++++++++++++++++++++++++++++

Songwriters

A songwriter or a team of songwriters is a major source of potential content for an artist. Many artists wear the songwriter "hat" and perform and record their own content. All songwriters are artists. A songwriter-artist is an individual who writes both the lyrics and music to a song. Many times, songwriters are also performers, singers, musicians or recording artists. Someone who solely writes lyrics may be called a lyricist, and someone who only writes music may be called a composer.

Although songwriter-artists of the past commonly composed, arranged and played their own songs, more recently the pressure to produce popular hits has spread the responsibility between a number of people. Popular culture songs may be written by group members, but are now often written by staff writers, who may be songwriters directly employed by music publishers.

Songwriting and publishing royalties can be a substantial source of income for songwriter-artists and music publishers, particularly if a song becomes a hit. Legally, in the U.S., songs written after 1934 may only be copied or performed publicly by permission of the authors. Permission is granted through a songwriter-artist agreement with a Performing Rights Organization and/or music publisher. The legal power to grant these permissions may be bought, sold or transferred. This right is governed by international copyright law.

Professional songwriters can either be employed to write directly for or alongside a performing or recording artist. Others may try to license songs to Artist & Repertoire executives at record labels, music publishers, and a music supervisor. Song pitching can be done on a songwriter's behalf by their publisher or independently by the songwriter them self. A songwriter who pitches their own song to their own band is wearing the publisher "hat."

Co-Writers

There's a reason why most music publishers encourage songwriters to collaborate. Look at the history of some of the best songs. Most of them were created by more than one individual. In the case of songwriting, one plus one does not just equal two. Smart songwriters know that the power of two is exponential.

++++++++++++++++++++++++++++

Arrangers

Another contributor to content creation is that of an arranger. Initially, song arrangement is completed by the songwriter who has built the song with some structure, such as the previously mentioned chord progressions or the order of verses, choruses and bridges. Song arrangement determines when the chorus or verses are to be performed. However, a performer may choose to alter the arrangement by adding an introduction or extend a verse or add a solo instrument as a part of a jam.

In the music business, most arrangers (other than the initial songwriter) are hired by a producer looking to record a version of the song or by a band performing the song. An arranger of music, who is preparing an arrangement of a song will review the song and may add harmonization, melodic paraphrasing, orchestration, or develop a formal structure for its sound.

Orchestration is limited to the assignment of notes to instruments for performance by an orchestra, concert band, or other musical ensemble. Arranging involves adding compositional techniques, such as introductions, transitions, or modulations, as well as endings or solo instrumentations. Arranging is an art and certainly a major part of content creation.

++++++++++++++++++++++++++++++

Creators within Product Development

Record Producers

The music producer's job is to create, shape, and mold a piece of music into a quality recording. The scope of responsibility of a producer may be one or two songs or an artist's entire album – in which case the producer will typically develop an overall vision for the album and how the various songs may interrelate.

In the U.S., before the rise of the record producer, someone from a record label's Artist and Repertoire Department would oversee the recording session(s), and assume responsibility for creative decisions relating to the recording.

A record producer oversees and manages an audio recording (i.e. "production") of a songwriter's music. Sometimes a music producer works for a record label and sometimes a record producer is hired by an artist. Sometimes a producer is an independent artist them self. Many times a songwriter-artist is also a producer or the performer-artist is also their own producer. Yes, being a producer is wearing another "hat."

A music producer may have many roles that may include, but are not limited to, gathering ideas for the recording project, selecting songs and/or musicians, coaching the vocalist and musicians in the studio, controlling the recording sessions, and supervising the entire process through mixing and mastering. Producers often take on a wider entrepreneurial role, with responsibility for the budget, schedules, and negotiations.

Today, the recording industry has two kinds of producers: executive producers and recording producers; they have different roles. While an executive producer usually oversees a project's finances, a recording producer oversees the creation of a sound recording.

With today's relatively easy access to technology, an alternative to the record producers, is the so-called 'bedroom producer.' With today's technological advances, it is very easy for a producer to achieve high quality tracks without the use of a single instrument; which happens in modern music such as hip-hop, electronic or dance. Many established artists also take this approach.

In addition, many times the music producer is also a competent arranger, composer, musician and/or songwriter who may be able to bring fresh ideas to a recording project. To make songwriting and arrangement adjustments, the producer often selects and/or gives suggestions to the audio mixing engineer.

In today's world, many artists wear the producer "hat." This may be good or it may be bad depending on the experience the artist has as a music producer.

Recording Engineers

Another major source of content creation for Product Development comes from the creative and scientific efforts of a sound production technician / engineer. A sound production engineer records raw audio tracks and then edits and modifies them with hardware and software tools to create a stereo and/or surround sound "mix" of all the individual voices, sounds and instruments. This recording is then given further adjustment by a mastering engineer.

An audio engineer is concerned with the recording, manipulation, mixing and reproduction of sound. Many audio engineers creatively use technologies to produce sound for film, radio, television, music, electronic products and computer games.

Audio engineering is concerned with the creative and practical aspects of sounds including speech and music, as well as the development of new audio technologies and advancing scientific understanding of audible sound.

Musicians

An important part of the creation process is how the content is interpreted and delivered. This, obviously, is done by musicians, singers and performers. A musician-artist (or instrumentalist) is a person who is talented in interpreting music through the use of their voice or musical instrument. A musician usually performs music creatively either live on stage or in a recording studio, or both.
Many musicians specialize in a musical style, and some musicians play a variety of different styles. Examples of possible musician skills include performing, conducting, singing, composing, arranging, and orchestrating music.

Technicians

Another important person in the area of musical content creation is an experienced technician. This is a person who helps the artist-musician communicate their art to their fans and customers via live performances. In addition to the recording engineers described above, there are other technicians such as sound technicians, lighting technicians, mastering technicians as well as stage technicians.

Technicians typically have intermediate understanding of music theory but expert proficiency in technique of their chosen field. For example, although audio technicians are not as learned in acoustics as acoustical engineers, they are more proficient in operating sound equipment, and they will likely know more about acoustics than other musicians or performers.

Technicians may be classified as either highly skilled workers or at times semi-skilled workers, and may be part of a larger (production) process. They may be found working in a variety of fields, and they usually have a job title with the designation 'technician' following the particular category of work. Thus a 'stage technician' is a worker who provides technical support on a stage when putting on a concert or a play.

Video Directors

A video or film director is a person who directs the making of a film or video and although video production is a part of Product Development, is certainly part of content creation. Generally, a video director controls a video's artistic and dramatic aspects, and visualizes the script while guiding the technical crew and actors in the fulfillment of that vision. The director has a key role in choosing the cast members, production design, and the creative aspects of the making of the film or the video.

++++++++++++++++++++++++++++++

Content Acquisition

If you are an artist who is a songwriter, who is also the performing musician as well as the recording artist, it may be easy for you to constantly create new content. An artist's decision of which content to use for their live shows (set list) as well as in their recordings is imperative to the artist's success.

In addition to a songwriter-artist writing their own material, many artists perform and record songs of other songwriters. This is especially true for new artists as they are more likely to start their careers by performing songs written by other songwriters and/or performed by other artists. In this industry, this is called "covering" a song. These performer-artists may be known as a "cover band." A cover band "covers" other artist's material (more on this later).

Publishing companies are an excellent source for this content. Publishers represent material, such as songs, lyrics and melodies from authors, songwriters, and more. As previously mentioned, some songwriters serve as their own music publishers, while others have publisher collaborators.

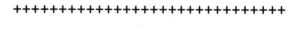

Public Domain

Another source of content for artists and musicians are works in the public domain. If content is not protected by intellectual property rights or, if the intellectual property rights are forfeited, or if the intellectual property rights have expired, they are considered to be in the public domain. Examples of content in the public domain are the works of Shakespeare, Beethoven or John Phillip Sousa. Anybody may use these artistic works without paying any royalties to those content creators. Derivative creations from works in the public domain are numerous.

Any works created before the existence of copyright and patent laws also form part of the public domain. For example, the Bible and the inventions of Leonardo da Vinci are in the public domain. However, keep in mind, copyright may exist in translations or new formulations of these works. For example, a Beethoven masterpiece symphony may be in the public domain but a recording of the piece may be copyrighted. In other words, producer-artists may not be able to use a "sample" of the recording without permission in their new recording.

Works of the United States Government and various other governments are excluded from copyright law and may therefore be considered to be in the public domain in their respective countries.

++++++++++++++++++++++++++++++

Derivative Works

Derivative works are new works created by an artist who uses another artist's work to create this new work. Sampling is a perfect example of a derivative work. The new work includes other work. Derivative works include translations, musical arrangements, and dramatizations of a work, as well as other forms of transformation or adaptation. Copyrighted works may not be used for derivative works without permission from the copyright owner, while public domain works can be used freely for derivative works without permission.

Works of art that are public domain may also be reproduced photographically or artistically or used as the basis of new, interpretive works. Once a work enters into the public domain, derivative works such as adaptations in books and films may increase noticeably. The plays of Shakespeare, all in the public domain, have been used in hundreds of feature-length films, for example. In addition to straightforward adaptation, they have been used as the launching point for transformative retellings, song ideas, movies and stories.

++++++++++++++++++++++++++++++

Creative Commons

According to their website (www.creativecommons.org) Creative Commons (CC) is a non-profit organization devoted to expanding the range of creative works available for others to legally build upon and to share. The Creative Commons organization has released several copyright-licenses, known as Creative Commons licenses, free of charge to the public. These licenses allow songwriters or other content creators to communicate which rights they reserve, and which rights they waive for the benefit of other creators. This distinguishes Creative Commons from other all-rights reserved copyright. Creative Commons creates a more flexible copyright model, replacing "all rights reserved" with "some rights reserved." Wikipedia is one of the notable web-based projects using one of its licenses.

The first set of Creative Commons copyright licenses was released in December 2002 and now there are hundreds of millions of works licensed under Creative Commons.

Creative Commons has been embraced by many as a way for content creators to take control of how they choose to share their intellectual property.

Finding Copyright Registrations

All United States copyright registrations and renewals registered since 1978 have been published online at the Copyright Office website. (www.copyright.gov) Registrations and renewals prior to 1978 were published in semi-annual soft cover Copyright Catalogs and are available at the U.S. Library of Congress.

Publishers

Another source of content for musicians is publishers. In the music business, a music publisher (or publishing company) is responsible for securing use of a song or songs by musicians, bands and recordings. They accomplish this by asking a performer to include the song in their set list during the artist's stage performance or by pitching the song for use in an audio or video recording. Publishers ensure the songwriters and composers receive payment when their compositions are commercially used. If a songwriter asks his or her band to perform or record one of his or her songs, then the songwriter-artist is wearing the "hat" of publisher. This happens all the time.

However, if the songwriter-artist collaborates with a music publisher to do this instead, the publisher pitches the songs for use and will receive a percentage of the total income royalties for doing the work.

++++++++++++++++++++++++++++++

"Cover" Songs

For recordings:
Once a song has been recorded by an artist, by law, any other artist may now record a "cover" version of that song. That does not mean that the use of a song for a new recording is free. This is where the compulsorily mechanical license comes into play. (There is more about this topic in other sections of the Artist Development Plan). There is a statutory rate established by the copyright tribunal for the use of another songwriter's song which has been previously recorded. It is adjusted from time to time. At the present time, the rate is 9.1 cents for every music recording that is manufactured or duplicated, whose length is less than 5 minutes. There are other variables. Songs longer than 5 minutes in length are charged at a different rate. If the artist is recording the song for a record label, the record label will pay the mechanical royalties associated with the recording. If the artist is producing their own recordings of the song(s), then the artist is wearing the record label or

producer "hat" and will have to pay the mechanical royalties associated with the recording of these song(s).

If the song has never been recorded, the artist-producer has to negotiate a fee for the song's "First Use" from the artist-songwriter or music publisher (more about this later).

> **Artists typically do not have to pay to use another songwriter's song unless they are their own promoter or are releasing their own recordings.**

For Performances:
If an artist performs the song on stage, then the venue where the stage is located pays a fee to a Performing Rights Organization for a license to use music in the venue. Usually a venue, such as a nightclub or concert arena, pays an annual "blanket" license which pays for all music performed in the venue during the entire year.

However, if the artist is wearing the promoter "hat" and is performing at a public park, for example, the park does not have a P.R.O. license for the use of music and the artist-promoter will have to pay the required fees for the use of the song(s).

++++++++++++++++++++++++++++++

Content Creation

Many artists are songwriters and these songwriters are the content creators. The old-style apprenticeship approach to learning how to write songs is being supplemented by some universities, colleges and music schools. Today, a good knowledge of modern music technology and business skills is seen as necessary to make songwriting a music career. Songwriter-artists not only have to be able to write quality songs suitable for licensing, they may also need to know how to make a demo recording of the song as well as knowing the current licensing options available for the song.

Following is a list of music genres where songwriters may earn income. Some artists are good at only one niche, while other songwriters are proficient at writing in multiple music genres.

++++++++++++++++++++++++++++++

> **A good knowledge of modern music technology and business skills is seen as necessary to make songwriting a music career.**

Music Genres

- Acoustic
- Adult Contemporary
- Afro Pop
- Alternative Rock
- Ambient
- Americana
- Avant Garde
- Ballad
- Ballroom
- Big Band
- Blues
- Boogie Woogie
- Bossa Nova
- Broadway Musical
- Cabaret
- Cajun/Zydeco
- Calypso
- Celtic
- Children
- Choral
- Christmas
- Classical
- Club/Dance
- Cocktail Culture
- Comedy/Novelty
- Contemp. Christian
- Country
- Crooner
- Dance
- Disco
- Dixieland
- Doo Wop
- Drum & Bass
- Easy Listening
- Electronic
- Electronica
- Ensemble
- Film
- Folk
- Funk
- Fusion
- Game Show
- Gospel
- Goth
- Hard Rock
- Hawaiian
- Heavy Metal
- Hip Hop
- Holiday
- Honky Tonk
- Horror
- House
- Industrial Rock
- Instrumental
- Jazz
- Latin
- Library
- Lounge
- Lullaby
- March
- Mariachi
- Mexican
- New Wave
- New Age
- Operetta
- Orchestral
- Patriotic
- Polka
- Pop
- Pop - Alternative
- Pop – Classic
- Pop – Dreampop
- Pop - Easy Listening
- Pop – Europop
- Pop – General
- Pop – Lullaby
- Pop – Religious
- Pop – Rock
- Pop – Standards
- Pop – Traditional
- Punk
- R & B
- Ragtime
- Rap
- Rock
- Sacred
- Samba
- Ska
- Soft Rock
- Soundtrack
- Spiritual
- Spoken Word
- Sports
- Standard
- Swing
- Techno
- Tin Pan Alley
- Torch Song
- Trance
- TV Movie / Series
- Urban
- Waltz
- World Beat

Songwriting Basics

Since this chapter is about content creation, we will cover some of the basics of writing songs. If you are interested in more about songwriting, it is suggested that you take a songwriting course, or five.

For an artist to write or select quality songs for their musical catalog, they should know a bit about what makes a song desirable to a listener.

```
Lyrics
Melody
Structure
```

There are three basic things a song needs to impress a listener. This, of course, is not true for all songs but overall, this is a good start.

First, and in no particular order because a song needs all of these, a song needs an interesting lyric to draw the listener in. Sometimes, the title of the song will generate some lyric ideas for a songwriter.

Second, the melody of the song needs to be "catchy," in order to have a better chance to be licensed for recordings and/or performances.

Lastly, a song needs to have a good solid structure. Standard song structures include 12-16 bars of blues or the combination of the 1, 4, 5 & 6 chords.

If all three of these song attributes are in harmony, then the song might have some success. If the song is weak in one of these parts, then the song does not have a very good chance at pleasing listeners.

Professional songwriters always continue to improve their writing skills in these three areas. Songwriting is a craft, yet an art. Aspiring songwriters should study songs and look at those three areas within songs that are successful.

Lyrics

Lyrics of a song are a set of words that are included in verses and choruses. The writer of lyrics is a lyricist. The meaning of lyrics can either be explicit or implicit.

Many times a lyricist will write lyrics that are abstract and almost unintelligible. Sometimes their explication emphasizes form, articulation, meter, and/or symmetry of expression.

Melody

A melody also known as a tune, voice, or line, is a linear succession of musical tones that the listener perceives as a single entity. In its most literal sense, a melody is a combination of pitch and rhythm.

Melodies often consist of one or more musical phrases or motifs, and are usually repeated throughout a composition in various forms. Melodies may also be described by their melodic motion or the pitches or the intervals between pitches, pitch range, tension and release, continuity and coherence, cadence, and shape.

Song Structure

In addition to lyrics and melody, another important ingredient of a song is its structure. Aspiring songwriters should study hits songs and search out study materials from several sources to begin continually improving their craft of songwriting. Treat songwriting as just that, a "craft."

Inspiration sometimes hits quickly and can be fleeting. Many times, a song is written quickly and ends up a successful song. This usually happens because the songwriter has studied and acquired knowledge long before that particular song was written.

Let's look at some basic songwriting terms and structure fundamentals.

Song Structure Fundamentals

Verse
Chorus
Bridge
Rhymes

A song is composed of several items. Many times a song will have multiple verses and a chorus, and perhaps a bridge or a tag.

Verse
A verse (or stanza) is similar to a paragraph in a book. It is a section of grouped lines and provides the details of the lyric. Typically, verses are 8 to 16 bars long and their melody repeats when the verse is repeated.

Chorus
A chorus is a section of lines that generally contain the catchiest part of the song and is known as "the hook." A hook is a phrase of words or music that catches the listener's ear. Usually, if the listener remembers anything of the song, it's the chorus. Many times, the hook is often the title of the song. In most cases, a song contains a chorus that is the same, or has only very small changes, to its content each time it's repeated. Some songs have no chorus, but most do.

Bridge
Some songs have a bridge. A bridge is usually of different length than a verse and usually has different music accompaniment. A bridge may "sum up" a song's message, or flash forward or backward in time, or often give a different perspective or surprise twist to a song.

A bridge is also called a "middle eight" and is often located about three-quarters the way through a song. It is typically 8 bars long. Hence the name "middle eight."

Rhymes
Rhyme patterns are simply the pattern of rhymes within a verse, chorus or bridge. The rhyme pattern in each verse may match other subsequent verses in the song. This pattern does not have to be the same in the chorus or bridge and is usually best to be different than the verses. Songs do not have to rhyme, but the vast majority of successful songs do rhyme.

Rhymes are generally categorized as "perfect" or "near." A perfect rhyme is not always the best rhyme; the name just refers to the way it is. For instance, the two words "grind" and "find" are considered perfect rhymes. The consonants following the rhymed vowel (in this case "I") are the same. The two words "find" and "line" are considered "near" rhymes because the consonants after the rhymed vowel are different.

Many songwriters use near rhymes as it is easier to tell a story because there are more potential words to use.

How Great Songs Become Great

1. A great song has interesting lyrics that draws a listener in.
2. A great song is "catchy" to again draw in the listener.
3. A great song has proper structure of verses and choruses.
4. A great song has quality rhyme patterns.

++++++++++++++++++++++++++++

Song Review

Before a songwriter considers their next hit song to be complete, they should review the song a way that music business professionals review a song.

Song Title: The title of the song may be the hook of the song. It should be easy to remember as well as accurately describe what the song is about.

Words by: A song reviewer may want to know who wrote the lyrics. Make sure credits are given.

Music by: As mentioned about, the reviewer may also want to know who wrote the music. Again, provide the credits.

Copyright: Was the song published? Is the song protected with a registered copyright?

Publisher: If the song has been licensed to a music publisher, who is it.

Verse Tune Quality: When determining the strength of a song, a reviewer will rate the quality of the tune(s.)

Chorus Tune Quality: The quality of the chorus is probably the most important part of a song. If the chorus needs work, the song will not be licensed.

Hook: Smart songwriters know where the hook is of their songs. It is the title or is it in the melody of the chorus?

Bridge Tune Quality: Not all songs have bridges, but if so, does the bridge provide a twist or new musical idea for the song?

Intro Tune Quality: The beginning of the song should be interesting. Many reviewers want a short intro. If the song intro has a 45 second guitar solo, the songwriter may want to reconsider the introduction.

Tag Tune Quality: The ending of the song is sometimes abrupt and sometimes fades out. What's the best use of a tag in the song being reviewed?

Lyric Quality: Are the lyrics the best they can be? Lyrics are the biggest reason a music publisher will send a song back to a songwriter for a re-write.

++++++++++++++++++++++++++++

CATALOG

Content Catalog

An artist is defined by the material that they record or perform or by the content that they create, such as songs. Professional songwriter-artists understand that their livelihood is dependent upon the quality of the content that they create. Many performer-artists know that their audience is there because of the songs they perform, whether they wrote them or not (as well as their "show" in some cases.)

If the artist is not a songwriter and covers other songwriter's material, they will need to catalog a list of all possible songs to perform and/or record. Much of this is pretty simple. It's just a list after all. As artists learn new songs, they may add them to their song catalog. If an artist can build their song catalog to about an hour's length, they can begin to think about performing.

However, if the songwriter-artist is paying attention to the entertainment market, as music publishers do, they are constantly looking for opportunities for their songs. They know who's looking for what. Other artists who are about to enter the studio to record a batch of new songs may be looking for material. Music supervisors may be on a new film assignment and looking for possible song to be included in the film. Songwriters who are also performers may or may not use their own songs. Look at artists-songwriters such as Bob Dylan, Carole King or Pharrell Williams. They not only write and perform their own material; they were licensing songs earlier in their career. The songwriter might find more exposure for their songs through film, television, commercials or through other artists.

A professional songwriter will catalog their songs and meta-tag them based on:

- Song Title(s)
- Copyright
- Songwriter(s)
- Release Date
- Publisher
- Performing Rights Organization
- Primary Genre
- Secondary Genre
- Song Length
- Tempo Feel
- Lead Vocal
- Moods 1
- Moods 2
- Subject Matter 1
- Subject Matter 2
- Similar Artist 1
- Similar Artist 2
- Language
- Era
- Lyric Credits
- Music Credits
- Short Description
- Long Description
- Story Behind the Song
- Recorded Format
- IRSC
- Score
- Fake Sheet

Building a Songwriter Career

As a songwriter-artist builds their career there are many stages of proficiency. Just like every other profession, songwriting takes passion and perseverance. A person who wants to become a songwriter doesn't need to know how to play an instrument, but it sure helps. Learning to play an instrument is another section of Artist Development. Theoretically, a person could sing or hum or whistle their song creation to a musician who then tries to interpret the songwriters' ideas to notes to become music.

As a songwriter-artist grows in the chosen career, here are steps to become a full-time songwriter:

1. Play guitar or piano or rhythm instrument
2. Write in 3 hour blocks at least once a week
3. Co-Write 3 hours per week
4. Get Involved in local songwriting organization
5. Stay focused daily to further your songwriting career
6. Visit a major music center (MMC) at least 3 times per year
7. While visiting a MMC, actively drop off songs to music publishers
8. Pitch songs in person
9. Perform songs 6 times per year or once every 2 months
10. Co-write with someone who has signed a single song contract
11. Sign a single-song publishing contract with a music publisher
12. Co-write with a songwriter who has a staff deal
13. Obtain exclusive songwriting agreement with publisher
14. Co-write with major label recording artist
15. Constantly encourage the publisher to pitch song(s) to major labels, music producers, talent managers and major artists

++++++++++++++++++++++++++++

Content Creation Tips

- every song has been absolutely improved repeatedly - every note/syllable crafted to be the best it can be
- vocal performance on the demo is not just perfect but head-turning, striking
- arrangement is everything it can be to bring out song/vocals
- arrangement offers a new idea to the world, and not just the usual paint-by-numbers
- photos/image are striking and amazing, and capture the essence of the music
- live show is so entertaining that even a deaf person would enjoy it
- artist has done this for a few years and still believes that this is their real calling in life, regardless of external rewards (or lack of)
- off-stage persona is sustainable (stamina, dealing with fans well, etc.)
- no addictions - to anything
- an unflappable healthy attitude to the immense amount of work it really takes to be successful at anything

++++++++++++++++++++++++++++

To Do

Notes:

Artist Development in the Music Business
Chapter 5 – Content Protection

Since songwriting and publishing royalties can be a substantial source of income for content creators, particularly if a song becomes a hit, smart songwriter-artists know how to protect this valuable asset. The royalties generated by one hit song could buy a songwriter-artist a modest home. It's like money in the bank, except it earns much more than bank interest.

Legally, in the U.S., songs written after 1934 may only be copied or performed publicly by permission of the authors and/or publishers. The legal power to grant these permissions may be bought, sold or transferred. This right is governed by international copyright law.

After creating content (songs, lyrics or melodies, music recordings, etc.), Artist Development turns to protecting the songwriter-artist's Intellectual Property (IP). After all, there is no sense being a starving musician. Content Protection is directly related to the financial success of a songwriter-artist. Smart artists know that this intellectual property of theirs is a major potential income source. The use of songs for audio recordings or for live performances is what the music business is all about.

Proprietary Rights

A company or any organization cannot effectively run without proprietary rights. It is the 'protective shield' of any organization.

Proprietary rights are a legal term and involve the rights given to the owner of intellectual property by the government to protect their ownership. In the music business, proprietary rights come in the form of copyrights and trademarks. These proprietary rights protect songs, lyrics, melody arrangements, recordings, logos and images. Yes, patents are also an intellectual property, but patents don't really apply to Artist Development as they mainly apply to new inventions, processes or technologies. Smart artists know the possible commercial value bestowed with having these rights. It is used in different ways by the legal community, but all the rights are directed towards defending ownership. These rights are sometimes structured in the contract of an artist with a third-party and all specifications of the rights are made clear through their agreement. They are also sometimes assumed by the owner. Owners can exercise their rights depending on the nature of their ownership.

Proprietary rights in a business ownership allow the owner to protect the name and brand of the business from duplication. The owner can file a legal suit on violation of the owned rights. Thus, he/she can protect their property with these proprietary rights.

Similarly, these rights give people the right to protect their intellectual property and determine when and how it can be used. It preserves ones artistic works, inventions, creations, songs, books, logos, etc., by legal means such as copyrights.

Intellectual Property

The term Intellectual Property (IP) encompasses various types of creations such as a music composition, a movie, book, painting or even a brand name. According to the concept of intellectual property, such 'creations of mind' are intangible or non-monetary assets which have possible commercial value. The owners of such non-monetary assets (creations of mind) are assigned some exclusive rights over their creation, of which they may financially benefit. However, it is not possible to recover or replace an intellectual property that is stolen. If stolen, the interests of the owner, over his/her creation will get affected. So, there must be laws to protect the moral as well as material interests of the owner over his/her intellectual property. The law that deals with the rights assigned to owners of intellectual property is called Intellectual Property Law.

Types of Intellectual Property
Here is a brief overview about the different types of intellectual property.

Types of Intellectual Property

1. Copyright
2. Trademark
3. Patent
4. Industrial Design
5. Trade Secrets

An intellectual property can be either artistic or commercial. The artistic works come under the category of copyright laws, while the commercial ones (also known as industrial properties), include trademarks, patents, industrial design rights, and trade secrets (trademarks are a separate section of the Artist Development Plan).

Intellectual property is like any other real property which is financially beneficial for the owner. The monetary benefits are said to encourage people to come up with new inventions and new creations.

Copyright

In generalized sense, copyright is an Intellectual Property. Copyright laws deal with the intellectual property of creative works like music, books, and paintings.

Copyright can be termed as, a provision by legal systems that empower the creator of a specified intellectual property with rights, over its use in public. The use of songs, or recordings of songs, by the general public can be in any form such as by direct copying or imitation or reproducing. Copyright is granted to artists, writers, scientists, architects, painters, and/or any person working or developing a useful element of science, technology or a piece of art. According to United States constitution, copyright is an instrument that is used "to promote the progress of science and useful arts, by securing for limited times to creators the exclusive right to their works."

A copyright is a right conferred on the owner of an artistic or literary work. It is an exclusive right to control the publication, distribution and adaptation of such creative work. The right lies with the owner-cum-copyright holder for a certain period. As the time lapses, the work can be republished or reproduced by others. Usually, in most countries, the time span of a copyright extends through the entire life of the copyright owner and lasts up to a period of about 50 to 100 (70 years in the U.S.) years after his/her death.

History of Copyright

The Copyright Act of 1709 or The Statute of Anne is considered to be the first full-fledged copyright law. This British law was established to encourage learning and maximize knowledge. The law provides the proprietor of content an exclusive right to print, distribute and copy the work. Anyone who wants to reuse the work has to have the owner's permission.

According to the law, as soon as any original work is created, the copyright is automatically given to its author. Though the author need not have to formally register the work, the registration makes the copyright more apparent.

U.S. Copyright Act of 1976

The Copyright Act of 1976 is a copyright legislation adopted in the United States. The Copyright Act of 1976 was designed to codify 'fair-use' practices related to new copyrights. The application involved consideration of the exact date of an author's death rather than some prior, fixed, renewal term and condition. Careful consideration of the technological advances led Congress to the formulation of the clauses of this act. Use of content for television, sound recording, radio and movies benefited from this agenda.

The Act was designed as a fair compromise between publisher and author. It cleared the air on the issue of payments on the death of the author. It was specified that the royalty is to be paid to widows and heirs, for a period of 19 years. Authors' rights are protected for a period of 70 years.

The Act determines fair use according to:
1. Purpose and character
2. Nature of work
3. Extent of original work used
4. Effect on the potential market

The Act also offers copyright protection to original, fixed authorship that may be developed to include a different perception and communication. This is applicable to authorships such as musical, literary and dramatic works, pantomimes, sculptural and choreographic works as well as sound recordings; each of which affects quality of motion pictures or other visual mediums of communication.

++++++++++++++++++++++++++++++

The Copyright Act of 1976, Section 102, specifies copyright protection to original work. It allows exclusive rights to all copyright holders.

Copyright's Exclusive Rights

1. Right to copy or reproduce
2. Right to generate derivatives
3. Right to lease or sell copies
4. Right to public performance
5. Right to public display
6. Right to digital recording

There are six (6) exclusive rights of a copyright owner:

1. **Right to copy or reproduce**
2. **Right to generate derivatives**
3. **Right to lease or sell copies**
4. **Right to public performance**
5. **Right to public display**
6. **Right to digital recording**

Content Protection

Part two of Artist Development is protecting creative content. One way this is done is by the process of copyrighting. According to the current copyright law, an original work is copyrighted as soon as it is in tangible form. Tangible form means it cannot be a thought unless it's written down. It cannot be an idea for a song if it has only been whistled. It must be either pen on paper, an audio recording or a text-message, but it must be tangible.

Another way to protect Intellectual Property is with trademarks. (More on trademarks later).

Copyright protection is acquired automatically when a work is "created." The definition of "created" is when a work is "fixed" (tangible) in a copy or recorded for the first time. A copyright has to be in tangible form to be valid. This, however, does not mean that the work is a registered copyright. It just means that there has been a copyright established. Proof of copyright is a different story.

Some of the works that come under the Copyright Protection Act are songs, stories, journalistic reports, theatrical scripts, computer software, architectural designs, multimedia digital creations, literature, and more. Copyright extends to books, dramatic works, audio visuals, motion pictures, pictorials and graphics, choreographic works, handouts, musical works, presentations and architectural works, dances, poems, and yes, sound recordings. All of these have potential to show copyright.

Remember, content is king. Owning or controlling content is where the most money is made in the music business. Protecting an artist's content is an important part of Artist Development.

Copyright Registration
One part of Artist Development is about protecting the "great" songwriter-artist songs by registering them with the U.S. copyright office. http://www.copyright.gov

++++++++++++++++++++++++++++++

Proof of Copyright Ownership

Proof of copyright ownership is achieved by registration of the copyrighted material through the U.S. Copyright office. This is done by filing a copyright form with the U.S. Copyright Office, with a check for their fees, and one copy of the unpublished song on a record, tape, CD, or lead sheet. If the song has been published, two copies should be sent. Registration by the U.S. Copyright Office becomes effective upon receipt of the application form, copies of the song, and their fee.

Registration of songs is necessary in order to protect a song from being used without permission, and is necessary to present in a court of law and, if needed, to sue for copyright infringement.

Copyright forms may be found in many published books, or may be obtained from the copyright office:

Copyright Office, Library of Congress
Washington, DC 20559

Or visit http://www.copyright.gov

Copyright Office
Library of Congress
Washington, DC 20559
www.copyright.gov

Registration of the copyright places on record, a verifiable date and content of the work. In the event of a legal claim, or case of infringement or plagiarism, the copyright owner can produce a copy of the work from an official government source and present it as evidence of ownership.

Who can claim a Copyright?

When the author creates a work, it becomes the author's property. The author, or those who derive rights from the author, is authorized to claim a copyright.

Protecting the Music

There are two types of copyrights in the music business: the C-Circle (©) copyright and the P-Circle (℗) copyright. The © copyright is the controlling copyright. This is the copyright that supersedes all other copyrights. For a producer to use a song for a recording, they must get permission from the C-Circle copyright owner. Once they get approval via a license from the C-Circle copyright owner, they may begin recording the song. When they are finished with the recording, they now own a P-Circle copyright.

For example: There are two songwriters. One is named Lennon and the other McCartney. They were in a band called The Beatles. These two (2) songwriters also own a publishing company called Northern Songs. The Beatles are signed to a record company called EMI Records. EMI desires to record The Beatles performing a song called Yesterday which was written by the songwriters, Lennon and McCartney and published by Northern Songs. The controlling copyright © is licensed from Northern Songs to EMI Records so that the song, Yesterday, may be recorded. EMI Records hires The Beatles to perform the song on the recording. The recording, which is owned by EMI Records, has a new copyright called a P-Circle copyright. Other record companies may also desire to record the song. The same process continues. There may be multiple P-Circle copyrights but only one C-Circle copyright.

Copyright Applies to:

- Audio Recording Copyrights
- Graphics Copyrights
- Photo Copyrights
- Song Copyrights
- Video Recording Copyrights

++++++++++++++++++++++++++++++

> **Copyrights May Be Granted to:**
>
> **Writers**
> **Painters**
> **Scientists**
> **Architects**
>
> **Any person working or developing a useful element of science and technology or a piece of art.**

This means that the creators of intellectual property, such as copyrights, are empowered with legal rights to their creation and can use these rights in multiple ways. They can sell the rights of the creation, like an architectural design or a painting. They can license their creation to another person or business, like a songwriter to a publisher or a publisher to a record company.

When writers permit publishers to sell (license) their content for them, the writer will negotiate a publishing royalty fee based on a percentage of sales as a consideration for their license.

Although international copyright protection does not exist, U.S. copyright protection is valid in many countries around the world. However, there are countries that do not provide any protection for foreign works, such as, Sweden, Ukraine, and Argentina. One has to ensure that one is reasonably comfortable with the copyright laws of different countries before throwing open the work to the rest of the world.

++++++++++++++++++++++++++++++

Copyright Infringement

Any unauthorized use of a work that falls under the copyright law is known as copyright infringement. Violation of copyrights include: a commercial imitation of intellectual property, and is punishable by law in many nations across the world. It is an act of violating the exclusive rights of the copyright owner(s). The illegal downloading of copyrighted material or sharing of music is a common example of copyright infringement. The secret copying of audio recordings or movies or unlawful use of text are other examples. Pirated copies of different media that are sold today are the 'best examples' of copyright infringement.

The law of the United States has provided a way of protection to the original works of authorship, both published and unpublished. The literary, musical or artistic works of the original authors are protected by means of copyright. The penalties for violation of a copyright can differ from case to case or jurisdiction to jurisdiction. The penalty can vary from a monetary compensation (that is given to the creator) to a prison sentence.

The owner of the work can hold these rights exclusively or may give these rights to others. In case of a work in the field of audio recordings, the owner of the work is also authorized to perform the work publicly by means of digital audio transmissions.

++++++++++++++++++++++++++++++

How does the content creator protect their creation from being copied, recorded, sold, or performed on stage by a musician who is getting paid for the use of the song, but the creator is not?

Copyright Protection

Copyright protection simply means protection of data from being copied. There are a physical ways and there are legal ways. It is actually the physical ways of the copy protection that deals with the mechanisms used to prevent data from being copied without the consent of the owner of the work. This type of copy protection, and copyright protection, is often used in the case of songs or data on CDs, DVDs, video games and computer software, thus resulting in decrease in the sale of original works. Casual copying relates to the copying of media formats on machines.

In addition to officially registering copyright with the U.S. Copyright Office, methods such as node locking, floating licenses, grid computing and tracking of software licenses have been and are being used to assure copyright protection. Copyright protection faces certain technical challenges. Logically a player that can read and play media is also able to write an exact copy of it. On similar lines, if an audio can be heard or a video can be seen, they can also be recorded. To fight this fact, some companies came up with various media formats, wherein; information is located in such a way that it cannot be rewritten. They devised software that requires for its use, the users' evidence of having purchased it. Media copyright protection uses other methods, which, in some way, binds the media to the machine that plays it. This may be done by means of encryption, registration keys, activation codes or serial numbers, which associate the data being used with its owner, thus achieving copyright protection. These types of methods don't prevent the duplication of work and safeguard copyrights but certainly make it more difficult for someone to copy the work(s).

++++++++++++++++++++++++++++

Work for Hire

There is a slight variation of copyright ownership in cases where the work falls under a term known as 'work made for hire.' For example, a 'work made for hire,' may be an employee during his/her period of employment who signs an agreement that his/her work made during their employment tenure should fall under this category. In this scenario, the employer becomes the owner of this work. If a piece of work is in the form of a contribution made to a collective work, it is also grouped under the status of 'work made for hire.' The owner(s) of the collective work will claim copyright.

Copyright Myths

Myth #1: "If I copy someone else's work and don't charge for it, it's not a violation of copyright laws."
Fact #1: It is still a copyright violation even if you give it away, as it is not yours to give. This is especially true if you hurt the commercial value of the work.

Myth #2: "The work is not copyrighted if it doesn't have a copyright notice."
Fact #2: This is not true anymore. In the USA, anything created confidentially and originally after April 1, 1989, is copyrighted regardless of it having a notice or not.

Myth #3: "You will lose your copyright if you don't defend it."
Fact #3: A copyright cannot be lost unless it is given up explicitly by the owner.

Myth #4: "If I make up my own songs, but base them on another work, my new work belongs to me."
Fact #4: This is called a derivative work. The U.S. Copyright law is quite explicit that making derivative work, i.e. work based on another copyrighted work is the exclusive property of the owner of the original work. Therefore, if you are writing a song using recording samples from someone else's work, you have to have that permission from that other content creator.

Myth #5: "I got to copyright the name of my band or the name of my song."
Fact #5: In fact, you can't copyright a name or even a title.

How to Get a Copyright

In most parts of the world, new creations are protected by a copyright as soon as the work is created in tangible form. In other words, copyright protection is automatic. However, if people register their work, they will receive a certificate of registration. This is called a registered copyright. This is useful if a person is seeking legal measures for copyright infringement. In the U.S., people who have registered original creations can introduce the certificate of registration in a court of law as evidence of their ownership. In fact, a successful plaintiff having a certificate of registration may have the right to claim statutory damages as well as attorney's fees.

To get a copyright in the United States, content creators can either go to the website of the U.S. copyright office (www.copyright.gov) and complete the application online and submit it along with their registration fee, or they can complete an online electronic form in PDF, make printouts and mail it, along with their fee. Yet another option through which a songwriter-artist can get a copyright is to fill out the U.S. Copyright's paper forms and then mail the application via the U.S. mail service.

++++++++++++++++++++++++++++++

Length of Copyright

Copyright laws are not uniform throughout the world. For instance, In the U.K., the duration of copyright protection depends upon the type of work. In case of films, literary, dramatic, musical and artistic work, the copyright is valid for 70 calendar years beyond the date of death of the last remaining creator (principal director, author or composer) or from the time the work becomes public. For sound recordings and broadcasts, copyright protection lasts for 50 calendar years from the date of an authorized broadcast or performance or after the death of the last remaining author of the work.

In the U.S., generally, for works that have been created after January 1st, 1978, the copyright protection lasts the lifetime of the creator and for an additional 70 years from the creator's date of death. Different copyright duration laws apply for works published before 1978. For more information about works prior to 1978, please visit the U.S. Copyright Office online at https://www.copyright.gov.

Fair Use

While the Copyright Act is aimed at protecting the creator of creative material from unscrupulous people who wish to use the material for commercial purposes, the fair use clause of the Copyright Act does not protect the copyrighted content from being used for non-commercial purposes. The fair use clause describes when the material can be used fairly, without the party who's using it to have to worry about being sued by the creator for copyright infringement.

Obtaining the permission to use copyrighted material from the creator is the best way of using it, and simply citing it does not amount to fair use.

Fair Use may be utilized in a few ways:

- Criticism and Comment: Quoting copyrighted material is considered "fair use" if the purpose for which it is used is for comment, criticism or review. One can quote copyrighted material for making a point in a wholly unrelated situation, with of course, the citation of the source. Even in the case of research and scholarship, the material can be quoted without any infringement issues.

- News Reports: An interesting instance of fair use of copyrighted material is in case of news reporting, where the reporter can quote it. So while this can be considered to be commercial use of the copyrighted material, it still comes under fair use.

- Non Profit Education: Since it is non-profit, and by that we mean that the teacher or the institution has no intention of making commercial benefit from the use of the copyrighted material, the material can be used for non-profit education, where only the student stands to benefit by gaining knowledge.

- Parody: A section in the "fair use" clause of copyrighted material is that the work can be used to mimic or otherwise make fun of the work publicly. Ironically, if one chooses to use the copyrighted work in an act of parody, it still amounts to fair use.

If there is any doubt whether the use is fair or not, ask these two questions:

1). Is the intention to copy the material or create something new with it? If the answer is yes, then it cannot be considered as "fair use."

2). Is the material being copied to compete with the source? If you intend on simply copying and are commercially competing with the source, then it cannot be fair use.

Song titles are not copyrightable

Copyright Symbols & Notice

Songwriter-artists and music publishers should put a copyright notice on all published copies of their content. A circle with a small 'c' in it is the usual mark ©, but the word 'copyright' is also acceptable. Follow the mark with the year and the copyright owner's name. For example: Copyright 2014 by Joe Doe.

> **Note: the year stated on a copyright notice is the year the song was 'first published' and not necessarily when the song was written.**

Unpublished works need no copyright notice, but it is still a good idea to put the mark and use the phrase, for example, "unpublished 2014, John Doe."

The use of the symbol is described in United States copyright law, and, internationally, by the Universal Copyright Convention. The C stands for copyright.

In the United States, the copyright notice consists of three elements:

1. the © symbol, or the word "Copyright" or abbreviation "Copr.";
2. the year of first publication of the copyrighted work;
3. an identification of the owner of the copyright, either by name, abbreviation, or other designation by which it is generally known.

What are these symbols? What do they mean? Most people would think they had an idea of the first one and very few would know of the second. If you are a songwriter-artist, musician, producer, performer of any kind these symbols should mean a lot.

With the rise of technology the once definite line between legal and illegal has become a bit shady. When can one copy a piece of music or sing a song at a local concert?

Many people get these two rights mixed up. Most think that when a singer puts out a song on a CD, it's the singer who would have to be contacted. But we have to remember that most of the singers we listen to didn't write the songs they sing.
So, not only would you have to get permission from the songwriter, you would also have to get it from the performer.

Writing and Producing Music
You see the two symbols above and they represent two types of copyright. Most people only think about or recognize one; but there are two:

The C-Circle is a symbol that represents creation copyright. This copyright basically covers authors, writers and composers. A composer has the rights to the song that he/she composed, and many times there is a music publisher who is assigned to 'sell' or license the song for commercial purposes.

The P-Circle is a symbol that represents a production of a recording copyright. This copyright may not necessarily belong to the performing recording artist(s) to their specific interpretation (production or performance) of the song. The owner of this type of copyright may not be the songwriter-artist either. The recording of the content is usually owned by a record company or a producer. Artists who record should ensure who owns the recording before they agree to being recorded.

Copyright Notice

In the United States, the copyright notice consists of three elements:

1. the © symbol, or the word "Copyright" or with the abbreviation "Copr."

2. the year of first publication of the copyrighted work.

3. an identification of the owner of the copyright, either by name, abbreviation, or other designation by which it is generally known.

Creative Commons Copyright

Story of Nine Inch Nails
When Trent Reznor decided to shake up the music business through a new distribution model, the Nine Inch Nails front-man used CC as an anchor point, releasing the Grammy nominated Ghosts I-IV under a CC.

While Reznor gave the first disc away for free digitally, NIN sold tiered offerings ranging from a $5 download of the full album to a $300 premium box set. Limited to 2,500 units, the box set netted $750,000 in profit for the band. Ghosts went on to become the #1 paid MP3 download on Amazon.com for 2008. NIN's next album, The Slip, was released for free under the same license, fueling a sold-out tour.

NIN fans could have gone to any file sharing network to download the entire CC-BY-NC-SA album legally. Many did, and thousands will continue to do so. So why would fans bother buying files that were identical to the ones on the file sharing networks? One explanation is the convenience and ease of use of NIN and Amazon's MP3 stores. But another is that fans understood that purchasing MP3s would directly support the music and career of a musician/band they liked.

The next time someone tries to convince you that releasing music under CC will cannibalize digital sales, remember that Ghosts I-IV broke that rule, and point them here.

++++++++++++++++++++++++++++

Copyright Tips

- ***When can one sing a song at a local concert?***

    Anyone can sing a song at a concert if the concert promoter has a license to present music. This license is assigned from the owner of a C-Circle Copyright. The license may be obtained directly from the song's music publisher or from a Performing Rights Organization who is representing the song for the songwriter and publisher.

- ***When can one record a song for a release on the Internet as a download?***

    As long as the song has been previously released, anyone may record their version of the song and release it on the Internet. However, the owner of the recording must get permission via a license from the owner of a C-Circle copyright. The license may be obtained directly from the music publisher or via a third-party such as the Harry Fox Agency.

- ***When can one use a recording of a song in a movie or video?***

    Anytime a song, or a recording of a song, is used in a film or video, the producer must obtain two licenses: one from the owner of the C-Circle copyright (synchronization license) and the second from the owner of the P-Circle copyright of the recording of the song (master–use license).

- ***Who can claim a copyright?***

    When an author creates a work, it becomes the author's property. The author, or those who derive rights from the author, is authorized to claim a copyright.

- ***What is copyright infringement?***

    Any unauthorized use of a work that falls under the copyright law is known as copyright infringement. It is an act of violating the exclusive rights of the copyright owner(s).

To Do

Notes:

_____

_____

_____

_____

_____

_____

Artist Development in the Music Business
Chapter 6 – Lessons and Coaching

Six months before Michael Jackson's last appearance of 50 shows at the O2 Arena in London, England. Michael was working 8 hours a day. He was working on dance steps, when to look at what camera and the overall quality of his show. He had choreographers working with him. He had people that knew dance. He had people that worked with him and his backup singers on vocals. There's a reason Michael Jackson was so successful. His years of practice made it look easy.

Music education is the learning of all aspects of music as a separate field altogether. It is also another part of Artist Development. Many artists have had no formal training and many may have received just a hint of experience to music instruction while in elementary school. Sometimes without formal training, artists have a difficult time expressing song ideas and song structures to other musicians, producers and co-writers. Music education consists of theoretical knowledge as well as practical experience. The main components of music education include everything from the history of music, the study of notable musicians, basic notes of music, different types of music, as well as the types of musical instruments, music theory, music composition, reading music and musical notations. That is just the basics. There's also learning how to find the groove, learning how to perform with other musicians, listening, and developing a feel for the music. Just as important, if not more so, is how it all comes together.

In addition to learning music, smart artists know that their success depends on much more than reading and performing notes. Many artists will want coaches for their vocals or their choreography, their business, or for pre-production before they get into the studio. If the artist cannot perform certain functions for their art, as well as handle their business properly, it may cost them both time and money as well as headaches and heartaches. To hire session players is not cheap. To hire a bookkeeper is not cheap. To run a successful business is not cheap. Many individuals don't have the know-how of music or the music business and may try and fail. The more knowledge and education that an artist may have about their art, their craft and their business, the better their chances at becoming successful.

Entertainment business coaches are knowledgeable about working with artists, writers, and other creative professionals. They are sometimes called creativity coaches. As creativity coaches, they have been specially trained to deal with the issues that creative work often brings, such as: where to find ideas, how to decide what idea to work on, how to develop an idea, how to market creative work, how to find an artistic community, how to deal with drama within a band, and so on. If an artist is largely focused on enhancing and optimizing their creative work, then they may want to consider hiring a qualified coach to springboard their entertainment career.

Now perhaps the artist has never taken a formal training on piano. Maybe they never took choir in elementary school. Maybe they've never considered owning and operating their own music business company. But they've had coaching, all their life. When studying the top stars, such as Justin Timberlake, Brittany Spears, Michael Jackson, Diana Ross, and Barbara Streisand; they all have, or have had coaches, even at the top of their game.

So for a musician who is in the garage, waiting for the phone to ring, telling me that he's not going to take any lessons 'cause he already knows what he's doing, I'm thinking… where's that attitude coming from?

It's been said many times that music is the universal language. As with any language, communication is what it takes to make it work. To learn to communicate with music, it takes trial and error and practice as well as feedback from other musicians and collaborators. One of the fastest and most effective ways to learn any new language is with instruction. Yes… lessons and coaching.

Music is a crucial part of life for many people all over the globe. It is probably the best and most creative way in which we can express our feelings. It is used in almost all parts of our life. From a very young age, we have experienced music in one form or another. Whether at church or on the car radio, we have all felt the power and emotion of music. Some people consider music as a hobby, some as a way to pass time, some dabble in it by performing occasionally on weekends while others perform regularly as a serious full-time profession. Those of us who have chosen to learn an instrument have also learned the joy of performing a new song or jamming with some friends. It's easy to learn a few chords and play a few notes but to become technically savvy on an instrument of choice may takes thousands of hours of practice and rehearsal.

> **The importance of music in life cannot be overlooked. Musicians and songwriters add more to society than bankers and lawyers… just ask them.**

A survey conducted by elementary schools and high schools found that students who were taught music, and had a good interest at it academically, found that they performed far better than those who were not into music learning. If students were given music education, they naturally tended to do well in subjects like science and math.

It is also a proven fact that students who had the knowledge of and interest in music tended to plan and organize actions more efficiently in their personal lives. Many schools who have music education have concluded that these students have a good discipline at school as well as home. And it is commonly believed that musicians are peace-loving people, and do not get aggressive as often as non-musicians. Children learning music are found to be fun-loving and are great at interacting with others.

Music education in schools also benefits the students emotionally, as a majority of students are satisfied and happy about learning music or playing a musical instrument. Good music education students also get a sense of personal achievement. A notable benefit of music education is that it is used as a stress reliever, considering a student's study routine. It has been observed that when a student gets bored or stressed out with studies, he or she listens to music or starts playing an instrument. The boredom ceases and the stress is relieved.

++++++++++++++++++++++++++++++

Learning Music Notes Fast

In reality, if a person really wants to study music notes properly and understand them thoroughly, then the first thing they need to do, is get rid of that word 'fast' from their vocabulary. The reason is, basic primary learning of musical notes may well be accomplished within a few minutes time; but if a musician-artist wants to perfect their knowledge, technique and their art, then it requires nothing but consistent practice and long hours of sincere hard work.

++++++++++++++++++++++++++++++

Technique vs. Groove

Can you keep a beat? Great! How long can you keep it going? Can you find the groove of the beat? Okay. How about technique? Within the beat, can you double the time or perform triplets? There is a big difference between technique and groove for an artist. There are plenty of musician-artists who are technically savvy but cannot find the groove. Finding the groove is more important than how fast the instrument is played.

++++++++++++++++++++++++++++++

As careers develop, artists may wish to improve their creative talents by investing in voice or instrument lessons or take master classes from more experienced musicians. In addition, workshops, clinics and seminars should assist artists with helpful tips about the music business.

++++++++++++++++++++++++++++++

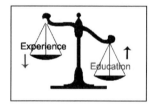

Education and Experience

What education qualifications does an artist need to get a career in the music business?

There's a difference between studying hard and working hard. In the music business, experience is more valuable than education. Now don't get me wrong, I strongly believe in education, but teachers can't teach emotion. They can't teach feel. They can't teach desperation. Experience is only valuable if a person learns from

their mistakes. Artists may not need a formal education, but it sure helps.
Colleges are the first to tell you that you need more than a degree to get hired, however graduates with work experience are more attractive than those without.

++++++++++++++++++++++++++++++

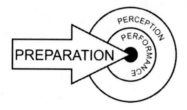

Preparing for Success

It's not the intention of the author to provide information in this book about learning an instrument or technique. Here we will focus on three (3) main instruments because these are used the most in popular music today: voice, guitar, and piano.

++++++++++++++++++++++++++++++

Alexander Technique

One type of instruction is called The Alexander Technique. It actually is a method of vocal training for performers like singers and actors from the 1890s. However, its theme is important for all areas of art and music.

The basis for all successful vocal education is an efficiently and naturally functioning respiratory mechanism. In this technique, breathing and vocalization are intertwined. It is based on the idea that "physical" habits or "mental" habits are all psychophysical in nature. During the entire process, the way we think about our daily activities actually determines how we coordinate ourselves to do those activities, therefore how long-held habits of excessive tension and inefficient coordination affects how we feel and think. The way an artist feels or thinks is reflected in the vocal performance as well as the way they play their instruments.

The difficulties most people experience in learning, is control of performance and in physical functioning which are caused by unconscious habits. These habits have a tendency to interfere with the natural poise and the capacity to learn. As per Alexander, when one stopped interfering with the natural coordination of the body, one would become capable of taking on more complex activities with better self-confidence and presence of mind.

++++++++++++++++++++++++++++++

Songwriters are much better at their craft when they know how to play an instrument. They don't necessarily have to play it well but knowing some basic notes, chords, and keys will help immensely. Most songwriters today, write while playing the piano or the guitar.

++++++++++++++++++++++++++++++

Learning Music Notes for a Guitar

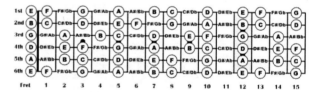

The acoustic guitar has six strings, namely, E, B, G, D, A and E (low). Here is a table which shows the different music notes corresponding to each fret on each guitar string.

++++++++++++++++++++++++++++++

Learning Music Notes for a Piano

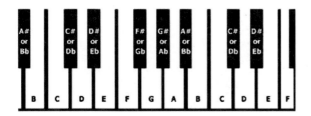

The traditional piano as well as all its modern forms such as the piano keyboard, synthesizer, etc. has a bunch of black and white keys. If you observe the key layout, you will notice that the black keys are grouped in two's and three's with white keys in between them. Starting from the left black key in the group of two, and moving ahead one key at a time till we reach the left black key in the very next group of two, here are the corresponding music notes for each piano key.

Key	Music Note
First Black	C#
First White	D
Second Black	D#
Second White	E
Third White	F
Third Black	F#
Fourth White	G
Fourth Black	G#
Fifth White	A
Fifth Black	A#
Sixth White	B
Seventh White	C
First Black (next octave)	C#

This is just some basic information regarding learning music notes using a guitar and a keyboard. To become a good musician, prepare for many hours of practice. In life, there may be shortcuts; but in music, there aren't any.

++++++++++++++++++++++++++++++++

Apply to Music Schools

In addition to learning how to sing, write a song or play an instrument through private or group instruction, many successful artists continued their music education through music schools and colleges. Music Business related degrees can be hard to come by, and good programs are even fewer and further between. Before you devote your time and money to a music degree program, learn what to look for so you'll come out with the best education possible for a career in the music business.

++++++++++++++++++++++++++++++

Notable Music Schools

Belmont University
Berklee College of Music
Capitol University
Columbia College – Chicago
Curtis Institute of Music
Eastman School of Music
Ferris State University
Full Sail University
Julliard School of Music
Loyola University
Manhattan School of Music
Music Recording School
New England Conservatory of Music
New York University
Oberlin College
Ohio University
San Francisco Conservatory
University of Hertfordshire
University of Miami
University of North Texas
University of Southern California

++++++++++++++++++++++++++++++

If an artist believes that school is not in their best interest, they may want to know: Brad Paisley and Leslie Womack attended Belmont University; Daniel Kellogg attended The Curtis Institute of Music; Herbie Hancock, Max Roach and Harry Connick, Jr. attended the Manhattan School of Music.

++++++++++++++++++++++++++++++

Music Business Conferences

In addition to formal training in music education, as well as how to run a business, many artist participate in music business conferences and seminars. Artists who are preparing their Artist Development Plan, as well as artists well into Product Development, will both benefit from attending and participating in music business conferences.

As music careers develop, artists may be inclined to attend a music conference to enhance their education as well as form new relationships. Music conferences are a great place to network and build relationships. As mentioned earlier, this business is all about networking and relationships. Music conferences are not only educational but a great place to meet other musicians as well as music business professionals.

Whether a person is a veteran musician and has attended music conferences before, or an aspiring artist, here are some steps to take to participate in an entertainment industry conference or seminar:

1. Review the conference's promotional materials to determine what the conference is about. There are some music conferences that specialize in songwriting and there are others that pertain to legal issues or booking performances. Pick a few that might benefit you the most.

2. Define the goals of attending the conference in the first place. Is the plan to gain more knowledge about the music business or perhaps strengthen some other qualities? Is the plan to learn more about something technical or legal? Many attendees are there to network with others and hopefully move up a notch in their field of expertise. Write down the goals and objectives and then refer to them as the schedule is planned. Often, panels or workshops are running concurrently and attendees have to choose between them. Many times an artist attends a music conference with a friend or two (or perhaps the whole band). If so, they can split costs and compare notes and resources later.

3. Determine a budget. Figure out the overall cost including travel, a place to stay, conference fees, food, etc. Start saving up and realize this is a career investment.

4. Book the hotel and configure the travel arrangements. Many times, the conference will have a block of hotel rooms reserved for the conference attendees and often at a reduced rate. It is always better to stay right at the hotel where the conference is taking place. It may cost a few dollars more, but it's well worth it. The extra costs of taxis and/or parking will cover that extra expense anyway. A great deal of the networking and connections that take place are during casual times between seminars or in the hotel lounge. If you need to run back up to

the hotel room to get another promo package or CD to give out, it's right there.

5. Prepare items to take. After an artist is set to go, prepare materials that may be needed for learning as well as for networking. Make a checklist and take a few weeks to gather them. If the materials are in electronic form, e-mail them to yourself for backup. They can be accessed in case the other materials have been distributed more quickly than anticipated or are lost in transit.

**Business Cards
Notebook
Audio Recorder
Camera
Promo Kit**

---

6. Upon arrival at the music conference take advantage of early check-in. Arrive the night before so you are rested. Get to know the hotel logistics and spend a few minutes in the lounge as other attendees will do the same. Don't be shy, say "Hi."

7. A good idea is to get the materials upon registration and go back to the hotel room to plot out a schedule. Leave time for regrouping. Non-stop seminars can be exhilarating and exhausting.

8. Networking is one of the main reasons why artists and music business professionals attend conferences. There are many people to meet and it's not always easy to remember them all after the conference is over. They have the same problem of remembering too. The single most important thing an attendee can do is collect and exchange business cards. Write a note about what was discussed, or if the person suggested a follow-up. It is suggested to refrain from giving packages out without being asked.

Many attendees accost the panelists after their presentation and unfortunately these promo kits get thrown into the garbage: not because the panelist is uninterested but because they don't want to carry it around with them. Instead collect their business card and ask if the material may be sent to them in a week or two. This again separates the artists stuff from the crowd. But use judgment and seize the moment. If an artist has the opportunity to hand deliver a package to the producer or potential collaborator that they never thought they'd be lucky enough to meet, they should take it!

9. Practice remembering names; it will go a long way to be able to address an attendee by their name. Everyone wants to feel valued. There are self-help books about the best ways to remember names. Read up on it before you go.

10. Find out where everyone is hanging out after the sessions. Definitely go to the "mixers" to talk to people in a more casual atmosphere. Sometimes there are informal "jams" late into the night. Participate.

11. In the question-and-answer session that normally follows a presentation, be conscious of not wasting the time of the panelists or other attendees with a personal request. Ask yourself if the question you have would benefit everyone, such as clarifying a point, or if it would be better to get to the speaker later privately. If your question has some merit, make sure you state your name as well as your band name and city. Branding never stops.

12. If available, take advantage of signing up for one-on-one critique sessions. These are invaluable and educational, not to mention making a personal connection with someone in the industry that may be

able to help you. This is where you can pick the brains of the experts. If you ask for a critique, take it graciously; don't challenge the reviewer's advice or become defensive. You want honest feedback of how to become better at what you do.

13. After the conference, if you can afford it, plan to stay one more day if possible so that you can really enjoy the last day and night. This is when you'll really feel connected to the other participants and start making plans to get together for follow-ups or collaborations.

14. Okay, the music conference is over and you are overwhelmed, but in a good way. When you get home, the real work begins:

    a. Follow up with thank you notes to the organizers and panelists of the conference. Your logo should be on the note (more branding).

    b. Organize the business cards and assign action steps to them.

    c. Put the packages together and send them to the people you said that you would (within a week or ten days while it is still fresh). Tailor them now that you know what they are looking for.

    d. Keep a log of your contacts, what you did to follow up, and then call in about two weeks to follow up on the packages you sent out.

    e. Schedule those co-writing or demo sessions you connected with.

    f. Order the publications and/or resources that you discovered.

To Do

Notes:

_____

_____

_____

_____

_____

_____

_____

_____

_____

Artist Development in the Music Business
Chapter 7 – Management

If you're an artist, chances are you've considered getting management. After all, everyone knows the names of talent managers who are just as famous as the artists with whom they work for. And it's definitely true that a band manager can help open some doors for the artist.

In any stage of an artist's music career, one of the biggest things a talent manager can offer is the chance for the artist to focus on their music. After all, they don't call it the music BUSINESS for nothing - there's a lot of hard work that goes into building a music career. For musicians, juggling all of the responsibilities of getting a career off the ground while trying to stay creative can be a struggle. Often, musician-artists find themselves chasing down promoters or pitching to journalists, at the expense of practicing, writing new songs or recording. A manager can take all of that pressure off by handling the business side of things, so that the musician-artist can focus on being creative.

A talent manager, also known as an artist manager or personal manager or band manager, is an individual or company who guides the professional career of artists in the entertainment industry. The responsibility of the talent manager is to oversee the day-to-day business affairs of an artist, and to advise and counsel artist concerning professional matters, long-term plans and personal decisions which may affect the artist's career.

The roles and responsibilities of a talent manager vary slightly within the entertainment industry, as do the commissions to which the manager is entitled. For example, a talent manager's duties in the music business differ from those managers who advise actors, writers, or directors. A talent manager may also be able to help artists find an agent, publicist or record label. In addition, they may be able to help artists decide when to leave their current agent and identify who to select as a new one.

Artist management is a crucial part of the success of any artist. In the early stages, many artists managed their own career. Their "BIG" picture is much smaller than a highly successful artist. At the beginning, an aspiring artist has much more to do, just to catch up. To do so, smart artist-managers jump-start their careers by thoughtful planning. Taking the time to organize will speed things up in the long run. The plans that a talent manager uses are the Artist Development Plan, The Artist Business Plan and the Product Development Plan.

As discussed in the section about expectations, other than self-management, there are other various "hats" of managers. A talent manager is in charge of the business side of being in an artist. Often, artists are great at the creative side of things, but aren't so great at promoting themselves, booking their own gigs, or negotiating deals. In a very general sense, the task of a talent manager is to take care of the day-to-day running of the artist's business, so the artist can focus on the creative side of their career.

A talent manager handles many career issues for bands, singers, musicians and performers. Occasionally, talent managers also assist producers and DJs. A talent manager is hired by a musician or band to help with determining decisions related to career moves, bookings, promotions, business deals, recording contracts, etc. Many times, the role of talent managers is extensive and may include similar duties to that of a press agent, promoter, booking agent, business manager (who are usually certified public accountants), tour managers, and sometimes even a personal assistant.

++++++++++++++++++++++++++++

Self Management

In the early stage of becoming an artist, most people do their own management. They may not realize it but when they are learning a new song, they are adding to their repertoire catalog. When they are trying to think of a stage name, they are working on their image. When they are learning how to book their first show, they are working on Product Development. All of these considerations for an up-and-coming artist is part of self-management.

The author recommends that artists manage their own careers until they can afford to hire one to do the job for them. Many times, parents are involved with artist management and can provide encouragement as well as a ride to the music instructor.

++++++++++++++++++++++++++++

Manager Collaborators

What an artist expects their talent manager to do really depends on where the artist is in their career. For new artists, their manager should be sure their Artist Development Plan is complete so that he or she may concentrate on the Product Development Plan as well as the Artist Business Plan. Soon afterward they should be promoting the artist to record labels, trying to get a recording contract, and generally trying to get things moving from one level to the next. If the artist is further along in their career, their manager should be making sure other artist collaborators are in synch to each of the projects, performances and recordings. Artists should simply be as clear as possible about what they need from a manager, and what they are willing to do.

For an artist to get into an agreement with a talent manager, they should both recognize that they are only collaborating in regards to activities the artist creates as a solo artist or band; not as a babysitter or drama coach. Managers assist the artist with numerous tasks and one of their primary objectives is to ensure that an artist has completed their Artist Development Plan. As that develops, managers then ensure that the artist has a good working team, including an agent, publicist, publisher and record label. After that, a manager must concentrate on the various projects of the artist, such as performances and recordings, and then making sure the team is in synch with each other.

Some artists collaborate with a manager that relates solely to activities as a musical artist and not to represent the artist in any other field of entertainment such as movies or television. This, however, depends on the agreement between an artist and a manager.

++++++++++++++++++++++++++++

Types of Managers

There are managers who solely work with an artist involving product development. In addition, there are talent managers and business managers.

- Talent Managers
- Business Managers
- Tour Managers
- Studio Managers
- Stage Managers

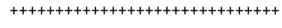

Management Duties

Responsibilities of a talent manager are often divided among many who manage various aspects of a musical career. With an unsigned act, talent managers have to assume multiple roles: booking agent, graphic designer, publicist, promoter, and accountant. As an artist's career develops, responsibilities grow. A talent manager becomes important to managing the many different pieces that make up a career in music. The manager can assist singers, songwriters, and instrumentalists in molding a career, finding music producers, and developing relationships with record companies, publishers, agents, and the music-loving public. The duties of an active talent manager will focus on developing a reputation for the musician-artist(s) and building a fan base. This may include mastering and launching a musical recording, developing and releasing press kits, planning promotional activities, and booking shows. A talent manager will gain access to recording studios, photographers, and promotions. He or she will see that CD labels, posters, and promotional materials appropriately represent the band or artist, and that press kits are released in a timely manner to the appropriate media outlets.

Talent Managers are expected to:

(a) use their best endeavors to promote and develop the artist and provide the artist with regular reports on their work.

(b) ensure all monies due to the artist are promptly collected and remitted directly to the artist by the parties from which they are due.

(c) refer all inquiries connected with the artist's work in areas which the manager is not permitted to, and to act directly for the artist.

(d) maintain their agreement with the artist and not have the right to assign or transfer obligations to any other person or company without prior consent from the artist.

The jobs a manager performs depends very much on the artist and where they are in their careers. For a new artist or band, a manager should:

- Complete the Artist Development Plan for the Artist
- Focus on the goals and objectives of the Artist Business Plan and the Product Development Plan
- Book gigs, if applicable, and invite record label executives and the media to the shows
- Network and talk to people about the artist
- Help book studio time and practice sessions
- Send out demos to labels, radio stations, local print media, and online publications
- Explore funding opportunities for the artist

The talent manager should be the mouthpiece of the band as well as their greatest ally. Managers make sure that everyone involved in the artist's career is working hard to promote the artist's success and doing their job.

For signed artists who are already collaborating with a record label, managers should:

- Advise and counsel the artist of new projects and opportunities
- Negotiate financial deals with the label for expenses like touring and recording
- Oversee other people working for the band, like accountants, agents, and merchandisers.

++++++++++++++++++++++++++++

Building the Team

As an artist-musician, the team they build to help them with their career is as important as the other musicians they perform and record with. From an artist's manager to an artist's booking agent and/or publicist, whom an artist works with, makes a ton of difference to their music career.

One of the most important jobs of a talent manager is to ensure that the artist is collaborating with the best team possible. (More about teams and collaborators in a separate section of the Artist Development Plan).

++++++++++++++++++++++++++++++

Finding Management

Before an artist hires a manager, they should ask them self this question - do I really need a manager right now? A good manager can be a vital part of an artist's music career, but they don't come for free. When artists are just getting started, hiring a manager may not be the best use of their cash. Before an artist goes manager hunting, they should make sure they understand what a manager does and why they may need one.

So, if an artist has decided to stop self-managing, they will need a talent manager to help them out. Now what? Finding a talent manager is not the hard part; it's finding a good manager that can be the real challenge. How does an artist find a good, quality talent manager?

Friend Managers

What does an artist need a manager to do for them? If the artist is looking for someone who can help book shows, send out some demos, set up some digital distribution and so forth - in other words, if the artist is at the stage of establishing them self - then the artist may already know their manager. Perhaps, artists need to look around their circle of friends. Is there someone who knows something about the music biz, who is organized and who loves the artist's music? This kind of manager can be someone who wants to get a start in the music business, and with the artist, can grow their careers together. A friend will gain valuable experience and make good contacts so they can move on to other management work in the future. The artist may also progress more quickly in their music career since they'll be shouldering some of the work with their manager-friend.

The downside here is that this person may need to learn as they go, but the upside is that the artist will have an enthusiastic manager who is eager and inexpensive.

However, believe it or not, an inexperienced manager may be able to bring even more to the table for an artist. Why? Well, they may not have the contacts in place, but they have one thing an artist is unlikely to find with the big dogs – boundless enthusiasm for the music and the time to work it like they are their only client (because, well, they are). Never underestimate the ability of someone combining enthusiasm and hard work to break down perceived music business barriers. In other words, a very motivated wannabe manager who is willing to learn the ropes while working on an artist's project, is going to get those contacts that the bigger name managers have - and they're going to be promoting the artist's music and brand all along the way.

Experience is not the end all, be all, when it comes to choosing a talent manager. Judge potential partners on a case by case basis. If an artist can see that someone is crazy about their music and appears to have the work ethic to match, this situation could be ideal. Tackling the industry together might just end up giving the artist more control over their career, and a friend for life.

Gather Recommendations

A manager has an extraordinary amount of influence over an artist's career, so hiring a manager is not something an artist will want to take lightly. If an artist doesn't know anyone who can serve as manager or if the artist is past the point where they can work with a manager-friend who learns with them, then they should ask around for referrals of good quality talent managers. They should ask fellow musicians and do some research to see who manages other acts. Perhaps, they should ask promoters and bookers whom they might recommend. If the artist is at the point where they need a professional manager, then they are at the point where they know people who can make these recommendations.

Approach the Short List

Getting a manager interested in working with an artist is much like approaching a record label, agent or promoter. Artists should be ready to provide the management prospects a few necessities:

- Music samples - not the whole catalog, just a few of the artist's best songs that show off their sound and their versatility. Artists can treat this sample much like they would a demo recording that they might send to a record label.

- Biography – who is the artist? What is the artist? Who are the artist's fans? Where is the artist located? What kind of music does the artist play?

- Press clippings, if any.

An artist's goal is provide their prospective talent manager with a good idea about the kind of music they make and how far along the artist has come in their career.

Follow Up

Quality managers get inundated with pitches from musicians, so artists shouldn't go calling them every hour or the day after they send in their info. Artists should give them a week or two, and if the artist hasn't heard anything then they should follow up. Ask if they have received the package and if they need any more info. It is okay to follow up at respectable intervals until an answer is received (or the impression that the perspective manager is not going to give an answer, which happens sometimes.) Just try not to come on too strong and be sure to respect the fact this person is probably busy. Patience is an artist's friend at this stage in the procedure.

Meet and Discuss
When an artist finds a person who is interested in working with them, their next step is to have a meeting with the talent manager-to-be to discuss the artist's goals. The manager should be able to discuss ways to help the artist(s) reach their goals. Artists also need to know the details of the financial arrangement that the manager is seeking.

In addition to being sure that this talent manager is on the same page with the artist in terms of direction, the artist needs to be sure that there is some kind of chemistry between them and their to-be manager. Artists may be spend a lot of time with their manager, and they need to be able to have open and honest communication.

Management Contracts

For the artist's sake and for the sake of the manager, artists should never enter into any sort of management deal without a contract. Any deal between artists and managers should be negotiated up front and revisited when significant events occur that could drastically increase or decrease the artist's income.

Even if an artist is working with a friend as their manager and there is no money involved for now, they still should write up an agreement. It doesn't have to be fancy or even supervised by a lawyer. They should both jot down what is expected of both manager and artist, and what the percentage of income for the manager will be, if any. Their agreement should also describe what happens if the artist and manager decide to part ways. Many new artists don't want to make their friends sign contracts. Forget that! When an artist is entering into a business relationship with a friend, a contract keeps their friendship safe. Everyone knows what's expected of them.

If the artist is working with a manager with more experience and the manager issues the artist a complex contract, the artist should get legal advice from a qualified entertainment attorney. Artist should never, ever, sign a contract they don't understand, and should never,

ever work with a manager without a contract.

(More about legal issues in a separate section of the Artist Development Plan)

A good talent manager can be instrumental in the success of any artist. Any contract an artist signs for any part of their career should be carefully considered, but perhaps none more so than the talent manager contract. Before an artist signs, they should brush up on their management contract basics so they can be sure they are making the right decision. Keep in mind that the information included here is general in nature and any potential deal may be different.

++++++++++++++++++++++++++++++

The Term
The term of a manager's agreement with an artist may be for a set amount of time, with the provision that the artist is entitled to terminate the term in the event that the manager does not complete the duties specified in their agreement such as, procuring the signature of a publishing or recording agreement by such date. Many times, after the term has expired, the now ex-manager may still be entitled to commissions upon the reason that they did the work prior to the end of the Agreement. Usually this is a step-down type structure where the ex-manager might receive 7.5% the year after termination and may be 5% the second year but nothing after that.

The artist or band should never agree to circumstances that cannot be terminated or negotiated within a short period of time.

(See more about the terms of legal agreements in the legal section of the Artist Development Plan).

++++++++++++++++++++++++++++++

The Territory
In addition to the term of the agreement with an artist, the talent manager may also define the territory where they represent the artist. The territory governed by their agreement may mean the United States, the World, or whichever country they mutually agree.

++++++++++++++++++++++++++++++

Exclusivity
Many talent managers represent and manage other artists. If this is the case, then many times the expenses of the manager must be related solely to activities of the artist and not as manager of the other artists. Some artists require that managers not manage other artists without prior knowledge and/or consent. Artists want to insure that the manager's activities with other artists do not adversely affect the manager's obligations to them.

Compensation

Artist managers are very handy to have around, but up-and-coming artists often forget one thing in their hunt for a manager - once they get one to work with them, the manager will want to be paid. Negotiating how an artist manager will be paid is VERY important. After all, not only is the manager going to help the artist start making money, but they're also going to be splitting the artist's income with them. Artists need to know exactly how and when their manager expects to be compensated for their work.

Usually during the term of the agreement between the artist and the manager, the artist is responsible to reimburse any expenses directly relating to the manager's activities, with the exception of office expenses i.e., telephone, staff etc., which is the responsibility of the manager. Many times any management or project expenses in excess of a pre-determined amount for any single item must be approved by the artist prior to it being incurred.

A talent manager should not be out of pocket for business expenses for promoting the artist, but artists need to reach an agreement on how expenses will be paid or repaid. Artists don't have to pay for their manager's phone costs or office costs, in most instances. However, artists do have to pay for business trips the manager makes on their behalf and reasonable costs like taking a record label representative out for cocktails. The best way to handle expenses is to pay them at set times, i.e. once a month. The manager should provide the artist with receipts for expenses.

It is recommended that the artist start off by negotiating a tentative compensation agreement with a talent manager that can be renegotiated after three or four months. The rate of pay is generally based on commissions of 20 percent of the net or 10 percent of the gross income. This amount obviously depends on the level of development the band or artist is at in their career and the experience, networks and resources of the manager The less developed the artist and more experienced the manager, the higher the commission that the artists pays the manager.

There are some things a manager should NOT get a commission. This includes songwriting royalties. Artists should be aware that there are many different kinds of management deals, and with the changing face of the music business, comes a change in management deals. Essentially, the way musicians make their money is in flux, and since the income of the musicians is directly tied to the income of the managers, managers try to make sure they are able to tap into any and all sources of money.

Managers typically charge for services by charging a commission of the gross income received by the artist. Many artists prefer to pay any commissions based on net income received by the artist. Everything is negotiable.

Commissions are usually payable based on income received by the artist. The manager may only be entitled to commissions of income derived from performances, recordings and compositions made in whole during the term of their agreement. Managers are responsible for paying their own income tax, insurance, and business tax.

Although sometimes a manager may get a wage (it has been done), the vast majority of management deals are based on commission. This means that a talent manager earns a percentage cut of an artist's income. What income they can charge a commission for is up to debate - and we'll get to that in a minute - but first, consider the amount of the percentage. The normal amount of commission is around 10%-15%, though some artist reps want 20%, particularly in the case of a new artist that is going to require a lot of upfront work before any money is earned. Often, this percentage is of the artist's GROSS income - which means that even if an artist loses money on a deal, the manager is still paid. However, some managers get a percentage of the NET, which means if an artist loses money on a show, the manager doesn't get paid for that project. Sometimes, managers get a gross percentage of some income and net percentage of others. It all depends on the contract between the artist and the manager. Other times, the percentage changes as certain earning thresholds are met. For instance, if a new artist agrees to 20% when they hire a manager, once they make a certain amount of money, the manager may agree to scale it back to 15%. Everything is negotiable.

Just as there are many ways the percentage can be calculated and applied, there are a number of ways to divide the streams of income. Some talent managers get a percentage of all income. Other deals are structured so that management gets a lesser percentage - or sometimes no percentage at all - on certain kinds of income, such as songwriting income. This may be true if the manager represents the artist as a recording artist. There are no hard and fast rules here - it's simply a matter of negotiating an arrangement that is acceptable to everyone. Do keep in mind that managers will want to maximize their earning potential by tapping into as much income as possible, and they should be compensated for the work that they do. Going back to the songwriting example - if the manager represents an artist as a songwriter and as a recording artist, then the manager should be paid as such.

Even when management gets a cut of all of an artist's income, there are certain things they shouldn't get a percentage of. For example, a manager should not be paid for things such as monies paid to the artist by a record label to pay for some other activity such as recording, producers, touring, or opening acts. This isn't income to an artist, but an expense. It all has to be paid back to the record label before an artist receives any recording royalty income. Once the artist starts receiving income from the record label, should they then pay their manager?

There are lots of different types of management agreements. The only rule is that both artist and manager need to come to terms BEFORE the work begins, so there isn't any confusion. By the way, many managers work on a handshake deal rather than a written contract. However, if that sound scary, there's nothing wrong with writing up at least an informal agreement so that everyone knows where they stand.

As previously mentioned, a standard management fee is usually around 10% - 20% of an artist's earnings but it's not unheard of for a manager to receive 50% commission of an artist's income, such as the relationship between Elvis Presley and his manager Colonel Tom Parker. An artist's manager takes a cut of proceeds from album sales, any label advances, and from the earnings from deals they have negotiated. Some managers do not get paid from merchandise sales, songwriting royalties, or from deals they have not negotiated (unless there is a prior agreement saying otherwise). Keep in mind that if an artist is a small band who hasn't started making an income yet, 10% to 20% of nothing is still nothing. Artists may want to keep this earning potential in mind when they are negotiating the details of the collaborator's job expectations.

++++++++++++++++++++++++++++++

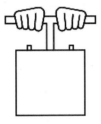

Words of Caution
Talent manager contracts can be very specific to the artist career circumstances, and so the advice above is a guide and does not represent hard and fast rules. The best thing an artist can do is be as clear and specific as possible, anticipating every bump in the road. If a small band has a manager who is going to grow with them, they should be sure to re-examine their agreement often to make sure it is still fair to everyone. If an artist already has a record deal in place and has a new manager who is about to come on board, the artist should seek legal advice to make sure their interests are protected.

Of course, in addition to being someone who can take care of some of an artist's business related responsibilities, a good talent manager is one who has some contacts that can help the artist move up their career ladder - contacts at labels, with promoters and agents, with the press, and so on. This is where it gets tricky in weighing up how important a manager could be for the artist. Finding a manager who meets both of these criteria takes one thing that is often in short supply for up and coming artists: money.

The bottom line is this: if the artist is just getting started in the music business, and they are still at the stage where they're starting to play shows, looking for a label, and so on, they shouldn't divert money from doing things like recording or promoting their music to hire a big money manager. An artist's best options for management are these:

• Work with a friend who is a fan of the music who is willing to help manage some of the business side of an artist's career.

• The second option for trying to find a good talent manager is by trying to find a more connected manager who is a big enough fan of the music to be willing to work for free at first, or for at least a very reduced rate. This type of arrangement is rare, but like lawyers and others, many people who are well placed in the music business might be willing to work pro bono if they really believe in the artist. That's another reason why an artist needs to be as much prepared as possible. The more an artist has completed their Artist Development Plan, the easier it will be for them to attract a bigger manager. Artists should be careful that they don't trade away their future to get this manager now. In other words, artists shouldn't sign away huge percentages of their potential future earnings to convince someone to help them out now.

Of course, these kinds of talent managers don't have to be mutually exclusive. An artist may have a friend on board helping them with detail work at the same time that the artist is looking for a bigger and more experienced talent manager. Artists should be clear about their intentions with friends, or if the artist is an established artist who is looking for new management.

For most musicians, this tricky question about artist representation rears its head at a time when A-list music management types aren't exactly blowing up their phone, which creates a quandary - should an artist wait it out for a big name manager to come their way? Should they devote more of their music making time to finding such a person, or should they give their wildly enthusiastic and overwhelmingly inexperienced friend the keys to the empire?

There's no doubt about it - experience counts in the music business, and music management is no exception. It's not so much the actual experience but it is the list of contacts that comes with experience that really makes an established talent manager important.

++++++++++++++++++++++++++++++

Experience

How Much Experience Does a Talent Manager Need?

Answer:
New musicians tend to take one of two views on artist management as they are launching their careers: either "I must get a manager now," or "no one will take me seriously," or "I've heard so many horror stories about band managers that I will never, ever get one and will only manage myself."

If an artist is trying to get a major label deal, yes, a manager (or at least an attorney) will be an important part of the process, but an artist won't attract a manager before actual work is involved.

++++++++++++++++++++++++++++++

Myths of Artist Management

The relationship between a talent manager and an artist is just about the most important (business) relationship either party will ever have. Misconceptions swirl around this oh-so critical connection. However, if an artist is thinking of hiring a talent manager or breaking into the world of band management them self, cross these music business myths off the list:

1. <u>No One Will Take the Artist Seriously If They Don't Have a Manager</u>
If an artist is a musician, managers are important because they free the artist to work on, well, music - and that is their real role in all of this. It is also true that

when an artist gets to a certain level, labels, promoters, agents, publicists and so on will prefer to deal with a manager instead of the artist. Sometimes these people need to say things about a musician's work that a musician might not like to hear - so they prefer to the let the manager do the dirty work for them.

However, in the early stages of an artist's career especially, artists shouldn't feel like they need to get a manager before they get enough songs to fill a set at a show or before they even have their first rehearsal. In fact, people within the industry will take an artist less seriously if they have one of those "managers" - i.e., a friend who calls themselves a manager and does absolutely no managerial work - than if the artist goes in representing them self.

2. Only A Connected Manager Will Do
There's a big difference between an artist's friend who decides they are a manager so they have an excuse to get a seat in the artist's van while they're on tour and the friend who decides they are a manager because they're so excited about the artist's music they think everyone should hear it - and they decide to make that happen. An enthusiastic, though inexperienced, manager with a solid work ethic can do big things for an artist, even if they have to fight every step of the way to establish contacts and get people to pay attention to them.

More established managers bring more connections, and they can often get things done more quickly. But they're hard to attract early in an artist's career, and an artist is unlikely to be their first priority. If an artist has a chance to get some enthusiastic hands on decks when they need some help, they should go for it.

3. Managers Tells The Artist What To Do
Artist-manager relationships should be collaborations, not dictatorships. When an artist is selecting a manager, it is critical to make sure that they share the same vision and have the same expectation about the music career that the artist is trying to build. If an artist's manager is trying to mold the artist into something they're not and pursuing opportunities that the artist is not sure they actually want, then they may have the wrong manager working with them.

Established managers surely do bring a world of experience to the table and definitely have valuable advice to give about how things work in the music business. However, that doesn't mean an artist has to sacrifice their sound and their ideas about their music to fit into some supposed framework. The right manager for an artist will help the artist maximize the things that they're doing to increase their chances of music business success. Smart managers know to not try to make the artist into a whole different act so they can get a record deal. Remember, a manager is a partner, not a boss.

4. Artists Don't Need to Communicate
The flipside of the above is that when an artist has a manager, they do need to include them in decisions. No manager likes to find out about a show, new song, interview or some other big thing through another party. It makes them look bad, and it makes them feel like they're being cut out of the artist's career. If an artist is negotiating for payment for something, the manager

should also be involved - after all, they get a percentage of the money their artist makes with an artist's music as payment for their work, so a manager should know about any little side deals an artist is trying to work (which can often be a bad idea, anyway).

Artists don't so much need their manager's permission to do music related projects - though they likely do need their OK to sign certain deals - but it's more of a respect thing. Again, remember, this is the artist's partner. Talent managers need to be in the loop, or they can't be effective.

++++++++++++++++++++++++++++

Tips about Talent Managers

1. If possible, when you get management recommendations from people, get them to make an introduction for you. Things will be a lot easier if you don't have to cold call people.

2. It is important to have the same sort of music business philosophy as your manager. If your manager is more experienced in the business than you, then you will be able to learn a lot from them. However, if, for instance, you're seeking chart music stardom and they're committed to the indie music scene, or vice versa, then the relationship is not going to work for either of you.

3. Remember that you are choosing a manager while they are choosing you. You don't have to sign with the first manager that comes along if you're not sure that it will work. A manager is almost like a member of your band. The best management relationships are valid on the professional AND personal level.

4. Before you approach managers, have a good idea of what you need from them. If you're trying to land a deal, then a manager who has lots of contacts at labels is a good choice for you. If you have a deal on the table and need someone to walk you through negotiations, then a talent manager with that sort of experience should be high on your list. Managers all have different styles, and some are more hands-on than others. Before you try to hire someone, make sure you have an idea of the job description.

5. When you're putting together information for potential managers, don't try to create a package that you think gives the "right" answers. Yes, you do want to put your best foot forward. However, if, for instance, you're a folk band and you're approaching a hip hop manager, don't go out and record some verses for your demo. You need a manager who "gets" what you're doing, and the only way to find someone like that is to give them an honest representation of your work. You'll find the right manager. Spinning things to try to match yourself to a particular manager is never a good call.

Artist Development in the Music Business
Chapter 8 – Ego, Attitude, Passion & Grit

Many aspiring artists fail because of ego and attitude, as well as lack of passion and grit. You wouldn't believe how many artists fail because of this.

Their failures are often caused by a negative attitude or uncontrollable ego. And yes, there are stories of artists becoming more successful because of their attitude or ego. But on the whole, success is fleeting when ego kicks in. And when ego and attitude gets mixed up, the artist fails. Ego can be dangerous. The importance of Ego, Attitude, Passion & Grit must not be overlooked as another part of Artist Development.

Ego
1. "Ego" is a Latin and Greek word meaning "I," often used in English to mean the "self" or "identity."
2. the "I" or "self" of any person; a thinking, feeling, and conscious being, able to distinguish itself from other selves.
3. egotism; self-importance
4. self-esteem or self-image

Ego separates us from each other. It's a conscious level of thinking which dictates everything in our life. Many times ego stops an artist from getting things done and getting people to work with them.

Ego is good for an artist in only one way: the artist must believe in them self. Ego is bad for an artist if it's too big to fit into the coffee shop; much less, a major world tour.

Self-Fulfillment

If you have happiness, excitement, true meaning in life, you create that.

If you feel misery, defeat, or that you are always a victim, then that's what you get.

Great entrepreneurs succeed because they're willing to do every job, ask every dumb question, and, above all, admit they can't do it alone.

Talent is God-given, be humble.
Fame is man-given, be thankful.
Conceit is self-given, be careful.
– John Wooden.

When an artist is successful, who gets the credit? When the chips are down, who's to blame? If an artist doesn't recognize people who shaped them as a young child, throughout their education, and at every step in their artistic and musical career, then their ego is out of check.

> **Conceit is a strange disease. It makes everyone sick except the person who's got it. – Harvey Mackay**

Generally, when we say someone has "a big ego" we really mean their ego is out of control, and gets in the way. They talk down to people, treat others as inferior, and their sense of self makes them unpleasant to work with. We may actually have bigger egos than they do, but we manage them better. Someone with "a big ego" is likely someone who, for whatever reason, is not self-aware enough to realize their lack of respect for others, or worse, realizes it but doesn't care

The goal should be to have a high opinion of one-self, and a high opinion of others at the same time. Namaste. Some might define this as a healthy psychology. We all know what we do well and are confident in our ability. It's all tied to the ego. Don't allow that sense of self to violate someone else's sense of self. We all know that if we are to grow, we have to do things we're not confident in doing. We have to put ourselves in situations where we're forced to say "I don't know" or "I'm afraid" and go to places an ego dominated mind would never have the courage to go. Being humble is healthy and creates opportunities that may never be found if an artist insists on only doing things they're confident in doing.

If happiness and fulfillment is the true goal, a big ego alone doesn't seem to be the way to get it.

Ozzy Osbourne has warned young hopeful musicians to embrace the first years of their success – before ego and business concerns get in the way.

The Black Sabbath frontman hopes rising stars can learn from his own experience, saying the years during which he recorded his first albums were the happiest of his career. "The early part of the success is so much fun. "The first two Sabbath albums were great for us because it was so new. Then all of a sudden it becomes deadly serious, because people start telling you what you should and shouldn't do."

With that added pressure of success came Ozzy's infamous reliance on drugs – leading to his dismissal from the band he'd helped to form. He remembers: "What happened with me and Black Sabbath was that, in the beginning we all had a purpose. But as it went along, that inevitable thing stepped in called ego."

> **Successful Artists Attacked by Ego**
>
> 50 Cent
> Axl Rose
> Don Henley
> Garth Brooks
> Gene Simmons
> James Brown
> Johnny Rotten
> Joni Mitchell
> Kanye West
> Lil Wayne
> Little Richard
> Michael Jackson
> Paul McCartney
> Pete Townshend
> Robert Plant

Overcoming Ego for Musicians

We will use the word "ego" to refer to that part of the consciousness that tells an artist that they are worth only as much as they succeed or possess. Additionally, their ego may make them feel that if they don't own the most current trends in musical instruments or electronic gadgets, they are somehow lesser, or the belief that they are defined by what other people think of them. In short; ego is the part of a person that makes them feel continually incomplete. Of course, the shedding of the ego (especially for musicians) is quite possibly one of the most difficult tasks that they may complete.

Here are a few techniques for getting rid of this pesky, mental, egotistic nuisance.

First of all, artists should stop comparing them self with other musicians (and this includes their peers). No more feeling incompetent or old before their time. Yes, the world is taken with "prodigies," they are impressive, and because they are so rare, they make for great press. But understand this: if an artist is able to perform a piece of music in a truly masterful way at age 25 or at age 50, people will take note. To be perfectly blunt: it is the sound that matters, not the vessel from which the sound comes. Therefore (and this is going to sound strange to those of us living in the western world) don't rush, there is time to be great.

Second, artists should support their fellow musicians. Many musicians, especially as teenagers, sit in recitals comparing themselves with fellow singers/pianists hoping that they sing or perform poorly. What they should be doing is to appreciate them and cheer them on. In the long run this would have opened their mind up to what they were doing right – and provided them with an opportunity to learn, and vice-versa. In short, an artist should do their best to be likeable. There is nothing wrong with having allies especially if an artist can keep these allies as they grow older. Their chances of success will be much greater.

> "Keep your thoughts positive because your thoughts become your words.
>
> Keep your words positive because your words become your behavior.
>
> Keep your behavior positive because your behavior becomes your habits.
>
> Keep your habits positive because your habits become your values.
>
> Keep your values positive because your values become your destiny."
>
> - Mahatma Gandhi

Third, artists should not judge themselves while they are performing. This includes performing for their instructor, in class in front of their classmates, or on a stage in front of fans and/or music business professionals. Artists should save all their evaluations until they are finished. Sometimes self-judgment seems like an involuntary occurrence, but the truth is, artists have control over it. During their performance, for better or worse, they should just power through – improvise if they forget or lose their place, sing "la" instead of words. Do whatever they have to do to finish the performance with confidence and performer-artists shouldn't let the audience ever see that they were shaken. Remember, the audience (for the most part) tends to take away the good things much more than the bad. If an artist fumbles on a note, or forget a word, but the rest of the performance is brilliant, then one error won't even be a distant memory. And if an artist has a serious problem during their performance; but they keep their cool and finish un-fazed; chances are, the audience will see them as a pro who just had a bad night.

Finally, remember that keeping the ego in check is much more than just maintaining a level head. It is about the artist knowing that they are complete without praise, without fame and without doubt. Having no ego isn't the defeat of self-esteem. It is the affirmation of it combined with the knowledge that they still have everything to learn. Ego is also there to remind artists that their technical abilities as a musician or songwriter come with the great price of monumental amounts of time spent practicing and rehearsing. Artists should not let their egos grow into areas that could be taken up by knowledge.

Ego can tear a band apart.

> **We make and design whatever we want in our lives. We have the ability to create happiness and we have the ability to create unhappiness.**

++++++++++++++++++++++++++++

Attitude

1. manner, disposition, feeling, position, etc., with regard to a person or thing; tendency or orientation, especially of the mind: a negative attitude; group attitudes.
2. the way a person views something or tends to behave towards it, often in an evaluative way
3. a theatrical pose created for effect (i.e.: the phrase "strike an attitude")
4. a position of the body indicating mood or emotion

Attitude for an artist is the approach, belief, mindset, mood, notion, opinion, perspective, philosophy, point of view and position.

Attitude is defined by bias, character, demeanor, posture, prejudice, reaction, sensibility, sentiment, stance, stand, temperament, view, disposition and inclination.

All of us have it, and all of us use it, but most of us don't know what it is. It is very clearly defined as the mental state of a human being to judge his or her likes or dislikes related to a situation, event, or a simple item around them.

Types of Attitudes

As humans, we tend to have different attitudes that may or may not change with time. An attitude is nothing but a point of view one holds for other people, situations, events, objects, places, phenomena, or even one self. It is essentially like an evaluative statement that is either positive or negative depending on the degree of like or dislike for the matter in question. An attitude reflects how one thinks, feels and behaves in a given situation. There are different types of attitudes and all are subject to change during the course of life.

There are two (2) sides of any particular attitude in psychology; the positive and the negative. This also defines the personality of that individual.

> **Positive Attitudes**
> **Negative Attitudes**

There are three (3) main components of the term attitude, which include an affective component, behavioral component and a cognitive component.

- **Affective Attitude**:
  The affective one refers to the emotional response that a person has to a particular situation which describes his/her attitude. Example: a musician, on stage, obviously having a bad day.

- **Behavioral Attitude**:
  The behavioral component is known to be the verbal response or the behavioral pattern in which the individual responds to a situation. To continue the example above: the musician-artist, who is having a bad day, expresses visual dissatisfaction with their performance.

- **Cognitive Attitude**:
  The cognitive component of an attitude is the judgment or perception of a situation that may be derived from it. To further the above example: As soon as the musician-artists recognize their error, they make a judgment call about themselves.

When these three (3) components come together, an attitude towards the "place, situation or event" is resulted.

Attitude Formation
When we talk about self improvement, there are many aspects of our personality which are considered. These aspects may be positive as well as negative, the results of these two sides of our mental development on our behavioral pattern and the way we deal with daily life. An individual's personality is defined as, any set of qualities found in him/her, which are very distinct for only that particular person.

However, attitude is a part of one's personality, and can't be used as a synonym for it. Unlike a person's personality, attitudes are temporary and can change according to experience. Many times a person's attitude is consistent with respect to their beliefs and values.

> **True nobility is not being better than anyone else... it's being better than you used to be.**

Attitudes of Music
A rebellious attitude is a commonly found negative type of attitude. People who have this attitude towards objects, are often in disagreement with most situations, people and other things around them. In a rebellious attitude, a person only thinks defensively towards most things, and reacts in very aggressive pattern like, bold actions, loud voices, high energy breakouts, etc. These can be harmful for people around him, as well as himself. Anger,

depression, loneliness, despair, disagreement, defensiveness, are a few more repercussions of this negative attitude.

In the broader sense of the word, there are only three attitudes, a positive attitude, a negative attitude, and a neutral attitude.

These were some of the attitudes that you may confuse with personality traits as there is a very thin line between the two.

Personality traits are more rigid and permanent, whereas, attitudes may change with different situations and experiences in life. Personality traits are what humans are endowed with whereas attitudes are learned and acquired. In simple words, attitudes are judgments or conclusions that we draw about certain phenomena in life including our own self.

Examples of Attitudes

Essentially, what you think, what you do, and what you feel is what forms your attitude. For example, if a woman says, "I like performing music," it represents positive thinking towards performing music. This attitude is formed because she believes that she likes performing music, or feels happy while playing music. Consider another example; when someone says, "I hate working on this project" it represents a negative attitude of that person towards the project. He either thinks so, or he believes that this work is boring. In both the cases, there could be numerous reasons for developing those attitudes. In the first case, the woman may think that performing music is good for health or it is 'cool' to perform, or she might be having fun while playing music. In short, the reasons could be numerous for her to like playing music or believe that she likes playing music. In a similar manner, take the second case; a man may hate working on preparing for a performance project due to numerous reasons that make him feel negative.

Attitudes take time to develop by various means. Sometimes, they are based on experiences and knowledge and sometimes they are acquired from other people. They are sometimes based on what is true or what we think is true. Humans manifest their attitudes through their behavior and actions. For example, in the first case, the woman may enroll in music classes. In the second case, the man may stop rehearsing his upcoming performance and leave the project.

Basically, there are three (3) components of attitude: emotional, cognitive, and behavioral that relate to feelings, information or thought process, and the course of action, respectively. All these things result in different people having different attitudes that may or may not change.

---

3 Components of Attitude

Emotional
Cognitive
Behavioral

It is possible for human beings to change or unlearn their attitudes as attitudes are learned. One needs to change the way he or she thinks, behaves, and feels in order to change the attitude. However, it is very challenging to change our emotions and feelings as they constitute a major part of our attitude and hence changing attitude is a difficult task. Though vague, feelings are powerful and difficult to control and hence, to change an attitude, a person must start with the other two components: thinking and behavior, as they are easy to control. By changing these components, it is possible to change different types of attitudes carried by different people.

> **Attitude is a little thing that makes a big difference**
>
> **- Winston Churchill**

The outcome of virtually every task in front of us is greatly impacted by our attitude about it. If we think positive thoughts, we attract positive energies and positive results are manifested.

Even though we devote so much time and energy into figuring out what to do to change our lives, what we should really pay attention to is who we decide to be each day, not what we decide to do.

The future of an artist is determined by the actions they partake in to create it. Artists engage in these activities not just for themselves, but for other people as well.

This is when the importance of attitude comes into play.

The worst situations in anyone's life are no match for the ability to capitalize on any turn of events. Artists must believe that what they want is worth the effort and then they will make it happen.

Attitudes

- Acceptance
- Authority
- Cautious
- Cheerful
- Condescending
- Confidence
- Considerate
- Cooperative
- Courteous
- Decisive
- Determined
- Faithful
- Flexible
- Frankness
- Generous
- Gratitude
- Happiness
- Hardworking
- Helping
- Honest
- Hostile
- Humble
- Independent
- Inferiority
- Jealous
- Kind
- Loving
- Modest
- Optimism
- Persistent
- Pessimism
- Realistic
- Reliable
- Respectful
- Responsible
- Sarcasm
- Seriousness
- Sincere
- Sincerity
- Suspicious
- Sympathetic
- Thoughtful
- Tolerant
- Trusting

Negative minded artists should also stop believing that the people in this world are there to get them. Artists should treat them good, and they'll get it right back in return. Some call it Quid Pro Quo and some call it Karma.

It's an artist's attitude that determines how they execute the actions that they contemplate each day. Their attitude determines whether they keep trying or they quit. A bad attitude is merely a mental message telling the artist that they need to change something, especially if they want the world to respond to their commands.

It goes in accordance with the law of attraction. If a person perceives the world as a hateful place, they will only receive hate in return. If they look for the most joyous aspects of life, however, they will discover them in excess more and more.

A person's attitude represents how they respond to the external world. It's the only world that matters, so artists should learn to view it in a positive and enlightening way.

Artists may be surprised to find out how much their world changes when they change the way they react to what's in front of them in every passing moment.

++++++++++++++++++++++++++++++

Positive Attitudes

Research shows that positivity can make a real difference to artist's success and well-being. In one study, researchers found that happy individuals are more successful in many areas of their lives, especially in their careers, compared with individuals who struggle with happiness and positive thinking. Other studies show how much of an impact positivity has on people's ability to think creatively, grow their careers, cope with challenges, and work with other people. Positivity is an essential ingredient for any successful artist.

How many bands that you know have broken up because someone's ego went way out of whack? Success will follow those who want to succeed. I truly believe this. You have to know, in your heart, that you are going to be sitting in that chair at the Grammy Awards. Artists have to feel it. They have to want it. They have to put them self mentally in that seat. And to go a step further, they have to mentally prepare of accepting that award by standing on that stage and saying "thank you." Success starts right there. You have to want it. Determine the goals. Focus on the ways and the means. Stay positive. Strive to improve. Learn from mistakes. But most importantly, keep your integrity. And that's means, integrity with the music, integrity with the song, the integrity of the production and the integrity of the quality of what an artist releases as their product or service.

When an individual has a positive attitude, it helps them cope with daily affairs of life, and help them make right and strong decisions. There are many results of a positive attitude and they are; creative thinking, positive thinking, motivational drive to achieve goals, success, constructive mind set, seeking opportunities, easy thought process of solving problems, and a stress free life.

It's up to each individual person to choose an attitude towards life.

Positive thinking brings inner peace, success, improved relationships, better health, happiness and satisfaction. It also helps the daily affairs of life move more smoothly. It also makes life look bright and promising.

Positive thinking is contagious. People around a person with a positive attitude will pick up on mental moods and will be affected accordingly. If a person thinks about happiness, good health and success, they will cause people to like them and a desire to help them because they enjoy the vibrations that a positive mind emits.

In order to make positive thinking yield results, an artist needs to develop a positive attitude toward life, expect a successful outcome of whatever they do, but also take any necessary actions to ensure their success. Artists need to think positive but also to take action on their positive vibration.

Effective positive thinking that brings results is much more than just repeating a few positive words, or telling oneself that everything is going to be all right. It has to be a predominant mental attitude. It is not enough to think positively for a few moments, and then letting fears and lack of belief enter back into the mind. Some effort and inner work are necessary.

Action Steps Toward Positive Thinking

Here are a few action steps and tips to help an artist develop the power of positive thinking:

- Always use only positive words while thinking and while talking. Use words such as, 'I can,' 'I am able,' 'it is possible,' 'it can be done,' etc.

- Artist should allow into their awareness only feelings of happiness, strength and success.

- They need to try to disregard and ignore negative thoughts. Refuse to think such thoughts, and substitute them with constructive happy thoughts.

- Before starting with any plan or action, visualize clearly in your mind its successful outcome. If you visualize with concentration and faith, you will be amazed at the results.

- Associate yourself with people who think positively.

- Always sit and walk with your back straight. This will strengthen your confidence and inner strength.

- Walk, swim or engage in some other physical activity. This helps to develop a more positive attitude.

- Think positive and expect only favorable results and situations, even if your current circumstances are not as you wish them to be. In time, your mental attitude will affect your life and circumstances and change them accordingly.

- When you expect success and say "I can," you fill yourself with confidence and joy.

- Fill your mind with light, hope and feelings of strength, and soon your life will reflect these qualities.

- Positive thinking is a practice. To get the full benefits of positive thinking you need to have a positive mental attitude and positive mindset.

- When you have a positive thinking mindset, you automatically have positive thoughts and you continually create positive situations.

- This process happens automatically because your subconscious mind is constantly responding to your positive thoughts. It creates your life based on your thoughts. If those thoughts are positive, then you'll have positive outcomes in life. This leads to more success.

- Positive thinking is a mental attitude that fills the mind with positive thoughts, words and images that allow you to grow, and enjoy greater success. It's a mental attitude which always expects or anticipates good, favorable and positive results.

- A positive mind is filled with happiness, joy, health and almost always gets a successful result.

- Whatever the mind expects, the subconscious creates.

- When you have a positive mindset, you instantly find answers to even the most complex problems and challenges. Positive thinking is an attitude that is geared towards automatically expecting things to work out. You always expect, believe and trust that things will always work out and they often do when you regularly practice and apply positive thinking.

- This is not to be confused with someone who simply says: "Think positive and everything will work out." Such a person does not have the proper mindset. They're simply turning to positive thinking when things go wrong – and by then it's too late, the damage has been done.

- Someone who has a positive thinking mindset naturally thinks positive and always foresees happiness, good health, success, and a positive outcome to just about every situation and event that takes place. They also trust and know that they will make the right decision and the right choices. Since they expect it – their mind and subconscious mind find a way to make it happen. This is the power of positive thinking.

- Not everybody thinks that positive thinking works, and often these are the people who use the concept of positive thinking sporadically or when they need to get out of a jam. If you try this approach don't expect results.

- Before you can develop a positive thinking pattern, you first have to realize that positive thinking is not something you do randomly. Positive thinking is a practice, one that you work with daily and apply regularly. By making it a daily habit you create a positive mindset that allows you to avoid negative and challenging situations. It also helps you resolve dilemmas quickly and easily.

- You will attract what you think about regularly.

- So if you regularly think that life is difficult you will attract situations that will make your life difficult. If you think that it's difficult to make money, you will attract situations that make it difficult for you to make money or make poor decisions about money.

- To have a positive thinking mindset, you need to have positive thoughts, and they should be in your mind constantly.

- The best way to get started is to change the way you think. So start paying close attention to what you think about every day.

- Is this thought positive or negative?

- Does it help me improve my life or does it make my life more difficult?

- If the thought is not helpful, if it doesn't allow you to succeed, if it doesn't make your life more pleasant, if you find that the thought is going to attract what you don't want, then change it. Create positive thoughts that lead to a positive thinking mindset.

- Create a thought that is positive and recite it regularly. These are better known as positive affirmations. I know some will say: "I've tried positive affirmations and got no results." Results with positive thinking and affirmations can vary. While they will help develop a positive thinking pattern it can take some time to see real results from reciting affirmations repeatedly. That's because it depends on what you want and where you are in life.

- For example: if you want to be a millionaire and you're currently earning 30-thousand dollars a year, it will likely take some time to earn a million and you may not see results as quickly as you want. Why? Because your current mind is programmed to making just 30 thousand dollars a year. To make a million you have to change the way your mind and subconscious mind operate. Working with positive thinking and affirmations will help but you'll have to do a lot more. You have to have a positive thinking mindset so that you always believe you'll succeed.

- Another reason why positive affirmations don't always create the results you want is because they are not phrased properly. To create a positive thinking mindset your affirmations should be said daily, should be in the present tense, and should be said in your voice.

- Visualize your success. See yourself succeeding at what you want to achieve. This will help boost the results of your affirmations and develop a stronger positive thinking pattern. There's no point saying an affirmation about making a million dollars and never have an image of you achieving that goal to support it. When you visualize, your subconscious associates the image with the affirmation and helps you achieve the success you want sooner.

Here are some simple steps that you can follow to begin applying positive thinking so that you enjoy greater success, more happiness and joy in all areas of your life:

- Be grateful. The more thankful and grateful you are, the more positive things will come into your life.

- Look for positive situations throughout the day. Think of something positive that took place in your life.

- Track your thoughts. Eliminate thoughts that are not positive and that do not help you succeed or enjoy life. Keep your thoughts positive.

- Create and work with Positive Affirmations. These will help you stay positive and keep the negative thoughts out of your mind.

- Visualize - see yourself succeeding and enjoying your life.

- Ignore the negative people. When you hear people saying negative things, avoid the conversation or try to steer it to being positive.

- Choose to say positive things and focus on positive situations.

- Always expect positive outcomes.

- Anticipate that things will get better regardless of your current situations.

> "A positive mental attitude is the starting point of all riches, whether they be riches of a material nature or intangible riches."
> - Napoleon Hill

Every person at some point or the other in life has to go through rough and tough times. It is understandable that in such a situation, an individual would be exposed to stress, depression, and other unhealthy mental conditions. The way a person thinks is believed to be the most important step for success. It is well said that if someone thinks they can do it, they can actually make it to success.

As the name suggests, a positive mental attitude is a mindset which only has positive thoughts backed up by motivation. Owing to the results from several surveys, medical professionals believe that this type of positive attitude aids in reducing physical and mental stress levels, contributing to a healthy life. A person with positive thinking will successfully be able to transform his negative perspectives into positive thoughts.

++++++++++++++++++++++++++++++

Developing Positive Mental Attitude

Be in a Positive Environment

In order to start thinking positively, you necessarily need to have an appropriate environment. Be in company of good friends and colleagues who have a positive mindset. Be with people who will always support, help, and encourage you to deal with bad thoughts present in your senses. This is the best way of changing the depressing negative thoughts to happy positive ones.

Work on Your Weaknesses

Be thankful for whatever good things you have that others do not have. Realize your strengths and sort down your weak areas in life. Work on your weaknesses and try to overcome your fear. Doing so will give you a base for starting to think in a positive manner. It will certainly help you to lead a healthy life.

In order to get motivated and create a positive mental attitude, you need to sort out the things to be done in a day. Write a day's schedule, and adjust the tasks according to your schedule. Sometimes, we can't do things because we don't try to do them. Make sure you do not keep time wherein you won't do anything. This will surely increase the level of satisfaction in living.

These are some general tips on developing a positive mental attitude. Practicing positive thinking for petty things will help you regain confidence for reaching new heights of success. This attitude has to be practiced with keeping the past mistakes in mind.

++++++++++++++++++++++++++++++

Negative Attitudes

This world in which we reside, is filled with both the positive and the negative. In fact, it is the existence of both that has now made us more open towards a 'gray' perspective of life. But to be really frank, looking at the gray side is just adjusting, isn't it? Lately, I have been listening to a lot of people who keep on emphasizing on 'positive thinking.' Trust me, I was a pessimist. I believed that thinking negative makes you more ready to face the worst. But I was wrong. Negative only takes away your ability to have faith, to be patient, to believe in achieving what seems difficult at first, to see the beauty of life, to see how mysteriously amazing life is... all these aspects being the most important pillars of true happiness and success in life. So, if life isn't in its best phase right now, just have a look at some of the quotes and phrases on positive thinking written below. They might not change the situation, but they will surely give you immense strength to face and conquer the difficulties of life.

Lots of people go through life without realizing that their failures and frustrations are due to their negative attitude. The following article defines the causes behind it as well as ways to combat it. Read on...

"It is our attitude at the beginning of a difficult task which, more than anything else, will affect its successful outcome." - William James

This is so true. It is the way we think and react to a situation that determines how much happiness and success we will find in our lives, both personally as well as professionally. For instance, for someone with a negative attitude, who has seen his business going bankrupt in the current economic slump, would mean end of the world. On the other hand, for people with positive thinking, the same scenario would be an opportunity to start something new, something different, in accordance to their choice!

We all hear this talk about being positive all the time and avoiding negativity. But, have you ever thought, what does a negative attitude mean?

Negative Attitudes

Anger
Jealousy
Greed
Frustration
Hatred
Bitterness
Shame
Pain
Inferiority Complex
Suspicion

There are a number of causes behind a person experiencing this in a band or personal life. The foremost amongst these is that a person is dissatisfied with the way their life is going or has shaped up. If a person is in an unfulfilling relationship, or if they find them self pursuing a profession they are least interested in, they are bound to feel frustrated and develop negative feelings.

Staying in the company of friends, colleagues or family members, who themselves think very negatively, can have an adverse effect on what an artist thinks. It is a known fact that the environment around a person is bound to affect them in some way or the other. Lastly, if a person has not had much exposure of life, if their view of the world is limited to their beliefs, such a narrow thinking can foster negativity in their mind and impede their personality development.

Tips to Change a Negative Attitude
You must have seen that people who have confidence and display a cheery, positive attitude, are much more likely to win friends and become successful in their career. That's why, if you display any of the negativity signs, it's time you change the way you think!

The first thing to do, is to try to look for positivity and goodness in every situation. For instance, if your car has suffered a break-down and you need to rely on public transport to travel to work, instead of feeling agitated, think that you are helping the environment by using lesser petrol and causing less pollution!

Have you ever heard of the adage that, "negativity breeds negativity?" Well, it does hold true. So, another thing that you can do to change your situation is to think about the long term consequences of such an attitude.

In the end, it would pay to know that such an attitude is not easy to combat. You cannot suddenly wake up one day and decide that from now on you will not get angry or feel jealous and will always display happiness. It does not happen that way. It would require a conscious effort, determination and patience on your part, to remove yourself from your negative thoughts. And once you are able to do so, the success will be all yours.

We are more and more afraid of sadness and moments of sorrow, despair, and loneliness. We tend to do most anything in order to avoid such moments in our lives, or at least to postpone them as much as we can. Nowadays, we hear all the time and most everywhere about positive-thinking, positive attitude, and so on and so forth, to such a great extent that we are in danger of forgetting that to be a complete person means to know how to manage your own issues and most difficult problems.

Positive emotions obviously are most pleasant and easy to handle but it is also quite normal to be worried sometimes, or utterly sad, or sometimes even feel miserable, disappointed or hopeless. If we are to be true to ourselves, we have to admit that all these emotions and states of mind can have the power to teach us new things about ourselves, they can make us stronger and more self-confident, if we go through such difficult times and still gain hope for the future. Without the negative emotions, feelings and thoughts that may naturally occur when we have to face difficult times in our lives, we may, in fact, never truly appreciate sheer and genuine happiness.

Of course, it can all depend on what we want to call "happiness" or positive attitude. We may refer to what certain famous philosophers understood by this word. The Greek philosopher Aristotle used to say that the ideal life is called "eudemonia" which, in translation, means "happiness." What now comes to my mind is a box of chocolates my mother gave to me recently, having the word "Happiness" written on it. Of course, we may find great pleasure in such a delight, but what Aristotle meant by happiness did not refer to any sensory pleasures and also he did not encourage a daydreaming life, in which one may have the illusion that things are (or they should be) better than they are in reality. "Reality bites," as the title of a movie once said.

Perhaps because of all that, human relationships have so many things to teach us. When we feel miserable and rejected, we may often think that life is unfair, uncertain and unpleasant. Therefore, in such moments, we are very likely in fact to consider happiness to be a justified, proper aim in our lives, or even a "natural state of mind." But this perspective may be wrong, as by it we ignore the fact that we are more complex than that, and that sadness is just as strong an emotion as intense joy. We have to admit also that feelings of joy, exaltation, enthusiasm and so on, can only gain their value by contrast with their opposite - disappointment, suffering or sadness.

Anxiety goes up when people go through dramatic changes, such as joining a new band, losing jobs, losing someone dear, divorce, a salary cut, or other such bad things, their level of anxiety goes up. This manifests by a lot of stress, sadness and sometimes even panic. We may in fact be in danger of seeing happiness as something that can and needs to be controlled by us. When we lose control over it, i.e. we lose our joy and tranquility, we simply freak out. So it's better to think positive than negative, but perhaps it's best to have a realistic perspective on life, to embrace all that we are, and LIVE.

++++++++++++++++++++++++++++

Law of Attraction

Your thoughts are creating your reality.

"Change your life. Change your thought." Instead of saying, "I can't do it," say "Of course, I can do it."

If you believe that you are what you do, then when you don't…
If you believe that you are what you have, that when it's gone….
If you believe that you are what other people think of you,
Your thoughts are creating your reality.

"Change your life. Change your thought."

We have the capacity, through the way we use our minds, the way we process things and events, to make our lives totally shift and change around.

It does not matter what age you are.

Which do you say? "I can't do it," or "Of course, I can do it."

Consider changing as you become God realized.

1. Change the idea that you cannot trust in your own nature

2. Trust in your own nature. No one else can do that.

Verse 38 of the Tao: The great master follows his own nature and not the trappings of life. A truly good man is not aware of his goodness and is therefore good.

No Where to Now Here and… where are you going… No where. Back to no where.

If you believe that you are what you do, then when you don't…
If you believe that you are what you have, that when it's gone….
If you believe that you are what other people think of you,

++++++++++++++++++++++++++++

Success

Success is only defined by the individual. Society may categorize people as successful but society cannot define what success is in the mind of the individual. Success is defined as a favorable or prosperous termination of attempts or endeavors. It is also the accomplishment of one's goals.

Smiles are contagious
Emotional state of smiles
Act of smiling makes us feel better
One smile and generate
Smiling makes you look good to others
More likeable
More courteous
More competent

Success is personal.

Artists don't follow their passion, they bring it with them.

Our own definition of success can make us happy or sad.

Everyone wants to be a success. That simple desire for success creates anxiety.

Loser is a failure of man-made rules. Success is deserved. Losing is deserved. Was Hamlet a loser? No, he just lost. All success involves choices. Succeeding in one area fails at another. Artists should strive to be successful but define what success is to you. Success is our own definition, our own ambition. Make sure our idea of success if truly our own. When you realize that you have enough, then you are truly rich.

Choice: What do we want to be successful at today?

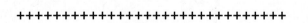

MUSIC

Passion

Passion (from the Latin verb patere meaning to suffer) is a term applied to a very strong feeling about a person or thing. In the case of an artist, they may have a passion for songwriting or singing. Perhaps their passion is performing or jamming for hours. Passion is an intense emotion, compelling enthusiasm or desire for anything. It's personal and addictive.

The term is also often applied to a friendly or eager interest in or admiration for a proposal, cause, activity or love – to a feeling of unusual excitement, enthusiasm or compelling emotion. It is a positive affinity or love, towards a subject.

Motivation

As a motivation in the entertainment business, there are different reasons individuals are motivated to do a certain job. One of these reasons includes passion for the occupation within the job. Many artists love the entertainment business. After all, it is a glamorous business. When an artist is passionate about what they do, the results are more work being done and more work satisfaction. These same individuals have higher levels of psychological well-being. When people genuinely enjoy their profession and are motivated by their passion, they tend to be more satisfied with their work and more psychologically healthy.

Passion and desire go hand in hand, especially as a motivation. Passion is an "intense, driving, or overmastering feeling or conviction." This suggests that passion is a very intense emotion, but can be positive or negative. It could involve pain and has obsessive forms that can destroy the self and even others. In the music business, when an artist is very passionate about their work, they may be so wrapped up it that they cause pain to their loved ones by focusing more on their job than on their friendships and relationships. This is a constant battle of balance that is difficult to achieve and only an individual can decide where that line lies. Passion is connected to the concept of desire. In fact, they are inseparable to many people. These two concepts cause individuals to reach out for something, or even someone. They both can either be creative or destructive and this dark side can very well be dangerous to the self or others.

As a Motivation for Hobbies

Hobbies require a certain level of passion in order to continue engaging in the hobby. Singers, athletes, dancers, artists, and many others describe their emotion for their hobby as a passion. Although this might be the emotion they're feeling, passion is serving as a motivation for them to continue their hobby. Recently there has been a model to explain different types of passion that contribute to engaging in an activity.

"A harmonious passion refers to a strong desire to engage in the activity that remains under the person's control." This is mostly obtained when the person views their activity as part of their identity. Once an activity is part of the person's identity, then the motivation to continue is even stronger. The harmony obtained with this passion is conceived when the person is able to both freely engage in or to stop the work altogether. It's not so much that the person is forced to continue, but on his or her own free will, is able to engage in it. For example if a woman loves to play guitar, but she has a rehearsal the next day and her friends invite her to out to a party, she is able to say no on her own free will.

The second kind of passion in the dualistic model is obsessive passion. Being the opposite of harmonious passion, this type has a strong desire to engage in the activity, but it's not under the person's own control and he or she is forced to engage in the hobby. This type of passion has a negative effect on a person where they could feel they need to engage in their art to continue interpersonal relationships, or "fit in" with the crowd. To change the above example, if the person has an obsessive passion towards playing guitar and she is asked to party with her friends, she will say yes even though she needs to practice for her upcoming rehearsal.

Since passion can be a type of motivation in art, then assessing intrinsic motivation is appropriate. Intrinsic motivation helps define these types of passion. Passion naturally helps the needs or desires that motivate an artist to some particular action or behavior. Certain abilities can be developed early and the innate motivation is also something that comes early in life. Although someone might know how to write songs, this doesn't necessarily mean they are motivated to do it. An artist's knowledge of their innate motivation can help guide action toward what will be fulfilling." Feeling satisfied and fulfilled builds the passion for the art to continue an artist's happiness.

++++++++++++++++++++++++++++++

Confidence

What is confidence except repetition, repetition, and more repetition? The more an artist rehearses, the easier it is and the easier it looks. Not only does it look easy, but the artist feels more confident with their artistic expression.

We make and design whatever we want in our lives. We have the ability to create happiness and we have the ability to create unhappiness. The more confident a person is as a performer, singer, musician or content creator, the happier they tend to be.

+++++++++++++++++++++++++++++

Grit

Grit is a passionate commitment to a single mission and an unswerving dedication to achieve that mission. Grit is the "never give up" attitude.

Grit Scale

Setbacks don't discourage me
I am a hard worker
I finish whatever I begin
I aspire for greatness
I get back up when I fall
I don't give up

Many artists seem to think that they should not struggle, fail, or have any obstacles to overcome. But when an artist looks back on their life, where have they learned the most? - From their successes or from their failures? Most people answer that they've learned more from their failures than their successes. If this is true for most of us, why then, are we so afraid to fail? Not that we would intentionally set ourselves up to fail, but what if some failures taught us the character trait of grit? If we simply learn from our mistakes and failures, get back on the horse, and then be able to say that "setbacks don't discourage me," we're in a good spot.

Is it the artist's disposition to pursue very long term goals with passion and perseverance?

Grit is living life as it is a marathon and not a sprint. Setbacks will happen and smart artists know this. They don't let setbacks disappoint them.

We adapt to our circumstances and if you've never had to try very hard then maybe you don't cultivate that capacity.

+++++++++++++++++++++++++++++

Quotes

Below are some of the best positive quotations and sayings that I came across. Though I was looking for them to assemble into an article, I actually realized how powerful an impact these quotes can have on an artist's mind and outlook.

"We are what we pretend to be, so we must be careful about what we pretend to be." - Kurt Vonnegut, Mother Night

"It isn't what you have or who you are or where you are or what you are doing that makes you happy or unhappy. It is what you think about it." - Dale Carnegie

"I am better than I think I am, and I'm pretty damn good. – Rob Davis

"The greater part of our happiness or misery depends upon our dispositions, and not upon our circumstances."
- Martha Washington

"There will be a few times in your life when all your instincts will tell you to do something, something that defies logic, upsets your plans, and may seem crazy to others. When that happens, you do it. Listen to your instincts and ignore everything else. Ignore logic, ignore the odds, ignore the complications, and just go for it." - Judith McNaught

"Don't waste your time with explanations: people only hear what they want to hear." - Paulo Coelho

"Our life is what our thoughts make it."
- Marcus Aurelius

"I've had it with being nice, understanding, fair and hopeful. I feel like being negative all day. The chip on my shoulder could sink the QE2. I've got an attitude problem and nobody better get in my way...I'm in a bad mood and the whole stupid little world is gonna pay!" - John Waters

"Every day one should at least hear one little song, read one good poem, see one fine painting and -- if at all possible -- speak a few sensible words."
- Johann Wolfgang von Goethe

"I love those who can smile in trouble..."
- Leonardo da Vinci

"Ability is what you're capable of doing. Motivation determines what you do. Attitude determines how well you do it."
- Lou Holtz

"Look on every exit as being an entrance somewhere else."
- Tom Stoppard

"Life is 10 percent what you make it and 90 percent how you take it."
- Irving Berlin

"A man is happy so long as he chooses to be happy." - Aleksandr I. Solzhenitsyn

"If you don't have time to do it right, when will you have the time to do it over?"
- John Wooden

To Do

Notes:

Artist Development in the Music Business
Chapter 9 – Business Set-Up

In the early stages of Artist Development, an individual thinks about becoming an artist and may dream about becoming a big star. Just so you know, big stars mean big business and big stars are business owners. You, the individual, the artist, must have an entrepreneurial spirit for your art to become your business. Many artists have a tough time thinking that their art is their business. If this is you, perhaps, you will want to wait to team-up with someone who is more business oriented.

Before we move much further, let's define what type of business that an artist is. As an individual person, an artist may wear the "hat" of a solo artist. As a solo artist, they may write their own material, perform their own material and record their own material. In this case, perhaps their business is a sole proprietorship.

Or perhaps, the artist decides to collaborate with another individual and wear the performer-artist "hat" of a being a duo or in a band. If this is the case, the artist will have to decide if they own the band or whether they are a partner and co-own the band.

In addition, the person, the individual, the artist, may be a soloist as well as a partner / collaborator at the same time. There are many artists who perform as solo singer-songwriters and then occasionally perform with a band. In this case, what's the business arrangement? Perhaps the person is a sole proprietor as a solo artist and also a partner as a co-owner of the band.

The important take-away from this is to remember to separate one's business from the other.

Remember, this is the music business. Successful artists know this. To set-up an artist's business, there are three plans that need to be considered:

1. The Artist Development Plan
2. The Product Development Plan
3. The Artist Business Plan

Artist Development is pre-release. It's the creating, the planning and the preparing. Product Development is implementing and producing: The making and the selling of music. The Artist Business Plan is the master plan of the who, what, when, where, why and how much of the artist's success. The Artist Business Plan brings all the components of the Artist Development Plan and the Product Development Plan together.

When a person (artist) begins to think of the business side of art, he or she will

**Individual
Artist
Business Owner**

start to wear another "hat": the entrepreneurial hat: The role of a business owner. This is when the person who is trying to establish themselves as an artist is also trying to establish themselves as a business owner; someone with whom others will want to do business.

> **Art is no less important than commerce for today's developing musician and artist.**

While contemplating the Artist Development Plan, the artist will realize the importance of setting up a bona fide business. If an artist truly wants to avoid playing local taverns the rest of their career, and wants to do business with others in the music business, then the artist should set up a business to do so; especially if there are more than one person on their team. Business. Business. Business.

++++++++++++++++++++++++++++++
Artist Business Plan

If a person is generating any income outside of a corporate salary or per-hour wage, then they are a business. What kind of business are you... a sole proprietor, partnership or corporation? What is your plan for long and short term success? Who owns the company? Is there one owner or a group of owners? Is the artist thinking in business terms? Artists need to develop and maintain an Artist Business Plan as well as an Artist Development Plan.

> **Plan Your Work & Work Your Plan**

An artist's Business Plan precisely defines the business, identifies the goals, and serves as the structure of an artist's company. The basic components of a business plan include a current balance sheet, income statement, and a cash flow analysis. An artist's business plan helps the artist allocate resources, handle unforeseen complications, and make good business decisions. Because it provides specific and organized information about the artist's company, the artist can make informed and educated projections for their goals and objectives. Additionally, it keeps the artist focused on their career. It informs personnel and collaborators and others about the business's operations and projects. As discussed earlier, this business is about projects. Planning and implementing actions toward those projects are identified in the Artist Business Plan.

The importance of a comprehensive, thoughtful business plan cannot be overemphasized.

> **Question: If you don't know where you're going, how are you going to get there?**

A good business plan can help in many ways, such as: securing outside funding, establishing credit from suppliers, managing projects and finances, promotion and marketing of each recording and/or performance, as well as staying focused on the artist's goals and objectives.

Despite the critical importance of a business plan, many artist-entrepreneurs drag their feet when it comes to preparing a written document. But just as a conductor won't begin the orchestra without a musical score, eager business owners shouldn't rush into new ventures without a plan.

Before an artist prepares and writes a business plan, they should consider four (4) core questions:

1. What are the services or products of the artist?
2. Who are the potential customers of the artist and why will they purchase from the artist?
3. Where will potential customers be obtained?
4. How will the business be funded?

A business plan is a tool with three (3) basic purposes: communication, management, and planning. As a communication tool, it is used to attract investment capital, secure loans, convince collaborators to hire on, and assist in attracting strategic business partners such as agents, managers, fellow musicians and record label executives. As a management tool, the development of a comprehensive business plan shows whether or not a business has the potential to make a profit. Some artists say that their art is not about making a profit. If the artist wants to continue making art on a full-time basis, they need to survive. To survive, they need to make a profit. The profit is defined in their business plan.

As a planning tool, a business plan requires a realistic look at almost every phase of an artist's business and allows the artist, as a business owner, to show that they have anticipated potential problems as well as alternatives to success before actually launching their business.

Purposes of a Business Plan

1. **Communication**
2. **Management**
3. **Planning**

The business plan helps track, monitor and evaluate an artist's progress. The business plan is a living document. It is fluid and changes as the artist plans new projects such as recordings and / or performances. Business plans are used to establish timelines and milestones. It can gauge progress and goals.

This is a good time to remember that an artist may have more than one business and each business may need a separate business plan. For example, some artists may release their own recordings, and therefore, may run a record label company. Some artists may act as the promoter for their own events, where they are the headline performer. Their production company may need its own business plan.

Parts of an Artist Business Plan

Executive Summary
About the Artist
Mission Statement
Company Summary
Management & Team
Product & Services
Customer Summary
Marketing Plan
Promotion Plan
Competition
Sales Plan
Intellectual Property
Technology
Relationships
Finance Plan
Resources

The many dimensions of an artist's company include:

- The Music - Repertoire, Rehearsals, Market Indicators
- Business - Planning, Office, Resource Mgmt, Networking, Publishing
- Legalities - Licenses, Contracts, Insurance, Taxes, Trademarks
- Marketing - Planning, Media Publicity, Internet, Co-Promotions
- Team Building - Band Members, Team Management, Delegation, Hiring / Firing
- Recording - Studio research, pre-prod, production, manufacturing, formats, gear
- Sales - Merchandising, Internet & Distribution

Artist Name / Business Name

(More about band names in the Image section of this book)

++++++++++++++++++++++++++++++

Business Names

The name of a business is an essential aspect of the entire marketing and branding strategy. The name of the band or artist may be the name of the company. The launch of any business, big or small, calls for detailed preparation prior to its launch. The existence of a concrete marketing plan to promote any business and this includes an artist's business. The marketing process often involves a plan to create a specific brand image or brand identity in the market. Using signature elements like a brand logo or a specific color scheme, one can create a brand image, but in addition to that, it is the brand name or the artist name that needs to stand out.

First of all, there are no surefire ways to come up with a successful and catchy name. More importantly, the name will only be a success if the artist's songs, performances and recordings are well received, and sales are soaring. There are many examples of artists with ordinary or even absurd names that are doing well in the market. Similarly, there are instances of artists with unique and well-thought names, which are not really successful. So, it is safe to say that while the name of the business does create an impression in the mind of the prospective customer, it is ultimately the quality of the artist products (songs, recordings & performances) that will decide the future of the artist.

Artist Name = Brand

Every artist has a unique thought process that goes into the making of the name. The company name is often the brainchild of the artist owner or creator and can be any name that the creator finds interesting and thinks is appropriate for the artist. Here are some of the ways that artists have used to come up with their business name.

Unique Words: There are several artist names which are unique words that are not necessarily related directly to the anything in the music business arena or the profession. In many ways, this creates a sense of intrigue in the minds of the potential fans and customers while keeping them guessing as to why such a strange name was chosen. i.e.: The Psychedelic Furs

Keywords: Some artist names make use of words which directly give an idea about the business. No frills, to the point and blatantly obvious. i.e.: The Singing Angels.

Acronyms: Some business names make use of one or several words to form the name of the company and then use the acronym of the name to form the brand name. i.e.: Of a Revolution is O.A.R or Orchestral Maneuvers in the Dark is OMD.

Compound Words: Some people like to combine two related words to form a unique company name, which may not be necessarily a valid word. i.e.: Smashmouth or Limp Biscuit

Non-English Words: Many business names have their origin in varied languages like Chinese, Spanish, Sanskrit and so on. I.e.: Los Lobos

Wrong Spellings: There are some business names that are words which have been intentionally mis-spelled to make the name sound more interesting and catchy. i.e.: Boyz 2 Men

In general, an artist's name should be catchy, simple to spell and easy to pronounce. It is always good to keep things clean and simple. So if an artist is planning to launch them self in the entertainment world, they should make sure they use these ideas to come up with a catchy name. Be careful though, it shouldn't be over-the-top confusing for the customers and fans to understand. Perhaps an artist might end up losing out on business simply because their name was too difficult to say, spell or understand.

Business Name Search
Select a few names to consider for your business. One of them may be available for you to use. If you are interested in a full international search, you may want to contact Thompson & Thompson to assist.

++++++++++++++++++++++++++++
Statewide Search

Example: State of Ohio
Go to: www.sos.state.oh.us
Go to: Business Services
Click: Businesses / Corporations
Click: Search Filings
Scroll: Search Database
Click: Search Database
Click: Business Name
Type: Desired business name
Click: Submit

- IF No rows returned, you may be OK within the State of Ohio
- IF Business names are listed, review for your specific name
- IF Found and active, repeat process with new name

+++++++++++++++++++++++++++++

National Search

Go to: www.uspto.gov
Click: Trademarks
Click: Search Tess database
Click: New Basic User Search
Type: Search Term

- IF No TESS records were found, you may be OK with the trademark
- IF Records Found, review your specific name and review Live / Dead status

If found, repeat with new name.

International Search

Search the World Wide Web your selected name. Use "Quotation Marks Inc" for better results.

+++++++++++++++++++++++++++++

Business Types

Sole Proprietorship
General Partnership (GP)
Limited Partnership (LP)
Limited Liability Company (LLC)
Corporation (C/S Corps)
Holding Company
Close Corporation
Personal Service Corporation

Business Entity Comparison

1) Sole Proprietorship

A sole proprietorship is owned and operated by no more than one individual. Sole proprietorships are often recommended for solo artists by accountants and attorneys because of their simplicity. From a tax standpoint, an artist who is a sole proprietorship does not have to file a separate business tax return. A Schedule C is attached to their 1040 and filed with the IRS. Gains (profits) and losses from the business are simply combined with other personal taxable items.

Issues to consider regarding a Sole Proprietorship:

With no legal distinction between an artist and their business, any business liabilities are also the artist's personal liabilities. If the artist is sued, they may receive a judgment against their personal assets. This may include their copyrights. In this scenario, an artist is risking everything they have for their business.

A sole proprietorship can find it difficult to raise capital, since it can only be accomplished if the artist can qualify for a personal loan.

Sole proprietorships have been historically limited in their ability to participate in such things as federally qualified pension plans and medical reimbursement plans that are available to other business entities.

Overall, sole proprietorships are risky entities that could cost an artist and their family all they own, especially considering that no other entity is more scrutinized by the IRS. As a result, the sole proprietorship is certainly not a long-term business solution for an artist.

Advantages of a Sole Proprietorship:
- Ease of Formation
- Pass-Through Tax Treatment (i.e., Simplicity of Reporting)

Disadvantages of a Sole Proprietorship:
- Personal Liability
- Lack of Continuity
- Lack of Investment Flexibility

2) General Partnership (GP)

This type of entity is formed when two or more people come together for the purpose of conducting a business. In the music business, this could be a duo or a band. It could also be a team of songwriters. It could also be used for an artist / producer relationship. In forming a partnership, all partners must agree on which duties they will each take on and what percentage of ownership they will each hold. Typically, this is done with a partnership agreement and should be put together by a lawyer.

Similar to sole proprietorships, general partnerships have many of the same advantages and disadvantages. Like sole proprietorships, partnerships are easy to form, but they are taxed according to the tax level of each partner. Likewise, no liability protection is offered.

Advantages of a General Partnership:
- Ease of Formation
- Pass-Through Tax Treatment (i.e., Simplicity of Reporting)

- Disadvantages of a General Partnership:
- Personal Liability
- Lack of Continuity
- Lack of Investment Flexibility

3) Limited Partnership (LP)

Limited partnerships are composed of a minimum of two types of participants; general partners and limited partners. General partners accept the responsibility for and take all risks involved in managing and conducting business. Limited partners, on the other hand, are investors who share some risk, depending on the amount invested, but who have no participation in the actual management of the entity. Limited partners simply enjoy the profits, and share in the losses (liabilities), on the basis of what is stipulated in their partnership agreement. These provisions provide limited liability protection, but they do not allow any privacy for the parties involved. Limited partnerships are often used for estate planning purposes. These vehicles allow individuals to control their assets, while still having the ability to pass ownership of those assets along to their heirs.

Advantages of a Limited Partnership:

- Pass-Through Tax Treatment (i.e., Simplicity of Reporting)
- Financial Flexibility
- IRS Discounting upon Death (e.g., Lower Estate Taxes)

Disadvantages of Limited Partnerships:

- Liability of the General Partner(s) (GPs)
- Lack of Control for the Limited Partners (LPs)
- Lack of Investment Flexibility

4) Limited Liability Company (LLC)

The limited liability company (LLC) is a unique form of business that blends the characteristics of corporations, partnerships and sole proprietorships into a simple and flexible business entity that many small business owners prefer.

The LLC entity can be used to hold property and transact any type of business. LLC entities are similar to partnerships, limited partnerships, S Corporations and trusts. An LLC is a pass-through entity. It passes all of the profits and losses directly to the members of the LLC. Individual members are therefore taxed at their personal tax rates.

LLCs are owned by members, which are like shareholders in a corporation. Unlike S Corporations, which are limited to 75 shareholders, the LLC can have an unlimited amount of members. A member's ownership interest in the LLC is referred to as a 'membership interest.' It is like stock in a corporation. All the members of an LLC can manage the business; management may also be delegated to fewer than all members or to a single manager. A manager can be an individual, a partnership, a corporation, or in some states, such as Nevada, even another LLC. This offers tremendous flexibility for artists and asset protection.

Advantages of an L.L.C.:

- **Asset Protection**
  As a completely separate entity, LLCs separate the owners from the business itself. There is no personal liability for any LLC debts, even if they relate to a contract or tort. The operating agreement can, for the most part, contain any procedures and their rules that the parties desire and once put into place can just sit there maintenance-free. The initial drafting of the operating agreement is very important because it must comply with state and IRS regulations so that the LLC will be taxed as a sole proprietor or partnership and not as a corporation.

- **Tax Advantages**
  An LLC legally separates the business from its owners (like a corporation), yet it can elect to be treated as a sole proprietorship or partnership for tax purposes. In this case, the LLC doesn't pay any tax itself - the income is passed through to the owners as with partnerships. The tax rules governing partnerships are more flexible, allowing for more flexibility in tax planning.

- **Ability to Raise Capital**

When an artist, or any person, starts an LLC, it is simple to bring new owners (called members) on board, and there is no limit as to how many can be involved. This may not be relevant to a band but it might be relevant to an artist who owns and operates a record label. These additional investors can be individuals, corporations, trusts and pension plans, none of which even have to be in the same state or in the U.S.

- **Easy to Run**
  The LLC entity was formed around the principle of the freedom to contract. This basically means the owners only have to agree among themselves how the company will be run and the agreement will hold up in court. As an LLC, resolutions, amendments, meeting minutes, and annual board meetings are not required by law, as they are with corporations. In fact, in most states, owners of corporations that do not comply with these requirements lose the asset and liability protection, typically provided by a corporate entity.

Disadvantages of a L.L.C.:

- **Federal Security Limitations**:
  The LLC is only available to privately owned companies. If a company were to go public, it would have to be a C Corporation.

- **Loss of Pass-Through Tax Treatment**
  This occurs when an LLC is viewed as a corporation, which happens when there is an election filed with the IRS and the LLC qualifies for three of the four criteria that defines a corporation. If it is taxed as a partnership, pass-through treatment still applies for taxes.

- **State Tax Treatment**:
  Some states impose an income or franchise tax on Limited Liability Corporations.

5) Corporation

The corporation is the most secure entity in business, because a corporation is considered a 'person' with rights of its own under the law, a stockholder is a holder of shares of stock in the corporation and is NOT IN LEGAL DANGER for the acts of the corporation. In addition, a corporation is a citizen in the state wherein it was created and does not cease to be a citizen of its state by engaging in business or acquiring property in another state.

The important point to remember is that, when someone owns a corporation, it exists as a completely separate entity or person. Owners live anywhere they choose, because it is the corporation's state of residence that dictates the requirements.

Different types of Corporations

"C" Corporation

- Allows for limited liability of the shareholders, directors and officers

- Runs on a fiscal year, which may be designated by the board of directors, rather than a calendar year
- Some states do not require corporate owners/shareholders to be on record - protecting your identity
- Profits are taxed at corporate rates on an 1120 return separate from the individual return
- Profits can be kept as retained earnings

Options available for business owners:
In almost every category, C corporations will pay less in tax than an individual. The C corporation tax table is the only one in which the tax rate drops when you start making millions. That's why every Fortune 500 company is a C Corporation.

C corporations have no limitations on shareholders. Shareholders can live anywhere in the world and can be any type of entity.

There are far fewer criteria for a C corporation, as compared with an S corporation, so you have the options you need to meet your objectives.

"S" Corporation

S corporation is a good option if you are incorporating a small business.

- Allows for limited liability of the shareholders, directors and officers.
- Typically runs on a calendar year
- Full disclosure of corporate owners.
- Profits pass through to the individual tax return 1040. No tax brackets separate from the personal tax brackets apply.
- All profits are taxed even if not distributed.

State taxes will apply for individuals who are located in a state with an individual state tax.

There are certain qualifications that the corporation must meet in order to elect S corporation status. To elect S corporation status, your corporation must meet all of the following:

- It must be a domestic corporation formed in the U.S.
- It may have no more than 75 shareholders
- It may have only individuals, estates or certain trusts as shareholders
- It may not have non-resident alien shareholders
- It may only have one class of stock
- It must be a small business corporation (financial institutions, such as banks, insurance companies, building and loan associations or mutual savings and loan associations, cannot take advantage of an S corporation election)
- It must conform to state statutory restrictions, which limit the transfer of shares/ownership of the company

C Corporation status is appropriate for:

- When owners live outside the country
- When owners live in a state with a state income tax

- When several individuals or other entities are involved in ownership
- When sales are greater than $60,000 a year

S Corporation status is appropriate for:

- Companies expecting start-up losses during the initial years of operation
- Companies with no intent of going public in the future
- Companies that do not expect to issue multiple classes of stock
- Companies that might be subject to the Alternative Minimum Tax
- Owners live in a state with no personal state income tax
- Sales are less than $250,000 per year

LLC status is appropriate for:

- When the business is a partnership
- When real estate is owned for investment purposes
- When several entities own the business
- When the owner is seeking company's protection from personal liability

The best entity for building business credit for your company is one that will:

- Separate you from your business
- Have its own federal tax identification number
- Separate your company's business debt from owners/officers

6) Holding Company

A holding company is a corporation that "holds" control of one or more corporations. The IRS defines "control" of another corporation as consisting of at least 80% ownership of its stock. At that point, the corporations are able to combine their income and expenses for filing a consolidated tax return or they can put together a consolidated financial statement to apply for financing. The company being "held" is usually called a subsidiary of the parent holding company.

7) Close Corporation

A close corporation refers to an entity designed for a small group of investors who act like a partnership, even though they retain corporate liability protection and the other advantages of a corporate structure. A company of this kind is "closed" to any outside investors by restricting ownership in the company and the disclosure of any corporate information.

8) Personal Service Corporation

A personal service corporation is designed specifically for small businesses such as lawyers, architects, accountants, etc. These corporations use a calendar year with a limit of $150,000 on accumulated earnings. The current tax rate for a personal service corporation is the flat corporate rate of 35%, instead of the graduated rate that currently starts at 15%.

Parts of an Artist Business Plan

Executive Summary
An executive summary, sometimes known as a management summary, is a short document or section of a document. It is the very last item completed on an artist's Business Plan. The reason is obvious: the Executive Summary is a "summary" of all the other sections of the plan. It is produced for business purposes, and summarizes a longer report or proposal. Although it's written last, it is the first item read when someone is reviewing the status of the company. As a summary, it is usually written in such a way that readers can rapidly become acquainted with a large body of material without having to read the whole document.

It usually contains a brief statement of the plan covered in the other main sections such as the marketing plan, sales plan or finance plan. It provides background information, concise analysis as well as conclusions.

It is intended as an aid to decision-making by artists, their managers as well as potential investors and/or collaborators. It is possibly the most important part of an artist's business plan.

Mission Statement
A mission statement is a statement of the purpose of an artist's company, organization or person and its reason for existing.

The mission statement should guide the actions of the artist's business, spell out its overall goal, provide a path, and guide decision-making. It provides "the framework or context within which the company's strategies are formulated." It's like a goal for what the company wants to do as a business.

Company Summary
A company summary is just that; a summary of the company. An artist's company is either a sole proprietorship, a partnership or a corporation. This, of course, depends on how the artist structures the company in the first place. This section also describes what the company does, where it is located and the types of products and services it has to offer.

Management & Team
This section of the Artist Business Plan identifies how the company is run. Who is in charge? Who's a part of the team? Artists need to identify the people involved with their organization. This is a good spot to do that.

Products & Services
Most artists have multiple products and perhaps only one service. In the music business, the products for sale include compact discs, music downloads, t-shirts, tickets as well as a plethora of other items. The service of an artist is their musicianship.

Customer Summary
Every artist has two types of customers: the fan customer and the music industry professional customer. The first type of customer purchases music and merchandise. This customer is the general public and purchases music downloads, compact discs, t-shirts, etc. They are those whom purchase tickets to the artist's performances. These are Fan Customers.

In addition to customers who are fans, there are also customers in the music industry. These customers are just as important and any other customer. These customers purchase the talent of the Artist for live performances or recorded products

Marketing Plan
A marketing plan is a part of an artist's business plan. Solid marketing strategy is the foundation of a well-written marketing plan. While a marketing plan contains a list of actions, a marketing plan without a sound strategic foundation is of little use.

A marketing plan is a comprehensive blueprint which outlines an artist's business's overall marketing efforts. A marketing process can be realized through a marketing mix.

The marketing plan functions from two points: strategy and tactics. In most organizations, "strategic planning" is an annual process, typically covering just the upcoming year. Many artists also may look at a practical plan which stretches three or more years ahead.

Promotion Plan
Promotion is one of the market mix elements of marketing. The marketing mix includes the four P's: price, product, promotion, and place. Promotion refers to raising customer awareness of an artist's product or brand, generating sales, and creating brand loyalty. Promotion is also found in the specification of five promotional mix or promotional plan. These elements are personal selling, advertising, sales promotion, direct marketing, and publicity. A promotional plan can have a wide range of objectives, including: sales increases, new product acceptance, creation of brand equity, positioning, competitive retaliations, or creation of an artist's image.

Competition Summary
A big part of the success of any business is that of competition. Fan customers as well as music industry customers have one thing in common: limited resources. After an Artist has determined their target customers, they will need to determine what other Artists are aiming at that same market. In the competition section of an Artist's Business Plan will identify exactly why a customer may choose to spend their money with the Artist and why they may not.

Sales Plan
A sales plan coordinates the efforts of sales, operations and finance for an artist. A sales plan is closely related to an artist's business plan and marketing plan. It is a road map designed to give an artist's sales team direction through specific sales goals and objectives. Sales plans can address long-term sales goals such as a five or 10 year plan, or short-term sales goals and objectives, such as annual or 90 day sales plans.

Intellectual Property
Intellectual property, as discussed in a previous chapter, is the area of law that deals with protecting the rights of those who create original works. It covers everything from original songs and novels to inventions and company identification marks. The purpose of intellectual property laws are to encourage new technologies, artistic expressions and inventions while, at the same time, promoting economic growth.

When artists know that their creative work will be protected and that they can benefit from their labor, they are more likely to continue to produce art.

Technology Summary
The Technology Summary of an Artist's Business Plan explores different ways that Artist's may utilize technology for their business. This not only includes the technology that an Artist may use on stage or in the studio but also the technology used in running the Artist's business such as hardware (computers, printers, telephone, etc.) and software (databases, e-mail, websites, etc.)

Relationships
The music business is dependent on networking and relationships. Music business professionals often look to those they know as opposed to working with someone they have never worked with. In this section of an Artist's Business Plan, Artists should identify the relationships that they have built as well as relationships they plan to garner.

Finance Plan
In general usage, a financial plan is a series of steps or goals used by an artist and their business. The goals of a finance plan are to estimate the probability of success for any of the artist's upcoming projects, whether it be recording, touring or purchasing new equipment. The plan often includes a budget which organizes an artist's finances and sometimes includes a series of steps or specific goals for spending and saving future. This plan allocates future income to various types of expenses, such as rent or utilities, and also reserves some income for short-term and long-term savings. In addition, a financial plan can focus on other specific areas such as risk management, assets, and/or project management.

Artist Development in the Music Business
Chapter 10 – Image & Branding

One of the cold, hard facts about the music business is that no matter how good a musical artist is, having a successful public career is not just about the artist's music, but also about their public image – their brand. In other words: how the artist is perceived by the public.

A public performer has a public image, a persona associated with his/her music. That, in essence, is part of the brand as an artist. For an artist to get their music "out there," they also have to get their brand "out there."

So let's talk about some basics to get an understanding of image and branding.

The idea behind image and branding is consistency. We're not talking about good girl/bad girl type of image here; we're talking about putting forward a consistent public image, so fans and customers can easily associate and remember the artist over time.

The overall brand of a musical artist is obviously a bit more complex than a Facebook profile photo. It has to do with all elements of the public presentation: logos, fonts, album art, merchandise, appearance, and the overall feel that is presented with all of these elements. All of it is part of branding. For that reason, it's good to remember that a good brand is not simply created–it is developed. The more consistently an artist develops their brand, the easier it is for the fans and customers to identify them.

The popular music business is an extremely image-conscious industry. The look and image of an artist, band or performer are often the first thing that the public comes into contact with, even before hearing the artist's music in many instances. The look and/or image can be crucial to the success of an artist. We only have to think of successful artists to appreciate how important image can be - Elvis Presley, The Beatles, K.I.S.S., Jay-Z, and The Boston Pops are some of the more obvious examples. Also take a look at stars such as Michael Jackson, with his moon-walking boots and gloved hand, or perhaps Madonna or David Bowie, with images that shift and change over time. Undoubtedly many pop-music icons first elicit interest as much for their "look" and charisma as for their music. These artist images are reinforced and manipulated through marketing and promotion by the artists, their publicists and/or the marketing departments of record companies. Clever use of design and visual imagery project the image of the artist to a wider public.

The importance of image and the way in which image is projected through an artist's promotional material cannot be ignored. An artist could improve the presentation of its image and visual material through a better awareness of how visual style complements live performance and recorded material. In addition smart artists know that design can be used as an important marketing tool in presenting their art and their music to their fans and to the public in general.

Right from the beginning, artists need to weave consistency throughout their whole branding and promotional campaign. To do that, artists start with their musical niche, and then grow their niche, as they expand into new markets.

Look, for example, at the Billboard charts of the hits and the artists whom performed those hits. Imagine any one of the artists. Each artist has an image. You get an immediate impression of a particular artist just by thinking of them. For this to happen, their marketing and promotion team did a great job. Whether good or bad, it doesn't matter. Pay attention to the image. That's the point. People may be able to determine the style of music just by looking at the name of the artist. They may be even able to mentally see the type of show the artist may perform just by looking at the photo of the artist. Image is a big part of Artist Development.

Look at the image of what an artist is communicating. People are going to want to hear the artist's music or they may choose a different artist based on their personal observation of the artist's projected image. Some people may even choose to listen to an artist's music because they like the name of the artist.

How do people pick what to listen to? When an artist, or someone from their team, sends an unsolicited link to some of their music, people have to make a judgment call of what they're going to pay attention to and what they are going to ignore. Many times, they pick the ones whose image appeals to their sense of quality.

They say a picture paints a thousand words. Human minds create much more than what is written in text. Combining our senses to focus on one brand or artist will increase the likelihood of the artist being remembered.

++++++++++++++++++++++++++++++

Niches

For artists to begin establishing their image, the first step they need to do is to recognize the niche into which their music fits. To do this, an artist needs to look at, and follow, their heart. Following the money doesn't always pay for artists who are fake. A true image will garner loyal fans. A fake image will fool some of the people, some of the time. However, when you look at the image of an artist such as The Gorilliz or The Count Basie Orchestra, image is not their personality. The fans who appreciate their style of music may also appreciate their style of dress or makeup or caricature. Many times, it comes down to perception.

Successful artists know that their musical niche needs to be communicated in their live shows as well their songs and recordings. In other words, their live show should show an artist's image and fit the mood and genre of their songs. Their collaborators are a big part of that. In addition, the lighting technician for an artist's live performance will blend the proper lighting with the mood of the song being performed. The sound technician will enhance the performance based on the intention of each song.

A niche market is the subset of the market on which a specific product is focusing. Entertainment has a sub-set called music. Music has a sub-set called rock. Rock has a sub-set call metal. Metal has a sub-set called death metal. You get the picture.

A market niche defines the specific product features aimed at satisfying specific market needs.

A market niche may be defined by:

- specific market needs
- the price range
- production quality
- demographics

Every single product that is on sale can be defined by its niche market. Products aimed at a wide demographic audience, with the resulting low price (due to price elasticity of demand), are said to belong to the mainstream niche. Usually, because of the amount of competition in the mainstream, prices may be lower. Narrower demographics lead to elevated prices due to the same principle. This is true with live performances as only a few artists can regularly deliver quality (or perceived quality) in their live performance niche. However, recordings of songs (no matter the style of the music genre) are within a much larger niche and therefore prices remain similar to other recorded songs as a file download or on a compact disc.

The niche market is the highly specialized market that tries to survive among the competition from the vast amount of struggling musical artists on the street. If this niche market gets large enough, other artists may look to add this musical niche to their product line. In some cases brand recognition with which the artist wants to be associated (e.g., quality, prestige, conscience, power, etc.) is the purpose of niche marketing.

Once a new musical niche has been tapped, many copycats will try to enter that specific niche: Some successful artists such as Brett Michaels who saw his involvement in an over-crowded "hair-band' market with his band Poison found a new niche for himself in country rock. Some artists were unsuccessful at their attempt to cross-over such as Pat Boone trying to capitalize on attracting metal fans by releasing an album of heavy metal songs.

Niche Audience
Technology and industrial practices changed with the post-network era. There is a new drive for niche audiences because audiences are now in full control of what they see, watch and hear. Audiences and potential fans have numerous options to pay attention to new music and new artists. It is very rare to have a substantially large audience pay attention to one artist at one time. There are a few exceptions such as artists appearing on "American Idol," the "Super Bowl" and/or the "Grammy Awards." They specifically target an audience demographic. Entertainment companies do this all the time. For example, MTV targets youth and the Lifetime television network targets women.

Some niches may become saturated with savvy marketers, increasing competition and thus, according to the economic law of supply and demand, reducing the slice of the pie available to each competitor. For example, when a new song with a new mood hits the top of the charts, many publishers and record labels as well as many professional songwriters may try to find or write songs that fit the same musical style. Artists, on the other hand, may not have the same motivation. Their style may or may not have the same mood or feel. If they release a song outside of their niche, fans may become confused and ultimately not believe in the artist. This happened when Bob Dylan turned "electric" at the Newport Jazz Festival where he was booed by the fans who were expecting to hear Dylan's folk roots.

++++++++++++++++++++++++++++++

Image and Brand Management

Brand management is an important strategy for every artist, and it can really determine its future prospects. Today, there are a lot of artists which are synonymous with their brands, and the prime reason behind this is their ability to manage their brands effectively.

In today's fiercely competitive music market, artists are known by their brands. Brand management should be a high priority for every artist that aims to develop a brand identity and create a loyal base of customers. With the advent of online social media, new avenues of brand management are now available to artists. Today, there is an increased interaction between consumers and artists. It is important for serious artists to invest time, effort, and capital to create a unique identity for them self.

Artists should always remember that their future of brand management lies in innovation as well as maintaining an open and honest relationship with their fans.

++++++++++++++++++++++++++++++

Image Importance in Branding
In addition to the many aspects of Artist Development, creation of brand identity is one of the most important parts of establishing the credibility of an artist. This was discussed briefly in the chapter about setting up a business for an artist.

A brand identity is very much like a personality of the artist. The artist's brand identity describes, the artist's ideas and describes with just one or two words, a look or image.

Brand identity has been defined as, "a name, term, design, symbol, or any other feature that identifies one seller's goods or services as distinct from those of other sellers." The sellers being artists. But, in the entertainment industry, specifically, the music business, brand identity is defined by the style of music itself. The legal term for a brand logo, design or symbol is a trademark (see section on trademarks). A brand may identify one item, a family of the items, or all items of the artist.

An artist's brand is the artist's identity and is usually unique and visually appealing. The combination of a brand name, a related tag line, an emblem or a symbol with specific designs, colors and fonts to suit the artist's identity and preferences will aid the artist's prospective customer base. Many times, the sound, or the songs of an artist becomes the basis for the perceived image of an artist. This is another reason why the quality of the songs is so important.

++++++++++++++++++++++++++++++++

Creating a Brand Identity
Once the process of establishing the artist's company begins, the owner(s) need to answer some basic management questions. What are the artist's goals? What are the strategies of the artist to achieve those goals? What is the nature of the prospective market that might help the artist achieve its goal? How does the artist currently fill that role? Does the artist's role and its image drive the market? These questions might seem irrelevant to a layman, but to an artist's promoter or manager, these very questions help to strategize the brand identity of the artist.

Artist Name = Artist Brand = Brand Name

Logos and Slogos

One part of building an image is through the use of a logo. A logo is a graphic design used as an emblem or a symbol to complement an artist's brand name. Marketing experts state that logos have a better recall value compared to any other component of branding. The customer's mind tend to retain the designs of a logo and can identify the artist just by viewing the logo design. A logo should be visually appealing and in colors suitable for the artist and artist's image. Managers generally opt for colors that are in sync with the current market trend, nature of the product or the age and preferences of target customers. E.g., logos of eco-friendly brands are mostly in green color. Logos for brands meant for youth are generally in bright catchy colors. Some unforgettable logos that speak a lot for themselves are the lips and tongue of the Rolling Stones or letters N I N for Nine Inch Nails.

Artists don't necessarily need masses of money to start their image or design concept. For some artists, this may be relatively simple, particularly where the look of an artist or their style of music offers obvious possibilities. An artist with a name like Nuclear Whiteout suggests some quite obvious visual ideas. However, where this is not the case, a band may need to think rather more carefully about its choice of visual imagery.

Brand identity often helps fans and potential customers perceive that the artist is selling the best quality products. It therefore puts a solid responsibility on the artist and its management to live up to customer's expectations by constantly producing and releasing quality products and performances.

Facts about Brand Identity

- It is first of all essential to select a brand identity that will continue to remain popular for years to come.
- A brand identity is treated as an artist's intangible asset. Its value increases as the artist's goodwill rises.
- The brand identity of an artist needs to be registered when the artists registers or incorporates the company.
- Artists are encouraged to create a trademark to discourage illegal use of their brand identity.

++++++++++++++++++++++++++++++++

The record industry spends millions of dollars marketing both new and established artists. For an unsigned band "image" can often be the crucial factor in securing that all-important record deal. Image on its own is not enough but it can be a very important element of an artist's overall package. Great songs, stage presence and visual style/image are perhaps the three (3) most important factors contributing to the success of any musical artist or performer.

The history of pop music has many examples using the power of the image. From Elvis Presley's hip shaking and duck haircut to Malcolm McLaren's Sex Pistols "Never Mind the Bollocks" marketing campaign, or U2's Zoo and Zooropa tours which were massive assaults on the senses with their multi-media presentations. On the other hand, some artists have made a virtue of deliberately cultivating a low-key image. In many cases this becomes as recognizable as a trade mark. A few examples of performers who have opted for an extremely low key image include Suzanne Vega, Eddie Reader and New Order. These artists cultivated a very distinctive low-key visual style through their use of simple but striking and innovative design images.

Once an artist has come up with a winning design, they should think about badges, stickers, T-shirts and other possible merchandise. Not only are these brilliant advertisements for the artist or band, they can be valuable sources of income. The most likely point of sale for an artist's merchandise is of course at the gig.

After the artist has developed an image in the form of a logo, they may also use it for letterhead, on band backdrops (extremely useful for advertising the band at support gigs or on out-of-town tour dates), stickers, badges and other publicity material. It is also useful for some artists to get a rubber stamp of their logo. This can then be used on basic publicity material and as a ticket stamp at gigs, etc.

++++++++++++++++++++++++++++++

Tips for Brand Building

One of the first steps in brand building is the artist's belief and confidence in his or her self.

1. If music business collaborators of an artist do not have a high regard for the values of the artist and/or the artist's organization, they will fail in performing to the best of their abilities. Brand building helps the artist's collaborators to relate to the artist and the artist's company as they feel that they are a part of it.

2. Taking steps for building the artist's brand alone may not alone bring results, so it is important that the artist measure and monitor their level of progress. Developing effective plans is one thing but it is important to ensure that what is written on paper is put to action. Monitoring the artist's brand building activity also helps them to get a feedback from their team and collaborators about what they think is working right for them, and what steps can be taken to improve their project or projects.

3. The artist's brand building strategy should be focused on creating a unique identity for itself. If an artist does not take their chosen name seriously, fans and potential customers may become skeptical about the name or perceive it to be a fake. This will definitely affect the artist's brand. It is important therefore, that artist's think creatively and put in an effort to differentiate their brand from others.

4. Brand building is carried out to create a positive perception of an artist in the minds of their fans and customers. The crucial point here is the relevancy. Every product is aimed at a particular market and it is important that artists always keep their target audience in mind. If the artist's product is aimed at a relatively smaller customer base, it is advisable to not stretch the brand too thin. Similarly, if an artist has a large target customer base, it is important that their brand is able to fit into a wider range.

5. Artists should know their strengths and then capitalize on them. Every artist is unique and each has their own strengths and weaknesses. It

is very important for an artist to know its brands weaknesses as well as its strengths - the qualities that set it apart from others. Rather than embarking on a holistic approach towards brand management, an artist may focus its products and performances in such a manner that it reflects the artist's outlook.

6. Deliver on promises. It is very important that an artist deliver on what they promise to their fans. These fans are the artist's customers. Advertisements, marketing campaigns and promotions would be of no good use if the artist's recorded sounds or live performances are not up to the expectations of the fan. It takes a lot of time for an artist to build a brand and leniency from the artist can seriously hamper all the efforts. It is important that the artist stay true to their word and deliver a consistent flow quality products to their customers. Every show should be the best ever. Every recording should be of the highest quality.

7. Be consistent with quality. One of the biggest mistakes that artists often make is taking their customers for granted. A brand which has created a niche for itself can't rest on its past laurels to sustain in the marketplace. It has to ensure that the quality of its products does not deteriorate over the years. A classic example of this is the artist who relies on past hits and instead of releasing a new album, issues a greatest hits compilation. Another example is the artist who tours and performs all old songs. These artists are not working on new composition, new songs or new shows. They are in a delusion that their old material will sustain forever. Big mistake.

8. Keep reinventing the brand. This may be difficult for beginning artists but as careers develop, new songs and sounds will be discovered by the artist. The brand will grow from that.

9. Ensure a great customer experience. For a brand to be respected, the after-sales experience of a customer is vital. In other words, to solidify a fan's loyalty, an artist needs to follow-up immediately. Fans come one at a time and they can be lost one at a time as well. Most artists spend a fortune on promoting their product and getting new customers on board, but fail miserably when it comes to after-sales experience. Retaining fans is as important as acquiring them. People have the power to hail or harm an artist through word-of-mouth feedback. It becomes imperative for an artist to train their support staff and customer service efficiently to ensure that the brand image doesn't take a beating, and their loyal fans don't lose interest in the artist.

++++++++++++++++++++++++++++++

Living Up to the Brand

Consider a band that promotes environmental issues with water, but uses plastic bottles on stage when they perform. Or the business that claims to be customer-centric, but reserves the best seats near the front of the stage for those who pay the most.

Brands have come to mean even more in our time-poor society. Why? Because great brands that we trust can save us time. Consumers tend to think: "If I can trust the maker, I can buy the product now and worry about its specific features and benefits later." In the world of complex products, brand trust is vital, as many products and services seem to have the same features and benefits. Many fans will buy a new recording from an artist because they know, from past experience, that they enjoy the sound of that artist. As previously mentioned, the sound of an artist is a part of its brand.

A brand worth looking at is Virgin. Sir Richard Branson, the entrepreneur behind Virgin, has developed one of the strongest and most respected brands worldwide. He can literally take the name Virgin and put it to most industries and create value over night. That's the power of his brand.

Branson has applied the Virgin brand to many industries - from a record label to airlines to financial services - each time bringing instant value to the new business, simply because of his existing power in the Virgin brand. This benefit alone provides reason for building a well-recognized brand name.

> **a brand = a product or service + a business relationship**

The brand itself is a valuable asset and may be represented on the business' balance sheet of the artist. In some cases the brand can represent considerable value in relation a brand = a product or service + a relationship to a business' overall market value or saleable value. So, what do image and brand really mean? Simply stated:

- Image is the perception (picture) fans and potential customers have about an artist at any one point in time
- Brand is the link (relationship) between the artist and the customer's values. For instance, when we look to buy a product, we want to know it will deliver on its promises, and will often select a brand because we feel we can trust it. This is referred to as goodwill.

Image and brand have everything to do with identifying an artist's target market, and identifying which values are important to that target market. Smart artists create an image and a brand which relate to those values, and then promote the brand and fulfill the promise.

Why does an artist need an image and a brand?

Some artists may think: "But we are not a huge artist, we are only a small business – we don't need to develop a brand name or an image. Besides, we don't have the money to promote and build it." Perhaps, but if the artist is generating any income from their performances then they are a small business. They may not be able to afford to spend like these major artists do. Keep in mind, though, these current stars started off as a small business too. Creating an image and a brand for a small or medium artist is not about flashy and slick advertisements. It is about ensuring the target market recognizes the art as their preferred choice for the products (recordings) or services (performances) provided by the artist.

Artists need to build their brand that's recognized by the public, even if it is only their local neighborhood. This helps to draw people to their performances as well as their website to download their recordings. It also helps build loyalty, goodwill and true sales value in the artist's business.

Branding forms part of a business' Intellectual Property (IP). (See trademarks section) IP is big business in today's business and entertainment world. It cannot be ignored by small, medium or mega-artists. An artist's small business can develop goodwill and an image that may develop into a brand recognized by the local community, city, state and country, or even worldwide. One of the major reasons for branding an artist's business is to encourage goodwill and therefore build its value.

Another reason for a quality image is to enhance a competitive advantage. An artist's brand is built from an artist's image. As fans and customers interact the art and the artist and the artist's business, they will form an image of what they like and dislike about it. If it fits their values, they are likely to become loyal fans. If it does not, chances are they are going to purchase tickets to another artist's show or download another artist's recordings. The most important steps in building an image and brand for an artist, and an artist's business, is to stop, think, plan and then act. The process of developing an image and brand requires artists to take a close look at the business and then plan for its future success.

Artists should be working on their business and developing it with intent. While it doesn't have to be expensive, branding can be a large investment both in time and dollars, so it is important to plan well.

If an artist thinks their fans and potential customers don't expect quality, they may as well get out of this business. Attention to the little things, or lack thereof, can communicate competence or ineptitude. It can communicate professionalism or scream amateur. It is the artist's choice. How many concert promoters are going to hire performers who can't perform? How many fans are going to buy a musical recording from an artist with inferior songs? Quality does not have to cost an artist a lot of money. It could, however, make a significant difference to the attitudes of an artist's fans and customers as well as their staff and collaborators.

Here are some ideas that may be helpful in developing an artist's brand:

- Simplicity – identify the vision and goals for the artist's brand name. These need to be easy to remember, popular, easy to pronounce and likely to stick in a potential fan's mind.

- Validity – public perception of the artist is very important. Consider how the public relates to the artist: what things represent the artist to the public?

- Distinction – the artist identity should make them stand out. Artists should be proud of it.

- Protection – before an artist makes the final decision on their name, they should seek expert legal help to determine if they can use or register the brand name. This is essential.

- Likeability – artists should seek feedback from their key fans and customers. See what they relate to. Artist should ask why, as this will inform them about the image that the brand is purveying.

- Extension – does it have longevity? Artists should make sure they can brand and be used in a number of visual executions and being able to stretch across a number of products without a complete re-design.

++++++++++++++++++++++++++++++++

Branding the Artist

Many of today's fans and customers think of branding as that creative thing artists do with the name of their product or service. It is the packaging of a product which includes the visual impression, logo, the jingle or tune that a customer's mind conjures up when they hear the artist's name. Branding can be as simple as designing a new t-shirt or it can be an exciting long-term media campaign for print and television that communicates the brand message.

++++++++++++++++++++++++++++++++

First Impressions

Today's buyers use their instincts to determine the worth of an artist's product or service, and it is based on visual impressions. Potential buyers make the subconscious decision of whether or not they want to do business within the first few seconds of exposure to the artist's music or image. This impression comes from the packaging of the product, the impression people have of an artist's web site, and presentation information, such as brochures or business cards. A successful image is the foundation of every successful artist. The image of an artist's brand determines their credibility in the mind of new fans, and establishes the value of their products and services.

An artist has only one chance to make a great first impression. Here are some of the areas that artists and companies use to make favorable first impressions.

- Logo Design
- Letterhead & Business Cards
- Web site and interactive design
- Flyers & Posters
- All Promotion Presentations
- Performance Presentations
- Product and packaging design
- Professional Customer Service

Branding is more than making a new logo or company slogan. It is the silent message that the buying public receives and motivates them to tell others about their purchase. Real branding increases the profitability and lowers the cost of getting new customers.

Image and Branding Tips

Now let's get down to some specific tips about developing an artist's image and brand:

1. Decide on an overall visual "look" for the artist's public information including colors, fonts, etc. The artist's website design, flyers, press material, album art, etc. should all start bearing that consistent look.
2. Choose fonts and colors that best reflect the overall theme and feel for the artist. (HINT: If your music style is pop/rock, a font named "Gothic Horror" is probably not going to convey the right idea about you.)
3. If the artist has a logo, they should begin putting it on anything and everything that has to do with them. They should make it so that when people see that logo, they know it's the artist, whether or not the artist's name is with it.
4. Register the artist's stage name and/or logo as a trademark. This ensures that no one else can use their name.

Here's a final thought about image and branding. Whenever an artist begins developing as their public persona, make sure it's real. They should make sure they're putting their true self into it. They shouldn't let their public image be a character they play that doesn't reflect who they really are. That might work for awhile, but fake public personas are very difficult to maintain for the long haul and the burden becomes too heavy after awhile. It's better for an artist to be honest, and let their public image be a reasonable reflection of who they are, as a person and as a musician.

---

10 Ways to Brand Your Band

1. Have a great logo
2. Make the website layout and design consistent with the artist's image
3. Say something with your fashion choices
4. Take cool band photos
5. Create amazing CD packaging
6. Do a vinyl release
7. Conduct free giveaways through your website, newsletter, and social media platforms
8. Blog
9. Shoot a music video that is worth sharing
10. Sell graphic T-shirts and merchandise

As an artist, the name you choose identifies you: you as a brand. All artists are brands. This is important to fans and customers as well as to music business collaborators such as agents, promoters, talent buyers, record label executives, and publishers, not including the vast amount of other ancillary companies or individuals. To continue doing business on a regular basis, your name (brand) must remain untarnished. Integrity in the music business is still important. In reality, the industry is relatively small. Everybody knows everybody. The music business is all about relationships and your name / brand should become synonymous with someone whom others will want to do business with.

Doing Business As = DBA

Shawn Carter owns the brand Jay-Z. Gene Simmons own the brand K.I.S.S. Justin Timberlake owns the brand Justin Timberlake.

What's a Brand?
It's an elusive concept but here's a simple definition: A brand is the sum total of the images, ideas and experiences people have regarding an artist, a company, product, person, etc.

The McDonald's brand isn't just their golden arches logo or their "I'm loving it" slogan. It's what we (you, me and everyone else who is aware of the company) collectively conjure up when we think about McDonald's. And what we think of McDonald's is based on our prior experiences at their restaurants and with their advertising, public image, etc.

An individual or organization will choose a name for the business entity when filing articles of incorporation. The name chosen must be distinguishable from the name of any other artist, business entity, corporation, trade name, Limited Liability Company, limited liability partnership, limited partnership or that which is currently registered in the office of the Secretary of State.

Before filing articles of incorporation, you should check the availability of the name you choose. It is a good idea to have two or three alternative names for your business entity.

The Secretary of State will make the final determination in the availability of your business entity's name once the forms are filed.

Band Name Ideas

You need to ponder over several ideas while coming up with a name for the artist: soloist or a band. While many may think it is a very easy task, this might not always be the case. There is a lot of thought and effort that goes into creating a great and unique band name.

Band names are, without a shadow of doubt, one of the most influential factors in a band's popularity. A band is a brand. While a band may practice for endless hours and possess the capability to produce great music, unless the band's name is one that instantly captures the attention of the audience, all its other efforts might go in vain.

In most cases, band names should be relevant to the kind of music being played and the genre in which it operates. There may be intentional exceptions to this case, but that does not work out too often. Many times, artists and bands use their names as a symbol or a message that they want to convey by their music.

If you are planning on starting a band, or already have one, but are yet to name it, or want a better name, here is a list of band name ideas divided into various types.

Cool Band Names

Cool band names are special! They're meant to establish the identity of the artist and give it a presence in the hearts of fans and customers. Some of the many famous musical artists of all times have crossed borders and entertained every nook and corner of the world. Depending on your bands type of music and the way you wish to present the artist or band in front of an audience, you can come up with some good names.

Choosing Creative Band Names

While choosing creative names for your bands, you have to do some brainstorming to come up a unique band name. For instance, you can choose a particular theme or a cause and name your band dedicated to that cause. You can choose some names from various popular books. For example, the name of famous band, Veruca Salt took its name from the famous book *Charlie and the Chocolate Factory*.

Just like various bands have named their bands on some geographical location, you to can pick up the name of some of landmarks in your area and name your band on that! Linkin Park, Chicago, Boston, and Soundgarden etc are some of the classic band names. You can also combine two words of any band and name your team. Simon and Garfunkel would be a good example of this. You can also use the first name of your favorite person or any of your team members (more specifically, the lead singers) and can form some cool names for a band.

Keep in mind that the name of an artist may be different that the name of the artist's company. For example, the band McGuffey Lane is a DBA of Invisible, Inc.

Takeaways:

- Image is the perception (picture or feeling) your fans and potential customers have about the artist at any point in time
- Brand is the tangible and recognizable link between an artist, their business and their image
- Developing an image and brand can create value for an artist's business
- Image and brand are all about an artist's target market and their values
- Image and brand are all about clarity of an artist's business values and their relationship / expectations to the fan / customer
- Image and brand may help an artist stand out from their competitors
- Image and brand often make the difference in a purchase.

First impressions count for a lot and they are often made within seconds of a fan or potential customer hearing the artist's music or seeing the artist's performance. Today's artists should think of their business through the image they emit:

- The design of posters or flyers
- The dress and presentation of performances
- The type and style of t-shirt that are sold at the merchandise table
- The presentation of musical recordings.

These can all send a message to an artist's fans and customers. If done well, it can help make a difference to the sales of an artist performances or recordings or merchandise. If done poorly, an artist may be sending the wrong message to their fans and customers. This, in turn, could be hurting the artist and their business without them really understanding or even knowing why.

To Do

Notes:

Artist Development in the Music Business
Chapter 11 – Legal Issues

The music business is very fond of contracts. The record, publishing, merchandising, and management sides of the industry are contract crazy. In the performance arena, there are indeed contracts. At the beginning of an artist's career, performance agreements may be either a verbal agreement or a handshake. As an artist becomes more established, it is almost guaranteed that written contracts will become the norm.

The next part of an Artist Development Plan that an artist needs to consider is the legal issues pertaining to an artist's career. It's good practice to begin thinking about the legal aspects early. At the very least, an artist should know their rights and priorities when starting to collaborate with others.

The legal part of any artist career is of utmost priority. You may have heard stories of an unscrupulous manager, publisher or agent who "stole" an artist's work. It's my contention that in these cases, the artist must not have properly reviewed the legal documents that they signed. If they had, I doubt there would as many stories.

No matter how proficient an artist is creatively, they need to think and operate like a business in order to remain successful. The legal aspects are a big part of any business; especially those dealing with intellectual property. Music-related careers are affected by legal matters on a regular basis: from artist contracts, band member agreements, recording and publishing contracts, copyright law, name protection and business organization contracts. Legal aspects of the music business include collaborative issues with artists, musicians, managers, agents, promoters, producers, publishers and many more.

It's important for an artist to take a real-world approach to understanding the legal issues of the music business today. A big part of this is learning what different collaborators, players and team members do and when the artist may need them.

Musicians, songwriters and artists should pay particular emphasis to band member agreements, management contracts, copyright law, recording contracts, as well as performance and publishing contracts.

++++++++++++++++++++++++++++++

Agreements Overview

We enter into contracts so many times in a day that 'contract' has become an indispensable part of our life. When a person purchases a newspaper in the morning or a ticket to a concert in the evening, they are entering into a contract. We give money and expect something in return.

It must be noted that a contract need not be in writing, unless there is specific provisions in law that the contract should be in writing such as a contract for sale of immovable property, promissory notes, or trusts.

A verbal contract is equally enforceable, if it can be proved. A contract can be enforced for compensation and damages for breach of contract which can be obtained through Civil Court.

A gentlemen's agreement is an informal agreement between two or more parties. It may be written, oral, or simply understood as part of an unspoken agreement by convention or through mutually beneficial etiquette. The essence of a gentlemen's agreement is that it relies upon the honor of the parties for its fulfillment, rather than being in any way enforceable. It is, therefore, distinct from a legal agreement or contract and is almost impossible to enforce.

In law, a contract is a legally binding agreement between two or more parties which, if it contains the elements of a valid legal agreement, is enforceable by law or by binding arbitration. A legally enforceable contract is an exchange of promises with specific legal remedies in case of breach. These can include compensatory damages, where the defaulting party is required to pay monies that would otherwise have been exchanged were the contract honored, or an equitable remedy such as specific performance, in which the person who entered into the contract is required to carry out the specific action they have reneged upon. For example, if a club owner cancels a contracted gig, he or she might be required to pay the scheduled performer any way.

Any agreement which is enforceable by law is a contract. Hence, we have to understand first what an 'agreement' is. Every promise and every set of promises, forming the consideration for each other, is an agreement. A person makes a proposal (offer). When it is accepted by the other, it becomes a promise. However, a promise cannot be one sided. Only a mutual promise forming consideration for each other is an 'agreement.' For example, Person A agrees to pay $100 to Person B and Person B agrees to give Person A a ticket to a show which is priced at $100. This set of promises is a form of consideration for each other. However, if Person A agrees to pay $100 to Person B, but Person B does not promise anything, it is not a 'set of promises forming consideration for each other' and hence, not an agreement.

It should be noted that the term 'agreement' as defined, requires mutual consideration. Thus, if Person A invites Person B to sit in on a recording session and Person B agrees to come, it is not an 'agreement,' because there is no mutual agreement between them.

> **Important Agreement Considerations**
>
> - Always think "win/win"
> - Negotiate only with those in authority to agree to your requests
> - Have a prioritized agenda. Start with the most agreeable items and work downwards to the toughest points
> - Put yourself in the other person's place and structure your arguments to address their concerns.
> - Anticipate the other party's issues
> - Never give ultimatums. This is bad form and sets up a defense position
> - Never concede a point, however small, without winning a comparable concession in return
> - Take notes and verbally summarize each point agreed to before you move on to the next point. Misunderstandings are a common problem
> - Follow up negotiations with a memo or letter summarizing what was agreed to, and ask for a written response within so many days or hours if any points are disputed
> - Make the other party feel good about the outcome

An agreement is said to be reached when an offer capable of immediate acceptance is met with a "mirror image" acceptance (i.e., an unqualified acceptance). The parties must have the necessary capacity to contract and the contract must not be indeterminate, impossible, or illegal.

As long as the good or service provided is legal, any oral agreement between two parties can be a binding legal contract. However, only parties to a written agreement have material evidence (the written contract itself) to prove the actual terms uttered at the time the agreement was negotiated. In daily life, most contracts can be and are made orally, such as purchasing a compact disc or a ticket to a show.

Agreements

Proprietary rights agreements are confidential agreements ensuring that certain information pertaining the company or the organization remain only between them. They are mostly related to copyright laws and trade secrets that are confidential and shared between companies and their employees.

However certain exceptions are also there in the confidential agreements regarding the disclosure of statements during the party's relationship. The confidential report has provisions to allow access of information under given guidelines and circumstances.

Proposal or Offer

A proposal is made when one person signifies to another their willingness to do (or to abstain from doing) anything legal, with a view of trying to obtain the consent of the other party.

Typically, a concert promoter may propose an offer to an artist to perform at a certain event on a certain date and time for a specific set of financial or promotional benefits. This would be considered a proposal or offer. Another example would be a publisher proposed an offer to a songwriter-artist for the use of a song in return for a specific percentage of income derived from the licensing of that song.

Promises

Acceptance of Proposal - Promise
When the person to whom the proposal is made signifies their agreement, the proposal is said to be accepted. When a proposal / offer is accepted it becomes a promise. As is clear from the definition, only persons to whom a proposal is made can signify their acceptance.

To continue the above scenario: if the artist agrees to the proposal of the concert promoter, the offer is considered as accepted, and as such, a promise is established.

Steps of a Contract
- Proposal of Agreement
- Acceptance of Proposal
- Agreed by Mutual Promises
- Contract Establishment
- Performance of Contract

Promisor and Promisee
The person making the proposal is called the "promisor" and the person accepting the proposal is called the "promisee." In the above case, the concert promoter is the promisor and the artist is the promisee.

Consideration for Promise
The definition of 'agreement' itself states that the mutual promises should form consideration of each other. 'Consideration' is essential of an agreement. A promise without consideration is not an 'agreement' and hence naturally, it is not a 'contract.'

Consideration

Definition of 'Consideration'
When, at the desire of the promisor, the promisee has done or promises to do something, such act or promise is called a consideration for the promise.

In order to convert a proposal into a promise, the acceptance must:

1. Be absolute and unqualified
2. Be expressed in some usual and reasonable manner

Acceptance of offer is complete only when it is absolute and unconditional. Conditional acceptance or qualified acceptance is no acceptance.

Contract Establishment

After an unconditional acceptance of an offer, both parties may then establish a written contract amongst themselves (which is recommended) or they may agree to a verbal contract.

Performance of Contract
The performance of a contract is the final stage of putting together an agreement. Both parties must complete their part of the agreement.

Voidable Contracts

1. An agreement which is enforceable by law at the option of one of the parties, but not at the option of the other or others, is a voidable contract.
2. When consent is obtained by coercion, undue influence, misrepresentation or fraud, it is voidable at the option of the party whose consent was obtained by coercion, fraud etc. However, the other party cannot avoid the contract.
3. When a contract contains reciprocal promises and one party to the contract prevents the other from performing their promise, the contract becomes voidable at the option of the party being prevented.
4. When time is of essence in a contract and one party fails to perform in time, it is voidable at the option of other party. A person who himself delayed the contract cannot avoid the contract on account of their own delay.

Agent and Principals

An "agent" is a person employed to do any act for another or to represent another in dealings with third persons. Yes, that means a booking agent, but in legal terms, it also could mean a manager, a publisher or a publicist. The person for whom such act is done, or who is so represented, is called the "principal."

The "principal" may be any person who is of the age of majority and who is of sound mind. Thus, any person competent to contract can appoint an agent.

An agent can be any person unless they are not of the age of majority or of sound mind. The agent must be responsible to the principal and the principal will only want a responsible person to be their agent.

With this in mind, an agent can act on behalf of a principal and can therefore bind the principal to an agreement.

An agent has duties towards a principal:

- Conduct principal's business as per principal's directions
- Carry out work with normal skill and diligence
- Render proper accounts
- Communicate with principal
- Pay sums received for principal

An agent's duty is terminated by agreement, the principal's death or insanity. As discussed in the management section of the Artist Development Plan, an artist may elect not to have their personal manager act as their agent. In this case, the manager may make referrals to the artists but cannot sign agreements or contracts as the artist's agent. This all depends on their agreement.

++++++++++++++++++++++++++++++

Licenses

The verb license or grant license means to give permission. The noun license refers to that permission as well as to the document recording that permission.

A license may be granted by a party ("licensor") to another party ("licensee") as an element of an agreement between those parties.

In particular, a license may be issued to a content provider to allow an activity that would otherwise be forbidden, such as copyright. It may require paying a fee and/or proving a capability. The requirement may also serve to keep the owners informed on a type of activity, and to give them the opportunity to set conditions and limitations.

A licensor may grant a license under intellectual property laws to authorize use (such as copying songs or using a (patented) invention) to a licensee. This will help the licensee form a claim of infringement brought by the licensor. A license under intellectual property commonly has several components beyond the grant itself, including a term, territory, renewal provisions, and other limitations deemed vital to the licensor.

A shorthand definition of a license is "a promise by the licensor not to sue the licensee." That means without a license, any use or exploitation of intellectual property by a third party would amount to copying or infringement. Such copying would be improper and could, by using the legal system, be stopped if the intellectual property owner wanted to do so.

It is undeniable that intellectual property licensing plays a major role in today's music business and economy. Licensing has been recognized as an independent branch of law.

Categories of Licenses
1. Bare licenses
2. Contractual licenses
3. Licenses coupled with an Interest

A bare license occurs when a person enters or uses the property of another with the express or implied permission of the owner or under circumstances that would provide a good defense against an action for trespass. For example, a person entering a nightclub to ask for tickets is a licensee and not a trespasser.

Contractual license provides an expressed or implied permission to enter or use the property in exchange for some consideration. For example, the purchase of a concert ticket allows the ticket holder a license to enter the venue at a particular date and time. Licenses that are acquired by contract may include the right to use property that is protected by copyright, trademark or patent. Another example of a contractual license is a person who purchases a compact disc of recorded music. This person does not own the music or the recording of the music.

They own a piece of plastic and are "licensing" the music.

A license coupled with an interest arises when a person acquires the right to take possession of property owned by another person or company. For example, when a grant by the holder of a copyright to another of any of the rights embodied in the copyright, short of an assignment of all rights, is a license coupled with an interest. Songwriters and publishers do this all the time.

> **All agreements are not contracts. Only those agreements which are enforceable by law are 'contracts.'**

The Need of Contracts

Yes, yes, yes, yes, yes. Contracts are an essential part of the music business. Not only do they protect an artist or band, they actually help get things done more efficiently. Musicians think of lots of great reasons why they shouldn't bother with contracts.

Here are a few truths about contracts:

- Working with friends can be very difficult. When something doesn't go right, not only is it frustrating professionally, it is frustrating on a personal level. Working together can destroy friendships. Having an agreement, though, will help foster those friendships.

- Beginning artists may not care about the money now – until they think that there is actually some money that was made off of their music. When that happens, they will care. They will want their proper share and they won't want anyone else taking more than their fair share.

Contracts let everyone know exactly where they stand. A contract spells out what everyone's role is; what their responsibilities are; and what they will be paid for their contribution or work. There is no room for disagreements. Contracts also protect the artist and ensure that the artist gets everything to which they are entitled.

Even if there is no money involved in the beginning stages of an artist's career, there could be sometime in the near future. Now is the best time to decide how that money will be handled and divided. Oh, and don't fall for that old "I don't care about the money" stuff. Artists need money, too. They need money so they can continue to make their art. Protecting an artist's financial assets is an investment in their artistic vision, not a step of "selling out."

> **Valid Contract Requirements**
> - Offer and Acceptance
> - Free consent of both parties
> - Mutual and lawful consideration
> - Enforceable by law
> - Parties competent to contract
> - Object should be lawful
> - Possibility of performance
> - Acceptance is absolute

++++++++++++++++++++++++++++

Contract Clauses

There are many clauses in a contract that artists should be familiar with.

The Term - The term is the length of time that an agreement with a music business collaborator is valid. Artists and their collaborators will need to agree upon a term and a contract cancellation policy. A fair contract term is a one year agreement, with an option to extend the agreement at the end of the year if both parties agree. At that point, artists can look at negotiating longer agreements, but a one year term is a good trial term for both parties.

Artists need to be wary of giving term and renewal options to extend their contract with a collaborator without an agreement. If an artist does, they may be forced to stick with a collaborator that they don't want.

> **Good contracts specify how either party may leave the deal.**

The term of a contract is the duration of the contract. (How many performances are expected? Any there any time constraints?) An event promoter may want to sign a performer for as long as possible and to book as many performances as possible.

What's the duration of the contract? How many records will be manufactured? Are there any time constraints?

A record company usually wants to sign an artist for as long as possible and to make as many recordings as possible.

An "option," is the record company's option whether the artist will make each recording.

Years are not recommended for the term of the agreement. If, however, agreements use years for the term, it should not go past seven (7) years on the delivery of product.

Territory – An artist's contract with any business collaborator (music business or not) should specifically state where the collaborator has the right to represent the artist or the artist's art (albums, bookings, etc). For example, an artist may already have bookings in a certain area and has a booking agent who books that area for the artists, an agreement with another agent would exclude the area already represented by the first agent. Another example is that of a record company who may release recordings of an artist in only certain sections of the world. If the artist has self-released a CD in the United States, a record label may only release their recording of the artist in Europe.

Compensation Clause - This is a crucial part of many contracts. Artists need to specify how and when they can expect to be paid and from whom. Many times, artists are musicians, it is important for them to know that they may not be paid until the collaborator, such as a record label or publisher, makes back the money it has spent on the artist or the artist's art (including the advance). The contract then needs to state how any profit after the collaborator recoups their expenses and how costs will be divided.

The following are just a few of the optional items that can be included on a contract between an artist and a music business collaborator. They may or may not apply on a case by case basis:

Accounting Clause - This gives the artist the right to audit the collaborator's finances and books relating to their collaboration at a given interval - say once a year. This can be as simple as meeting for a cocktail and reviewing some quick and easy numbers, or it can be as formal as having an accountant complete a full audit. Smart artists will reserve the right to audit the books of their collaborators. This is especially true when there's a door deal or a percentage deal for a performance. It a promoter's responsibility is to report financially to the artist (usually occurs after the performance. It's also true for recording artists to audit the books of their record label. The label's responsibility is to report financially to the artist (usually occurs every six months; i.e., if an accounting period lasts from January until June, the label will report to the artists approximately in September).

Licensing Clause – For example, if the label licenses the album to a label in another territory, or if the label licenses a track from the album for use in the media, how does the fee get divided?

Acceptance and Delivery Clause - This clause is a major label contract staple that is seldom used by indie labels. Basically, this means that the label does not have to release a record that deviates from the kind of music they thought they would be getting from the artist, and that the music has to recorded in a format that could be played on the radio (i.e., not on a 4-track in someone's bedroom). This clause can be controversial.

Reclaim Fee Clause - Some promoters reclaim their investment in the gig before they pay the performer(s). The venue rental, sound and lights, technicians, rider, gear rental, hotels - these things can all be reclaimed from the fee. The contract should clearly state which expenses a promoter can reclaim from the show proceeds.

Spending Cap Clause - Recording artists usually don't make money until the record label makes back all the money it has spent on the album (with the exception of mechanical royalties, which labels have to pay songwriters and publishers no matter what). That doesn't mean the artist is required to let the label spend and spend and spend. It's good to include a spending cap in record label contracts that says the label must consult the artist after spending X amount of cash. It will save loads of hassle in the long run when the artist is complaining about money and complaining that the record label has overspent on their release.

Advances Clause - How much (recoupable) recording money will the artist receive? Recoupable costs will have to be paid back by the recording artist from the royalty rate as applied to actual sales.

How much (living) money will the artist receive that is recoupable? What about other advances, such as videos, and touring? Advances are also paid back to the label.

An advance to an artist should pay for the recording and to help support the artist during the process. The advance is a loan from the record label that will be deducted from money that is earned from the artist's record sales. In other words, if the artist has a $10,000 advance and earned $10,000 in royalties, the artists would not receive any money. For that reason, some artists recommend keeping the advance (and recording costs) as low as possible. This enables the artist to turn a profit sooner.
On the other hand, some artists say that the higher the advance, the more commitment from the label. Others say that, since the failure rate is so high with new releases, an artist should seek the highest advance possible so that if the record underperforms, artists can at least enjoy the money from the advance.

Exclusivity Clause - Many event promoters includes a provision stating in the performance agreement that the deal is "exclusive." In other words, during the term of the agreement, artists can't perform for other promoters within a specified time period or location perimeter. Therefore, an exclusivity clause in a contract refers to the fact that artists may only contract with one promoter in one area during a specific time or date.

Record labels may require that artists agree that during the period of their agreement, they will not perform for any other person, firm or corporation, for the purpose of producing commercial sound records. In addition, the record label may require that after the expiration of the agreement, the artist will not record for anyone else any of the musical selections recorded by the record label.

Every record contract includes a provision stating that the deal is "exclusive." In other words, during the term of the agreement, artists can't make records for another record label.

Creativity Clause - Who will control the style of music and the quality of the delivery? Promoters, record labels and artists want as much creative freedom as possible. Who will control the amount of product and the quality of the product? Both record labels and artists want as much creative freedom as possible. The record label often maintains a veto power when letting an artist choose the producer, engineer, studio, etc. This certainly changes when the artist becomes more successful.

Publicity Clause – Promoters, publishers and record label executives will need permission from the artist for the use of their name, likeness and voice of the artist in order to publicize their collaboration. Also, ownership of the artist's website URLs may also be a point of negotiation.

Merchandising Clause - The term "Merchandising" may refer to various items for sale including compact discs, t-shirts, DVDs or downloads.

Key Man Clauses - If a significant band member resigns, or leaves the band, the collaborator may terminate the deal.

Departing Member Clause - Often one or more band members decide they want to leave the band. Sometimes (very often) this is the lead singer and primary songwriter in the group. A Departing Member clause spells out what will happen if and when one or more members leave the group or the group disbands entirely.

When this happens, the record company typically has the right to do the following:

- Terminate the recording agreement with the leaving member AND the remaining members;
- Terminate the recording agreement in regard to some of the leaving members and/or remaining members, while retaining the rights to other leaving members and/or remaining members;
- Require any leaving member to record anywhere from 2 to 5 demos for their review. After submitting the demos, the record company has an additional period of time (usually 30 days) to drop or retain the members.

Royalty Clause - There are various clauses about royalties. The money paid from a record label for the artists' service as recording artists for each and every recording sold is called a royalty. Royalties are also paid to publishers for mechanical licenses for the use of the material such as music and lyrics.

Video Clause - Who controls the music video and how are the costs apportioned? Record labels will want to have 100% of the cost recoupable. Does a concert promoter have the right to video an artist's performance?

Assignment Clause - A record company may reserve the right to sell the contract with the artist to another record label. Major labels sometime shuffle acts around from one affiliated label to another within their family of labels and this assignment gives them permission to do so.

Controlled Composition Clause
How the label will pay mechanical royalties? Standard practice is that the label will only pay on 10 original songs on the artist's record, and at 75% of the current statutory mechanical license fee.

Delivery Clause – The label may have some say over what type of material will eventually be released by the artist. Hence, there exists what is known as a delivery requirement in recording agreements.

Delivery means that the record company has to accept the recordings which are brought to them by the artist as adhering to the terms of the record deal. The contract will specify what standard the record company will use to test how acceptable the recordings are.

The most common standard is that the artist must deliver commercially satisfactory recordings. In essence, this means the company will only accept recordings which it believes are hit records. This ambiguous standard can cause many problems, including: (a) the label suspending the contract period until acceptable tracks are delivered; (b) putting the artist deeper in debt to the label because additional recordings cost more money; and (c) allowing the label to terminate the deal under the argument that the artist was late in delivery and thus breached the contract.

Another delivery standard is known as delivering technically satisfactory recordings. Under this standard, as long as a recording is done using the proper sonic equipment, the company does not have the same leeway to reject the tracks. This standard is usually reserved for midrange and superstar artists.

Sideman Clause – A sideman's clause allows an artist to do studio work. The artist still needs permission from the record company; however, they can't say no unless they have a very good reason. Under normal circumstances -- without such a sideman's clause – artists would be prohibited from performing for any other band/label under the terms of an exclusive contract.

Reserve of Right Clause – Many venues reserve the rights to agreements such as the age of a ticket buyer (especially if they sell alcohol).

Miscellaneous Clauses – Along with the standards set forth above, labels generally add other delivery requirements to the contract. Some of the most common are the following: (a) tracks must be recorded during the term of the contract, (b) songs must be new (not previously recorded by the artist), (c) tracks are studio recordings, (d) material does not infringe upon someone else's copyright, (e) songs must have a minimum length (normally at least two minutes), (f) recordings feature only the artist's performance, and (g) recordings are not completely instrumental.

+++++++++++++++++++++++++++++++

Artist Development Agreements

Band Member Agreements
Collaborator Agreements
Confidentiality Agreements
Manager Agreements

Product Development Agreements

Performance Agreements
Record Label Agreements
Publishing Agreements
Merchandising Agreements
Consignment Agreements
Producer Agreements
Booking Agent Agreements
Studio Agreements

Agreement Types

As mentioned at the beginning of the chapter, the entertainment industry is gaga about contracts and agreements. Artists may need a band member agreement. If management is a part of their team, they're going to need a management agreement and the same holds true for publishing. These are just the agreements that should be considered when preparing the Artist

Development Plan. When an artist gets into Product Development, they will be inundated with other agreement types such as record label contracts and performance agreements.

Band Member Agreements
Other than an agreement with a qualified entertainment attorney, the first agreement that an artist may need is that of a band member agreement. If an artist is performing or recording with one or more individuals, they should have an agreement amongst them. Many times, bands are a bunch of friends. To remain friends, it is best to have an agreement. Misunderstandings are a poor excuse for ending a friendship.

Band agreements may define the issues related to running the artist's career as a business as well as how artists will work with others within the band.

Who are the content providers: the songwriters? Are there co-writers? Is there an agreement between them? What is the agreement between the members of the group? Who owns what? Does the band own a trademark? Is it owned by an individual member or the band? What happens if the band breaks up?

If the artist is a solo singer-songwriter and they work all the functions of an artist as well as running their business, certainly there is no agreement. If he or she is co-writing with another writer, then that's a different story. Every music professional that the artist works with will want to know who the artist has an agreement with, if any. Record company executives and publishers will want to make sure that those agreements are completed.

Writing up band agreements should define the issues related to running the artist's career and their business as well as how the artist will work with people within the band and those on their team.

What about contracts between members of the band? Is that really necessary? Well, it could be. Are there band members who do all of the creative legwork, and other band members who just show up and play? If the band starts to make money, is everyone paid the same, no matter what their role? Or does the songwriter or singer or band leader make more money? What about money that goes into the band fund? Does everyone contribute equally? How and when will that money be paid back? What if a member decides to leave the band and wants to take their share of the band's assets with them? Who owns the name of the band? These kinds of questions can easily be addressed by a contract; answering them now can save an artist from some nasty headaches in the future.

> **Hint: Details in any contract can be changed to suit an artist's needs. Artists should not hesitate to propose changes to any of them.**

Collaborator Agreements
After the agreement between the band members, the artist should begin to understand potential agreements with their manager, their producer, their agent, their publicist, and their collaborators. The entertainment

business is full of collaborators and hence, more agreements.

What an artist expects their music business collaborator to do really depends on where they are in their career. Artists simply need to be as clear as possible about what they need from a collaborator, and what they are willing to do.

Confidentiality Agreements
Confidentiality Agreements are between an owner of information or data and where it is shared with another person or entity. This could be song ideas, project ideas such as a recording or tour. It could also mean business ideas such as growth plans, sales incentives or market penetration. In the music business, confidentiality agreements may be needed between an artist and a record label or an artist and a tour manager. In these agreements, the owner of the idea of data proposes to disclose certain of its confidential and proprietary information to a recipient. Confidential information may includes all ideas, data, lyrics, compositions, demos, products, technology, business plans, marketing plans, financial information, and many others disclosed or submitted.

The recipient will agree that the confidential information is to be considered confidential and proprietary to the owner and that the recipient shall hold the information in confidence and will not use the confidential information other than for the purposes of its business with the owner. The recipient usually may disclose it only to its officers, directors, or employees with a specific need to know.

Confidential Information furnished in tangible form by the Owner may not be duplicated by the Recipient (copyright infringement) except for purposes of their Agreement. Upon the request of Owner, Recipient must return all Confidential Information.

As with most agreements, there is usually a term limit placed on the confidentiality.

It must also be explained, that a confidentially agreement is nothing more than that. All further agreements should be granted under a separate contract.

Talent Manager Agreements
If management is a part of the artist's team, the artist is going to need an Artist Management Agreement.

As discussed in the management section of the Artist Development Plan, a good talent manager can be instrumental in the success of an artist. As a matter of fact, a talent manager may be the most important aspect of an artist's career. In some cases (N'Sync or Backstreet Boys), the manager is the most important. Any contract, including a Talent Manager's agreement, that an artist contemplates for any part of their career, should be carefully reviewed and evaluated by the artist and the artist's attorney. Before an artist signs a contract with a talent manager, they should brush up on their talent manager contract basics so they can be sure they are making the right decision. Keep in mind that this info is general in nature and all deals may be different.

Here are a few basics to keep in mind about talent manager contracts.

- It Doesn't Have to be Complicated! - Especially for an indie artist. Skip the "therefore" and the "hereunder" talk, and write a simple document that covers money, division of labor, and the length of the agreement.

- It Should be Mutually Beneficial - Even if the talent manager has been involved with the music business a long time, Artists shouldn't sign their life away for a crack at the manager's expertise. A manager who really believes in an artist won't expect them to do so.

- It Should be Signed in Good Faith - If either party is looking for loopholes before they sign, there is a problem.

- Contracts are best negotiated when the end game is to remain friends when the project is over.

Songwriter-Artist Self-Publishing Agreements

For each song that a songwriter releases to another performer or recording artist or TV show or radio station, there should be a license from the artist (copyright owner) to the other party.

The copyright owner may give a record label a non-exclusive right to use the musical work, either words or music, or both. The record company then may record, manufacture and sell the recording of the song to the public. In return, the record label will agree to pay a royalty to the publisher for every record manufactured.

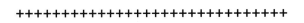

More About Product Development Agreements

Concert & Event Promoter Contracts

Music promoters who work with big money concerts would never dream of booking a show without a contract (nor would the artists with whom they work for consider playing a show without a contract). However, in the indie music world, performance contracts are probably the most overlooked. Relationships between promoters and performing artists at this level are often casual. Even if there are not huge sums of cash involved, a contract or an agreement lets everyone know their roles and responsibilities.

Promoters and bands alike can use these steps to create a fair contract that will help the gig go more smoothly.

Before an artist even gets started working with a concert or event promoter, they should make sure they understand the nature of the relationship between the artist and a promoter. The reason the same rules apply to writing contracts for both sides is because both the artist and the promoter are actually on the same side, especially if the artist is in the building stages of their career. If a promoter makes money, then the band makes money, and vice versa. The goal is to work together, not apart. Artists and promoters are on the same team. They should come to an agreement that gives everyone the tools they need to play their part in making the performance a success AND give everyone the best shot at going home with a profit.

Performance Contract Basics
The date and time of the performance
- The venue (name, address)
- Capacity of the venue
- The length of the set(s)
- Sound-check times and lengths
- Accommodations (if any)
- Charge-Back conditions
- Merchandise selling possibilities
- Backline provisions
- Contract riders
- Deposits (if any)
- Admission fee (ticket price)
- Act of Nature (Force Majeure)
- Cancellation fees
- Recording possibilities
- Promotional commitment
- Last but not least, the deal: who's paying whom? How much? For what? And when?

> **Who's paying whom? How much? For what? And when?**

The verbal contract between a promoter and an artist may simply be an agreement that the artist will perform on a certain date, at a certain time, for an agreed upon length of time, with what specific other act, and how much will be paid. Many promoters require some kind of written confirmation or a verbal agreement made over the phone.

> **4 Common Performance Deals**
> 1. Percentage Deal
> 2. Flat Fee or Guarantee Deal
> 3. Versus Deal
> 4. Plus Deal

Here are the four (4) most common performance deals an artist may encounter:
1. Percentage Deal
   Example: the performer receives no guarantee and will be paid a percentage of ticket sales
2. Flat Fee or Guarantee Deal:
   Example: the performer will receive a flat fee of $300
3. Versus Deal
   Example: The performer will receive $300 guarantee or 30% of the ticket sales (whichever is higher)
4. Plus Deal
   Example: The performer will receive a guarantee of $300 plus 30% of ticket sales

Both parties should always be absolutely clear about what deal is being negotiated. What are the expectations? Be clear about dates and times, about responsibilities and logistics. Use a confirmation letter if possible, and don't delay in confirming any arrangements or contracts.

The Musicians Union has a number of specimen performance contracts which cover most types of appearances. These are available from the Musician

Union offices and it would be wise to be familiar with the types of contracts that an artist might be asked to agree.

Door Deals

When an artist books a gig with a promoter or with a venue, the words "door deal" or "door split" are likely to come up, especially for indie artists and/or up and coming bands. Agreeing to a door split deal means that the artist is giving up the chance to be paid a set fee for their performance and instead will share in the proceeds from ticket sales with the promoter. In most instances, the promoter will first recoup the costs he/she spent renting the venue and promoting the show from the ticket proceeds, and then the remaining money gets split between the band and the promoter at a pre-agreed percentage rate. Promoters often weigh these percentages in favor of the band, so common door split rates are 80%/20% splits or 70%/30% splits (both with the band coming out with the largest percentage). However, a 50/50 door split is not unheard of and may certainly be fair, depending on the circumstances. Hint: Performing artists should be wary of splits that give the promoter the largest share of the profits.

Many times a promoter is the owner of a nightclub and the door split is 100% / 0%. Sometimes, the cost of production (sound & lights) is paid from the door proceeds and then the artist-performer receives their percentage. Sometimes the venue owns and provides the production for the performances and there are no deductions from the amount that the artist-performer receives.

Of course, with a door split, if the show doesn't sell many tickets, there is a danger that the artist won't get paid anything at all - in fact, the promoter may not even make their investment in the show back. If an artist is an up and coming band trying to create a buzz for themselves, it is usually worth playing these shows. Even if the artist doesn't walk away with money in their pocket, they may walk away with a few new fans, maybe some press coverage, and the respect of a promoter who will book the artist again in the future. Hint: Artist should look at their long-term career goals and not be afraid of these deals.

++++++++++++++++++++++++++++++

Record Label Contracts

A record label typically enters into an exclusive recording contract with an artist to market the artist's recordings in return for royalties on the selling price of the recordings. Contracts may extend over short or long durations, and may or may not refer to specific recordings. Established, successful artists tend to be able to negotiate their contracts to get terms more favorable to them.

A contract either provides for the artist to deliver completed recordings to the label, or for the label to undertake the recording process with the artist. For artists without a recording history, the label is often involved in selecting producers, recording studios, additional musicians, and songs to be recorded. They may also supervise the output of recording sessions. For established artists, a label is usually less involved in the recording process.

Although both parties allegedly need each other to survive, the relationship between record labels and artists can be a difficult one. Many artists have had albums altered or censored in some way by the labels before they are released—songs being edited, artwork or titles being changed, etc. Record labels generally do this because they believe that the album will sell better if the changes are made. Often the record label's decisions are prudent ones from a commercial perspective, but this typically frustrates the artist who feels that their artwork is being diminished or misrepresented by such actions.

For this type of agreement, the artist grants to the record label the right to manufacture, advertise, sell, lease, license or otherwise use or dispose recordings embodying their performances, either recorded or soon to be recorded. In addition, the artist grants the record label the right to use their name, likeness and photographs, in connection with the exploitation and promotion of the recordings.

In return, the record label pays the recording artists a royalty for each recording manufactured and sold throughout the world, for the rights granted and the services rendered.

In addition, the record company pays the songwriter (or songwriter's publisher) for the use of the songs on the recordings.

If the artist is a performer as well as a songwriter, they will be paid for each "hat." Payments of accrued royalties are made semi-annually, however, the record label usually reserves the right to deduct from the amount, any expenses or royalties previously paid or recordings returned, either as defective or on exchange.

In this agreement, the artist will warrant that they have no oral or written obligations contracts, or agreements entered into prior to the signing of the agreement which would in any way interfere with carrying out the agreement with the record label to its full intent and purpose.

Many times, the record label may have an option to extend the agreement for a period equal to the terms of the original agreement by giving the artist notice in writing of its option.

++++++++++++++++++++++++++++++

360 Deals

In the music business, a 360 deal is a business relationship between an artist and a music business company. The company agrees to provide financial support for the artist, including direct advances as well as funds for recording, marketing, promotion and touring, as an investment to the artist's lucrative potential. The artist agrees to give the company a percentage of all of their musical interests, including sales of recorded music, live performances, publishing, merchandising and any other income.

The 360 deal reflects the idea that the artist's team is consolidated and more likely to use synergy from all aspects of the artist's brand, including recorded music, as well as live performances and merchandise.

++++++++++++++++++++++++++++++

Music, Entertainment and Intellectual Property Attorneys

When getting into any contract or written agreement, artists should always consider hiring a qualified entertainment attorney or intellectual property attorney (depending on the circumstances) to review the documents and consult for legal opinions. Musicians and artists should hire a lawyer who specializes in the music business. These attorneys know many aspects and nuances of the music business and know what may be missing in the fine print. Remember when negotiating a contract, it is not always about what's in the agreement but also, what's not included.

Intellectual Property Lawyers
In today's age, intellectual property rights have to be established, processed and often defended. Intellectual property lawyers are those people who have specialized in intellectual property laws and help process transactions and litigate such claims in the court of law.

- Copyrights are a legal form of protection provided by law for original works of authorship which have been fixed into a physical form.

- Trademarks are a form of legal protection provided for words and symbols which help consumers identify the origin of goods.

So if an artist is looking for an intellectual property lawyer, they first need to identify why they need one such lawyer in the first place. For example, if an artist just needs to register a trademark, then they need a lawyer who undertakes transactional work. If the artist is suing someone over a copyright violation, then they will need a lawyer who will litigate in a court of law.

There are different methods in which most lawyers will take their fees. Depending upon the kind of work you have, the lawyer will either charge you on an hourly basis or will take a percentage.

++++++++++++++++++++++++++++++

Legal Tips

- If you're unsure about a deal, don't sign anyway - ask for help! If the other party has a legal team behind them, you will need legal advice. If they don't, it can be as simple as asking another music friend, "hey, when you booked that show, did you..."

- If things are moving a little too fast for you, don't be afraid to say you need to take a breather and think about things before you go ahead with a deal. Likewise, if you don't like the way something is going, you can say "no" - doing so will not impact your ability to work with quality people in the future.

- The deals you make when you hardly have anything going on can come back and bite you in a big way if you make it, so treat every deal as if you know you are going to sell millions of records some day.

- The music business lends itself to working with friends, which is fabulous. But when you are working with your friends and assuming you want to STAY friends, make sure you are on the same page on every point.

- When considering hiring an attorney, check the lawyer's background such as bio, and relevant work experience with cases similar to yours.

- Ask around for attorney references from your friends, family and colleagues. Often musicians or other people in the industry may know good lawyers.

- When you do find a lawyer, do an Internet search with their name, and then review potential articles, news items, etc. about them.

- Visit the website of your state's bar association and check the lawyer's registration and relevant information.

- See what associations and organizations the lawyer is affiliated with.

- When negotiating an agreement always think "win" / "win."

- Negotiate only with those in authority to agree to your requests.

- When you start negotiating, start with the most incontestable (i.e. agreeable items).

- Take notes and verbally summarize each point agreed upon before you move on to the next issue so that there's no misunderstanding.

- Pay attention to the length of term when negotiating an agreement.

- Written agreements are stronger in court than oral agreements.

- When preparing to negotiate an agreement, anticipate the other party's concerns.

NOTES

_____
_____
_____
_____
_____
_____
_____
_____
_____
_____
_____

Artist Development in the Music Business
Chapter 12 – Finance & Funding

With self-distribution and access to worldwide marketing, the artist can now wear many "hats": the performer, the songwriter, the publisher, the record label executive and the merchandiser. While wearing all of these "hats" at once, artists are now uniquely positioned to profit from the best possible contractual distribution terms and highest revenue generation via the sale, use, or streaming of their music. The challenge is that many artists don't know what these rights are, or how to collect the money they've earned from these revenue streams. There is not a comprehensive infrastructure that enables every artist who is owed money to easily collect it.

There is active income and there is passive income.

Financial planning is an important part of Artist Development and is directly related to an artist's business.

The importance of finance management is such that no artist can ignore it and so, here is an attempt to help the artist become aware about the importance of finance and how much that financial health is important for the artist's well-being.

Finance plays a very important role in the day-to-day lives of every artist or band. It is a very wide term and is really the study of the science of managing funds. Finance is related to lending, spending, projects, budgets, saving and funding.

How do artists fund their projects? Self Funding? Fan funding? Loans? Partners? Collaborators? Investors? Endorsers? Rich Uncles?

Setting up a Payment System

After an artist has registered their business with the state, they may apply to the Internal Revenue Service (IRS) for a Federal tax ID number. This tax ID number may be used to open a business account for the artist.

Every artist should have their own bank account which can be easily audited. In addition, it's easier if all payments flow directly into these accounts electronically.

The Income Reality

When looking at the income of individual musicians. A new survey of 5,000 U.S. musicians of different genres finds that:

- six percent (6%) of the average musician's income comes from recorded sales
- copyright law mostly affects the revenue of the highest-income musicians

- revenue from live performances is significantly larger with 28 percent.

The income stream for successful artists is different than income for struggling artists.

The survey collected data on the incomes of participating musicians and made it possible to compare the revenue streams per income group. Recorded sales are below 10 percent of the income for all groups. Interestingly, the lowest income bracket of musicians earns relatively the most (9%) from recorded sales.

The top earning musicians, earning an average $330,000 a year, earns by far the most from compositions, which make up 28% of their music-related revenue. The lowest earning musicians makes most revenue from live performances, more than 40%.

Revenue streams by income
Those who focus their activity on composing rely on composition revenue and are much more vulnerable to harm from copyright infringement such as file sharing or downloading from the Internet. The same goes for recording artists who rely on sales of sound recordings.

Musicians differ in earning money from music relying on several revenue sources.

The main finding is that the largest revenue category for musicians in the U.S. on average is live performances, which accounts for 28% of the overall annual income from music.

Another important income source is teaching (22%), followed by salaries from orchestras, bands and chamber ensembles (19%) and session work (10%).

Revenue from songwriting/composing and sound recordings is less important, accounting for 6% of the annual music income each.

Income Percentages

Live Performances	28%
Teaching	22%
Salaries	19%
Session Work	10%
Compositions	6%
Sound Recordings	6%
Merchandising	2%
Other	7%

Basic Musician / Artist Demographic
A "full-time" musician is often defined as someone who derives more than 75% of their income from music and spends more than 36 hours per week on music.

1. Money from songwriting / composing including publisher advances, mechanical royalties, collecting societies' royalties, commissions, jingles and soundtracks, synch licensing, ringtone licensing, and sheet music sales
2. Salary as an employee of a symphony, band or ensemble
3. Touring/shows/live performance fees earned as solo performer or as band/ensemble member

4. Money from sound recordings including sales of physical or digital recordings, payments from interactive streaming services, Internet radio, SoundExchange royalties, master use licensing for synchs or ringtones
5. Session musician earnings, including payment for work in recording studios or for live performances, and freelance work
6. Merchandise sales
7. Teaching
8. Other

Active vs. Passive Income

If a musician-performer-artist gets a gig to perform at a local venue, the musician performs, gets paid and then goes home. The money that the performer-artist earns is called Active Income. The artist does something actively to earn the income, hence active income.

If the musician-artist in the above case is also a songwriter-artist and performs songs written by the songwriter-artist, then the songwriter-artist may receive additional income from the use of the song in an establishment that pays a license for the use of music. These venues pay their license fees to a Performing Rights Organization who, in turn, pay the songwriter (and publisher.)

If the songwriter-performer-artist puts on the producer hat and records the performance and then posts that recording as a MP3 file to be downloaded on the Internet, the songwriter-performer-producer-artist may receive income for the rest of his/her life. Hence: Passive Income.

So in the above case, the artist may receive active income as a musician performing at a gig and also passive income as a songwriter whose songs were used in a venue who pays a license to a Performing Rights Organization for the use of music in a commercial establishment.

This is another main reason why an artist who is a songwriter needs to join a Performing Rights Organization. In the United States, there are three: ASCAP, BMI and SESAC.

If you are already a member of a Performing Rights Organization and are not receiving income from the use of your songs in licensed venues, then you are not playing the game correctly. After every gig, songwriters should notify their PRO the name of the licensed song performed, the name and location of the venue and the date that it was performed. If you do not do this, you may not get paid. Again, this is another income source. Artists need to capitalize on every income source in order to survive.

++++++++++++++++++++++++++++
Band Fund

It's important to understand the finances of an artist. Is there a band fund? Is there a day that something's not going to go right? Perhaps the vehicle breaks down on the way to a gig. Maybe the artist has an opportunity to showcase for a major music business collaborator but doesn't have the funds for gasoline or hotel. There's always something that may go wrong or is an emergency. It's better to be prepared. Something's going to go drastically wrong at the worst time, just as things will go unbelievably great at the right time. Are there funds to cover potential pitfalls? Insurance… basically. No, not auto insurance, but funds insurance. What happens if…?

In the band member agreement, artists know, up front, what the each member's split of any performance income that each musician receives when they do a gig. However, sometimes a portion of the total dollars brought in, goes to the band fund, if any? Let's start there. Before we talk about how much money you're going to make, let's discuss the band fund.

Many times artists are eager to build a band fund and may agree that twenty percent of any payments made to the artist should be contributed to the fund. Is this a good number? Perhaps. On the other hand, artists need to survive. If too much money is put into a band fund, then the artist may not have enough to survive, especially in the beginning years. If 20% goes into the band fund, the artist may have the funds available when they are needed.

++++++++++++++++++++++++++++++

Income Sources for Artists

- Merchandising
- Performing
- Publishing
- Recording
- Teaching
- Internet
- Salaries

Income Sources

Merchandise
    License
    Sales

Performances
    Live
    Recorded
    Salaried Player
    Session Work

Publishing
    Mechanical Royalties
    Performance Royalties
    Synch Royalties
    Foreign Royalties
    Print Royalties

Record Label
    Sales Royalties

Teaching

Internet

Income from Performing
On average, the largest revenue stream for musicians comes – unsurprisingly – from live performances, which account for 28% of the total annual income.

Income from Salaries
Salaries from orchestras, bands and other ensembles account for 19% of most musician's income.

Income from Session Work
Working as a musician in a recording session as a work-for-hire may account for a further 10 percent of an artist's income.

Income from Teaching
Teaching is another important income source for artists and nationally teaching is 22% of an artist's income. In other words, if you are not teaching, multiply your annual income by 1.22 to see what your income would be. For example, if the artist made $30,000 last year without the income source of teaching, the artist could have made $30,000 x 1.22 = $36,600 by including teaching. That's an extra $6,600 for beer money.

Less important are revenues from compositions (6%) and from sound recordings (6%). However, the smallest contribution to the annual musician's income comes from merchandising sales (2%). Other revenue sources account for the remaining 7% of the musicians' earnings.

Income from Publishing
Publishing income comes from so many different sources and over such a long period of time. There's a whole bunch of passive income in music publishing. The Billboard charts deal with fixed CDs, each with its own product code. But music publishing deals with the songs on the CDs: The actual copyrights, also known as intellectual property. And while a hit CD might have an average sales life span of anywhere from six weeks to six months, or even longer as a catalog title (if you're lucky), the copyrights go on... and on... and on. Copyrights last 70 years beyond the death of the author - which, if you write a song when you're young and live to a ripe old age - can translate to over a century of earning power.

There are three (3) types of musicians' income that have a different relationship to copyright law. Whereas revenue from compositions and sound recording has a direct relationship to copyright, revenue from teaching, live performance, salaries and merchandising sales has an indirect or no relationship to copyright. Session work is considered by the author to have a mixed relationship to copyright, since the payment in studio sessions is indirectly based on copyright law.

A song's copyright holder (either the songwriter or the songwriter's publisher) owns several important rights, including the right to copy the song, distribute copies of the song, prepare derivative works from the song and perform the song publicly. (For more information, see the chapter on Content Protection.)

A song generates revenue for its owner when the owner issues permits, (or "licenses"), to allow others to use these rights, for a fee or royalty. They allow this through the use of a license. When a song is written, the composer is the song's copyright holder and will remain the owner of the copyright until they assign the rights to a publisher. In order to get the song to generate revenue for the composer, it may be necessary to affiliate with a quality music publisher. A music publisher licenses songs, (and the copyrights), from songwriters and then exploits the songs commercially. Music publishers come in all shapes and sizes. Smart composers will want to affiliate with a good music publisher that will be able to find users for their song(s), issue licenses to users, collect the revenue, and then share the money with the composer. The songwriter/publisher contract should specify how any money generated by the song will be shared between the composer and the publisher. Depending on the bargaining power of the composer, the publisher may give an advance against future revenues.

As background, you need to understand exactly what kind of money a song generates for its copyright holder. A song earns money for its copyright holder from five (5) main sources: mechanicals, public performance, synchronization, printed song-sheets and foreign royalties. The way a composer gets the money, and how much of it is generated, depends on its source.

5 Sources of Publishing Income

- Mechanicals Royalties
- Public Performance Royalties
- Synchronization Royalties
- Printed Sheet Music Royalties
- Foreign Royalties

Mechanical Royalties:
Mechanical royalties are one of the main sources of income for music publishers. Mechanical royalties are moneys paid by a record company to a song's copyright holder for the right to use the song in "devices serving to reproduce the composition mechanically," i.e., vinyl, compact discs, MP3 players.

The record company pays the publisher a mechanical royalty based on a license fee determined by the number of phonorecords that are replicated. The publisher then pays the songwriter 50% of the income received. If the record label sells 1,000,000 units, they pay a statutory rate (currently $.091) for every song duplicated, replicated or downloaded. So, 9.1 cents X 1,000,000 units = $91,000 X 50% for publisher = $41,250 for the writer(s).

The Statutory Rate is a legislative safeguard for songwriters/publishers for protection. It is set by the "Copyright Royalty Tribunal," a 5-man crew born of the 1976 Copyright Act, who use the Consumer Price Index to adjust the rate in September of every even year against inflation.

The current statutory rate for mechanical royalties is 9.1 cents per song per record for recordings of up to 5 minutes in length. For recordings over 5 minutes in length, the rate is 1.35 cents per minute, or portion thereof. The statutory mechanical rate is subject to change, and should be checked before any project. So, it is beneficial to the song's copyright holder to negotiate a provision that the rate will be calculated as late as possible, i.e., the date of a commercial release, rather than the date of a contract.

With the FIRST release of your song, the publisher/songwriter can use it as a bargaining chip because on the first release you can set the rate wherever you want it.

Additional Publishing Income
In addition to the sources of income already covered, there are many other royalty-generating areas, many of which can - depending on the composition - generate substantial writer and publisher royalties. These include:

Lyric reprints in books
CD-ROM/Multimedia Audiovisuals
Karaoke
Musical greeting cards
Singing fish
Music boxes
Video games
Singing dolls
Commemorative plates
Ringtones
Sampling
Jukeboxes
Podcasting
Musical fountains

Income from the Internet
Internet service providers, websites, search engines, digital rights management, broadband, encryption, subscription and non-subscription services, compression, fingerprinting and watermarking, downloading and streaming, podcasting - these are but some of the many words and concepts that creators and publishers must understand if they are to enjoy the many benefits and opportunities available in the area of digital distribution of music.

There are two types of income for an artist from the World Wide Web. One is online distribution and the other is from affiliate marketing.

Whether audio or audio-visual works are downloaded, streamed or otherwise distributed, transmitted, or communicated, the concepts of performance rights, mechanical, statutory, compulsory, synchronization, territorial and durational licenses, etc., all continue to play a role in the royalty process regarding transmissions of copyrighted music over the Internet.

Personal Finance
Personal finance budgeting is an important part of an artist's long-term plans to gain financial stability. Artists need to have a clear idea of what they want in the future such as the amount of money they may need for retirement, the location of a place to live in, etc. (Retirement? Yikes, I'm just getting started). Artists need to have a plan and goal of translating these ideas into reality.

Hint: Do yourself a favor: place 10% of everything you earn into a savings account for retirement.

Endorsements

Endorsements are another potential income source for artists. Endorsements are not necessarily cash income but may be trade income: a potential expense that has been paid in advance.

This is where the artist needs to think again about finances. The best way to do this is to try to get endorsements for products and instruments which the artist is already using.

Leveraging an artist's brand takes a certain amount of pre-existing fame for potential endorsers to be enticed to participate. The fact that only a small percentage of artists earned money in this way shouldn't be a surprise given the high hurdle it takes to get there. And, in some instances artists don't necessarily see the endorsement money in their pockets, but notice it when it pays for tour expenses or provides them with free goods in exchange for their support.

So if the drummer in the group that you're representing on your record label, plays only Zyljian cymbals, why not try to do an endorsement deal with Zyljian so that the artist that's playing the Zyljian cymbals can stand up on stage every night and say "Hey everybody, I play Zyljian. Hope you like 'em, go buy some," and then sit back down and play.

That little ad pays for him getting new cymbals and sometimes cash. And that cash can keep that performer alive.

++++++++++++++++++++++++++++++++

Royalties

Synchronization (or synch)" royalties are income for songwriter-artists from granting rights to use songs in connection with video, such as TV, movies, and commercials.

Grand Rights Royalties (aka dramatic performance) are income for songwriter-artists from granting rights to perform music compositions publicly in a dramatic setting like a play, Broadway musical, or ballet.

Print Royalties are income for songwriters-artists from the sale of music in print (i.e. sheet music).

Foreign Royalties are income for songwriter-artists generated from outside the songwriter's country.

Mechanical Royalties are income for songwriter-artists from the replication of recordings of their songs – CD's, MP3s.

Performance Royalties are income for songwriter-artists from the performance, either live or recorded, of their songs.

Merchandise Royalties are income for performer-artists from the sale of merchandise bearing their likeness, logo or trademark.

Master Use Royalties are income for the owner of a sound recording such as a record label. The record label then pays the performers on the recording their recording royalty.

Recording Royalties are income for performer-artists paid by record labels when they sell a recording of a song of which uses the talent of the performer.

Of all the royalties that a songwriter-artist may receive, Mechanicals and Performance Royalties are the BIG ones. They generate the most income for a songwriter. This income is not for the performers on a recording or for the musicians on stage. It is for the songwriter and the songwriter's publisher. Certainly, if the musician is the performer and the performer is the songwriter, then the musician, as the songwriter, gets paid.

++++++++++++++++++++++++++++++++

> **Royalties**
>
> - **Performance Royalties**
> - **Synchronization Royalties**
> - **Print Royalties**
> - **Foreign Royalties**
> - **Grand Rights Royalties**
> - **Master Use Royalties**
> - **Mechanical Royalties**
> - **Merchandise Royalties**
> - **Recording Royalties**

++++++++++++++++++++++++++++

Controlled Compositions

Most record companies don't want to pay full statutory rate (75% is usually what they will offer) so try to get concessions elsewhere in your deals for dropping that rate. On later remakes and releases, the rate is law. If a songwriter only writes one big infectious hit in their lifetime (a.k.a. one-hit wonder), the mechanical royalty income could just go on and on and on.

Record companies routinely ask their recording artists who write their own songs for a mechanical license at 75% of the statutory rate on self-written songs ("controlled compositions"). Ideally, the record company and the song's publisher work out the details of the mechanical license before the song is recorded and placed on a compact disc or other mechanical reproduction. Even then, it is a monumental task to keep up with the number of copies sold and the calculation and collection of the mechanical royalties due. Many U.S. publishers use the Harry Fox Agency to monitor and collect mechanical royalties in return for a commission of up to 5% of the mechanical royalties collected. The revenues from mechanical royalties, or "mechanicals," are generally divided equally between the publisher and the songwriter.

Performance Rights Organizations collect fees from the licenses they issue to businesses (nightclubs, radio stations, etc.) using songs for live or recorded performances. They then pay their songwriter / publishers members their portion of the monies received.

Public Performance Royalties
Public performance income is the second largest source of income to a song's copyright holder. Almost every time any version of a song is performed publicly, whether live or on record, in concert or on the radio or television, the copyright holder is entitled to public performance royalties. There are a few narrow exceptions, (for example, educational use in a classroom setting).

Songwriters and publishers affiliate with a performing rights society to keep track of air play and other public performances of their songs, and to collect and distribute the resulting license revenue. ASCAP, BMI, and SESAC are the major performing rights societies. They issue blanket licenses to radio and television stations, nightclubs, restaurants, and even retail stores, which allow those users to play songs of their affiliated writers and publishers. The license fees vary, depending on the revenue of the user. The societies then monitor airplay and public performances and, using various formulae, distribute the money from the license fees, (less a commission), to their affiliated publishers and songwriters, separately. Both the publisher and writer should be members of the same organization, although co-writers may be members of different societies.

As to which organization is best for you, there is no single answer. They use different formulae in arriving at payments to their affiliated writers and publishers. As to which organization pays more, the common wisdom is that it evens out in the long run. If one PRO paid significantly higher rates than another PRO, every songwriter would join the PRO who paid the most. Talk to your friends. A payment formula that is best for the writer of a platinum smash may result in no payments at all to the writer of a song with only minor air play. It's probably more important to affiliate with the organization that has better personal contacts for you. While they can put songwriters in touch with publishers and vice-versa, their strengths and weaknesses in this area seem to vary with the genre of music and the particular regional office of the society.

Synchronization Royalties
A synchronization license is a permit to use a song in a movie or television show. The producer must obtain a "synch license" from the copyright holder, often for a onetime fee. The publisher usually splits that income with the writer 50-50. These onetime fees vary tremendously--anywhere from free, (for the exposure), to a few hundred dollars for a television show, to tens of thousands of dollars for a movie, to a hundred thousand dollars or more for a commercial. It depends on how much of a song is used, how important the song is to the show, whether it is merely background, etc. The first broadcast of a "live" show does not require a synch license, but re-runs would. The live broadcast would require the public performance license described above.

Print Royalties
Print revenues come from sales of sheet music. The relative importance of print revenue has decreased over the years as consumers have come to prefer records to sheet music. However, it is still a source of serious money and many industry watchers predict an increase in its importance with the growing popularity of detailed transcriptions (or "tabs") of heavy metal guitar licks, synthesizer programming, and the renewed popularity of acoustic music.

Print royalties vary. Copyright holders typically earn 20% of the retail price of single song sheet music and 10-12.5% on songbooks, pro-rated to reflect the number of songs in the songbook owned by that copyright holder. For example, if there are 40 songs in a songbook, or "folio," and you wrote 10, you, (or your publisher), would get 1/4 of the 10-12.5% royalty. Historically, publishers and writers don't split print income equally. For single song sheet music, the writer only gets 5-10 cents per copy and only about 10% of the wholesale price on folios. I am beginning to see publishing contracts which call for a 50-50 split on all income, perhaps in an effort to keep things simple. This is great for you as a songwriter, because it results in higher print income.

Many contracts limit your payments to what is specifically set out in the contract. That seems reasonable enough, but as technology continues to develop, new income sources may develop as well--revenue sources that we can't even begin to imagine. You don't want to be shut out from those sources of income. Insist on a "catch all" phrase providing that you will receive 50% of any and all other money sources not specifically referred to in the agreement.

In addition to these four (4) main sources of income, there is foreign sub-publishing. In a way, that's just the non-U.S. version of the income sources discussed above. Depending on the contract, your U.S. publisher may only acquire U.S. rights or may be authorized to sub-license outside the U.S., splitting the net income with you.

++++++++++++++++++++++++++++

Harry Fox Agency

The Harry Fox Agency assists songwriters and publishers by being a middle-man between them and others who want to use their song or songs. The Harry Fox Agency issues licenses for the owners of the song for a small fee (last I checked 4 1/2%) and then pays that license fee to the publisher who then shares it with the songwriter.

In addition, the Harry Fox Agency will audit record companies for the publisher of the song or songs. Their fee comes from whatever they recover from the record company.

++++++++++++++++++++++++++++

Income from Content Licensing

For licensing to occur, there needs to be a license. The license is a legal agreement between two or more parties expressly giving permission to use a song. The use of the song includes performing it on a stage or performing a recording of the song. A license of a song may also include the use of its lyrics in a book or movie or the use of its melody in a television commercial. Either way, a license is required. Before an audio recording or a video recording can be produced, the user must get permission from the song owner in the form of a license. Before a nightclub owner hires a band to perform a song, a license must be obtained from the owner of the song. Before a radio station performs a song over the airwaves, they must obtain a license from the owner of the song. All terms and conditions for use (especially how much and in what form is paid for the use of the song) are spelled out when a license is issued.

Before a song is released, a license should be granted for the use of that song. Large music publishers usually have a licensing department that handles these requests and negotiates and issues these licenses.

If a songwriter / artist is self-publishing, or working with a music publisher, it's a good idea for them to learn about negotiating and pitching songs. This is an important income source. Songwriter-artists should be getting the best possible deals for their songs.

Other Income from Song Use
Don't stop at getting re-released by other artists and thinking mechanicals

and performance royalties will be the only income for the song's use. There's literally a whole world out there to conquer. Film and TV producers might want the song for their projects; songwriters / publishers could issue a synch license and earn a modest fee which might include concessions from the premiere of the work or future considerations such as eventual video release. An ad executive may love the song and wants to have it in all his commercials. In this case, songwriters / publishers might be looking at commercial royalties for a long time. The local theater might want to add the song to their regular shows; songwriters / publishers could negotiate a nightly or weekly fee in licensing grand rights to them. Let's not forget the foreign royalties too.

Clearing House Libraries
These companies host a library of content that is "pre-cleared;" meaning the songs and the recording of the songs are ready for licensing. These Clearing House companies act as agents for others (like the film/TV producers, for example) by contacting the publisher and asking for the rights to use the song in their client's project.

They can do all the negotiating and researching for their client and get a license issued which "clears" the busy producer to use the song.

Income from Sound Recordings
Whether on vinyl, Compact Disc or via digital download, income from the sale, license or performance of sound recordings has been a core part of many musicians' income streams for decades. But there's no doubt that income from sound recordings — perhaps more than any other — has experienced significant challenges and undergone serious changes in the past 10 to 15 years.

While the existing music marketplace was fundamentally disrupted by peer to peer file sharing, we have also seen the decline of brick and mortar stores, and the development of legitimate download stores like iTunes and Amazon, and licensed subscription services like Rhapsody and Spotify. We've also seen the rapid growth in a new revenue stream for sound recordings — the digital performance royalties that are generated when sound recordings are streamed on any webcast service like Pandora or played on satellite radio.

When people think of "sound recordings" they may incorrectly assume that term is synonymous with "CDs, LPs and digital downloads." For the purpose of his research, we mean something more precise.

It's important to remember that a recorded piece of music embodies two copyrights: 1) there's the copyright for the composition (the lyrics and notes), and 2) a separate copyright for the sound recording (what gets captured in the studio). There are separate revenue streams earned by these two copyrights: 1) the composition earns mechanical royalties when it is licensed for reproduction, and 2) the composition also earns public performance royalties when it's performed publicly or played on the radio.

Income from Sound Recordings
This one focuses specifically on the money that sound recordings can earn when they are sold, licensed or performed. This includes:

1. Income from physical retail sales (brick and mortar, Amazon, mail-order)
2. Income from digital sales (iTunes, Amazon MP3, Bandcamp)
3. Income from sales of recorded music at shows/merch table
4. Interactive streaming services (Spotify, Rhapsody, Slacker)
5. Digital performance royalties (Pandora, Sirius XM, via SoundExchange)
6. Master use license for synchs, ringtones, etc.

Income from Merchandise
The sale of merchandise for performing artists is only relevant for a small number of musicians. Those who tour benefit the most from merchandise sales and many times supports the band on the road.

Revenue from merchandise such as t-shirts, hats, and posters, account for about two percent (2%) of performing artist's revenue. There are certainly differences of sales depending on genre. Jazz and classical artists typically earn less than one percent (1%) of revenue from the sale of merchandise where rock and hip hop artists earn up near seven percent (7%) from merchandise. Although small, it an income source that artists should not ignore.

Income from Other Sources
Corporate sponsorship and fan funding is filling in where labels have dropped off. It's no secret that label budgets have been going down. As a result, musicians are seeking other sources of money to support their work.

Some artists are turning to corporations to support tours, or projects.

Other artists are engaging their fans in the funding process.

++++++++++++++++++++++++++++++

Finance Plan

As part of the Artist Business Plan, the Artist Finance Plan helps an artist focus and increase the likelihood of success for each project.

The Finance Plan works in combination with other parts of the artist Business Plan such as the Marketing Plan, Sales Plan and Projects Plan.

Segments of an Artist Finance Plan
- Use of Funds
- Important Assumptions
- Key Financial Indicators
- Break Even Analysis
- Projected Profit and Loss
- Projected Balance Sheet
- Goodwill
- Accounting
- Independent Account Report
- Forecasted Finances
- Forecasted Balance Sheet
- Forecasted Cash Flows
- Forecasted Operating Expenses
- Forecasted Assumptions
- Forecasted Revenue
- Risk Reduction
- Risk Management
- Exit Strategy
- Spending Strategy
- Return On Investment
- Budgets
- Ratios
- Accounts Receivable
- Accounts Payable

Corporate Finance

As discussed in the chapter on business set-up, an artist should form a company and the company should plan for financial success. Yes, this is the music business.

Corporate finance deals with financial decisions which an artist makes, whether it's investments, analysis of credit, selling of assets or products or acquiring assets. Maximizing the artist's value and at the same time managing risks associated with investing in a particular product or project is the main aim of corporate finance. Moreover, corporate finance also studies the short-term and long-term implications of a decision and looks into matters related with dividends to shareholders' debt or equity. Matters related to taxes which a corporation has to pay are also taken into consideration when dealing with corporate finance. The artist's Financial Plan is more detailed in the Artist Business Plan.

Business Finance

Finance for an artist's business can't be undervalued. It can be regarded as the lifeline of a business which is required for its well-being. Finance acts as a lubricant to help keep the artist's business running. It doesn't matter if the artist's business is small, medium or large. They will always need finance, right from promoting and establishing their product, acquiring assets, employing people, encouraging them to work for the development of their performances and recordings and creating a brand name. In addition to that, a current business may need finance for expansion or making changes to its products as per their market requirements.

The finance area of Artist Development is of utmost importance as it is responsible for financial planning, thus ensuring that adequate funds are available for achieving the objectives of the artist and the artist's organization. The finance section of an Artist Development Plan is the pre-cursor to the Finance Plan of the artist's Business Plan. Many times, the business manager of the artist is the person primarily responsible to make sure that the funds are controlled, looks after the cash flow and controls profitability levels. One of the most important jobs of the business manager / accountant is to identify the necessary financial information such as the return on assets or the net profitability of selected projects which should be revealed to talent managers so that they can make informed decisions and judgments. The business manager is also responsible for making financial documents and preparing the final accounts so that they can be presented in the annual general meetings of the artist's company.

Start-Up Summary

A start-up summary for an artist or an artist's company, as a part of the Finance Plan, includes an estimate of start-up costs including the expense of consultants, advertising, office supplies, legal costs, and expenses associated with opening their first office. Much of the start-up costs will need to be financed by a direct owner investment: the artist.

Spending Strategy

We want to finance growth mainly through cash flow. As we expand, public offerings will be considered.

Budgets

While thinking of a long-term plan, budgeting and savings becomes an important part of an artist's finance. Savings may help an artist make investments in the future so that they may have a secure life. Smart artists know to be frugal and to keep their expenses to a minimum.

Finance is such a thing that can't be substituted by anything, so artists need to make sure they use their finances in the proper order, so that they can secure their future.

Establish a budget for each project that the artist is planning such as gigs, tours, recordings and/or merchandise. Include everything that is a planned cost for the project as well as expected sources of revenue. This information should be shared with the artist's team as well as the artist's bookkeeper and/or accountant. This way, everybody on the artist's team is on the same page.

Use of Funds
If the artist has the funds to get started, how will use the funds complete the initial business structure? Will part of the funds be used to develop strategies for attracting investors?

Once the funding request has been completed, begin working on Financial Projections.

+++++++++++++++++++++++++++++++

Important Assumptions
The Financial Plan depends on important assumptions. The key underlying assumptions may be such items as:

- Assumption of a slow growth economy, without major recession.
- Assumption that there are no unforeseen changes in music technology to make products or services immediately obsolete.
- Assumption that costs are high and income is low.

Key Financial Indicators
Collection days are very important. Artists don't want to let their average collection get above 45 days under any circumstances. This could cause a serious problem with cash flow, because our working capital situation is chronically tight for most artists.

Another part of an artist's plan might be to maintain gross margins of 75 percent and hold marketing costs to no more than 10 percent of sales.

Break Even Analysis
The Break Even Analysis provides the artists a good balance of fixed costs and sufficient sales strength to remain healthy. Artists can estimate their breakeven point on a monthly basis.

Projected Profit and Loss
On the Finance Plan, the projected profit and loss will help the artist see the road ahead. It's always a good idea to keep estimated expenses high and estimated income low.

Projected Balance Sheet
A Projected Balance Sheet may indicate to artists and their management, an expectation of healthy growth in net worth.

Financial Projections

Artists should develop the Financial Projections section after they've analyzed the market and set clear objectives for the project. That's how the artist may allocate resources efficiently. The following is a list of the critical financial statements to include in an artist's business plan.

Historical Financial Data
If an artist has an established business, they will be requested to supply historical data related to the company's performance. Most creditors request data for the last three to five years, depending on the length of time the company has been in business.

When putting together the historical financial data, include the company's income statements, balance sheets, and cash flow statements for each year that the company has been in business. This is usually up to three to five years. Often, creditors are also interested in any collateral that the business may have that could be used to ensure the loan, regardless of the stage of the business. This collateral may be equipment, instruments, vehicles or copyrights.

Prospective Financial Data
All businesses, whether startup or growing, will be required to supply prospective financial data to anyone interested in participating financially with the artist. Most of the time, creditors will want to see what an artist expects their company to be able to do within the next five years. Each year's documents should include forecasted income statements, balance sheets, cash flow statements, and capital expenditure budgets. If this is the artist's first year, they should supply monthly or quarterly projections. After that, stretch it to quarterly and/or yearly projections for years two through five. Perhaps an artist may want to consult with their business manager or accountant during this phase.

Make sure that the projections match the funding requests; creditors will be on the lookout for inconsistencies. If assumptions are made in the projections, be sure to summarize what is assumed. This way, the reader will not be left guessing.

Finally, include a short analysis of the financial information. Include a ratio and trend analysis for all of the financial statements (both historical and prospective). Since pictures speak louder than words, add graphs of the trend analysis (especially if they are positive).

Next, you may want to include an Appendix to the plan. This can include items such as credit history, resumes, letters of reference, and any additional information that a lender may request.

++++++++++++++++++++++++++++

Project Finance

We all know the entertainment business is project based. So, when looking at the long-term career of artist, it is important to look at the success of each of the artist's projects. Projects may include: writing a song, recording a song, performing a gig, touring or selling merch, etc. Whatever the artist's project is, the finances, funding and budget should be addressed prior to starting the project.

One of the best projects in the music business that doesn't take any money to accomplish and can generate a big portion of a songwriter-artist's income: songwriting. However, as soon as the song has been completed, the need for cash becomes apparent. There is cash needed to bring the song to market. Recording a demo may have costs such as renting a studio, hiring a producer or purchasing the recording equipment.

Consider who is going to fund the artist and the project(s). Usually, in the early stages of an artist's career, it is the artist themselves who do the funding. Even prior to that, parents often enroll their children in classes to learn to play an instrument or how to sing properly.

Many artists, early in their career, have day jobs and earn enough to purchase their own instruments. One instrument can be used to start making money in the music business. Learn to play it and people will pay to hear you play.

If the artist is not funding the projects then who is?

The artist should review their goals and objectives as well as their proposed projects and then estimate the funding required to complete each of the projects. The financial plan should generate ideas for the person, persons or company that will assist with the funding of the project or projects. Many times a publishing company will fund the recording of a demo that will be used to pitch the song to artists to perform or record. A record company will fund a recording session as well as the pressing and distribution of the product. Many businesses in the music business, such as record companies and publishers, are like banks. They fund projects and basically loan the money to the artist. The funds of the project must be repaid before royalties to the artist are distributed.

Financing of artist projects is much like financing other types of projects in terms of the calculus of investors, the drivers of costs and revenues, and the amount and sources of subsidy. That said, performance and studio projects are regarded very differently, and typically have different costs, revenues, and subsidy profiles, than do performance projects.

Working in music can mean an almost constant struggle to find the money to keep things going. Whether you're a band in need of money to tour or a label in need of cash to press some CDs, it seems like it is ALWAYS something. Music Business funding is never easy, but there are options. Find out how to uncover the cash needed to fund each and every project.

Time Required: Ongoing

1. Identify Your Needs

We all know we need money to get a musical endeavor or entertainment project off the ground, but one of the most important steps in getting the money is figuring out just how much of it is going to be required. Hint: the answer is not "as much as possible." Figuring out a realistic budget for the planned project will help keep everything running smoothly and will help when it's time to start applying for loans/grants. For instance, artists don't need $100,000 to do an indie release - ending up with more money than needed, leads to bad spending. Start each project off right with an understanding of the costs and expenses with the proposed project.

2. Write it Down

If you're going to apply for a small business loan or for a grant from an arts council or other funding body, you're going to need a business plan. An artist's business plan helps the artist focus on goals and objectives. Even if you're planning on financing your music project with your own credit cards, writing a project plan forces you to think about the potential for achieving the goals and objectives. The project plan shows how to make it happen. Your project plan should include:

• Overview of the project
• Project manager
• Project dates - begin / end
• Market / consumers projections
• Estimated cost
• Projected returns
• Expected length of time
• Marketing plan for the project

3. Investigate Funding Sources

The available sources for music business funding vary from location to location to location. For instance, people in the UK are fortunate to have a network of arts councils provide grants to get musical projects started. In the U.S., there are fewer grants available and most artists apply for traditional small business loans. The best way to learn about what types of local funding might be available is to ask fellow musicians and colleagues. Also many local governments have programs available. Check their websites for more information.

4. Approach Your Sources

After you've identified the people most likely to help you with funding for your project or company, it's time to start preparing your sales pitch. Hint: One thing artists should keep in mind is that yes, they're trying to work in the music business, which can be a bit more laid back and casual than a traditional industry - but the people whose money is needed will almost always be more "business-y" types. Showing up late to a meeting, wearing last night's clothes and smelling like you bathed in lager is not a good first impression. Be professional and give the impression that you are capable of succeeding with your proposed venture.

5. Get Ready for the Long Haul

Getting funding for any business can be tough, and the creative industries are a special case (largely because the people who control the purse strings are secretly convinced that artists can't be trusted to manage the money). Finding money can take a long time, and artists may have to apply for money from several sources to fund one music project. When planning the project, make sure to build in plenty of time to secure the right funding sources.

++++++++++++++++++++++++++++++

Project Funding Requests

The funding request should include the following information:

- The current funding requirement

- Any future funding requirements over the next five years
- How will the funds be used? Is the funding request for capital expenditures? Working capital? Debt retirement? Acquisitions? Whatever it is, be sure to list it in this section.
- Any strategic financial situational plans for the future, such as: licensing, capital investments, debt repayment plan, or merging of businesses. These areas are extremely important to the artist and any future creditors, since they will directly impact the ability to repay the loan(s).

When outlining the funding requirements, include the amount needed now and the amount needed in the future. Also include the time period that each financial request will cover, the type of funding, equity or debt, and any terms of the deal. Funding a recording session may be expensive but promoting the result of the recording may be cost prohibitive. Do your homework. Don't hurry up and do it wrong,

To support the funding request be prepared with historical and prospective financial information. This is where the Artist Business Plan comes in. The artist's Financial Plan is located within the artist Business Plan. Yes, a plan within a plan. Both plans (as well as the Sales Plan, Promotion Plan and Long-Term Plan) will keep the artist focused on the goals and objectives.

++++++++++++++++++++++++++++
Investors

When you're struggling to pay the bills at your music related business, the idea of a music business angel or other investor swooping in with arms full of cash sounds like a dream come true. However, that dream could turn into a nightmare really quickly if you don't proceed with caution. However, learn how to make sure your music business angel investor stays an angel and how to make the deal beneficial to the both of you.

If you think your business needs money, then make sure you know why, how much, and how much you think you can make. Not only will thinking in this way help you focus your thoughts and show an investor you're serious, it also sends the message that you're prepared to stay in control of your business.

Financial Business Investors vs. Music Business Angels

A bank may be willing to make you a loan in return for some modest rate of interest. An investor/music business angel wants more. They're making a high risk investment in your business with hopes that the gamble will pay off, and they'll want to do everything possible to make sure they don't lose their money. That means they may want a controlling stake in your business, and they may want to be involved in your business decisions. A music business angel may be more likely to "get it" since they have industry experience. Other investors, well, your creative vision is not their priority. They want to make money.

Artist Vision vs. Investor's Money

When an artist's vision interacts with an investor's money, great things can happen. Mozart would not have been able to survive writing and performing music had it not been for the funding of the royalty that believed in him. A perfect combination is when the investor lets the artist do what that artist is good at: create art. However, some investors may want to steer the art to be more commercially acceptable. The idea of an artist giving up some control in their music may give them anguish, and rightly so. But, the right investor may actually bring some valuable business know-how to the table. That may be especially the case if the investor made their money in the music business. The best way for an artist in this situation to walk this line is to be very clear from the outset about the compromises they're willing to make versus the amount of input the investor wants to have. Know up front who holds the creative reigns.

Sometimes, the perfect music business investor can provide an artist with both capital and good advice about achieving their goals.

An investor, whether a financial investor or a music business investor, will want the artist to spend their money wisely.

Hint: Never take money from any source without a clear idea of what you need it for, and how you will pay it back.

++++++++++++++++++++++++++++++

Artists, Bands, Brands and Revenue

For this, income from "brand" could include any of these:

- Merchandise sales
- YouTube partnership program: revenue-sharing program that allows creators and producers of original content to earn money from your videos on YouTube
- Ad revenue: or other miscellaneous income from your website properties (Google AdSense, commissions on Amazon sales, etc.)
- Fan funding: Money directly from fans to support an upcoming recording project or tour (Kickstarter, Pledge Music)
- Fan club: Money directly from fans who are subscribing to a musician's fan club
- Persona licensing: payments from a brand that is licensing a musician's name or likeness (video games, comic books, etc)
- Product endorsements: payments from a brand for a musician endorsing or using their product
- Acting: in television, movies, commercials
- Sponsorship: corporate support for a tour, or for band/ensemble
- Grants: from foundations, state or federal agencies
- Essentially, it's income tied to a musicians' creative self, but ancillary to what they earn based on their sound recordings, compositions or performances.

++++++++++++++++++++++++++++++

Artist Funding Tips

- Look for the RIGHT Funding Source - Sure, when an artist wants to get their project off the ground, it can be tempting to take an "I'll worry about that later" attitude towards loans and debts that are being racked up. In the long term, if funds are spent unwisely at the beginning, there won't be anything left to make sure the project gets the push it needs. High interest loans and credit cards might seem like a fast and easy way to get things rolling, but they should be the last resort. If an artist has take on some debt, take the time to make sure it will be manageable enough for it to be paid off and keep the project going.

- Get Help When You Need It - Even where there are no nice arts councils or arts grant sources, there usually are groups to help small businesses get their stuff together. If you need help writing a business plan or coming up with a budget, do a quick internet search for small business assistance groups in your area. You may be able to get free (or very cheap) assistance in putting together a professional proposal that will help get the cash needed.

- Do Your Homework - This is especially important if you are looking for funding to start a business like a record label - make sure you REALLY understand your market and what you are getting into. Just because you're a music fan and read a lot of music magazines doesn't mean you really know how the business side of music works. If you don't have any specific experience in the part of the music business you want to get into, investigate before you take the plunge. Seek out other people who are doing what you want to do and get their input so you have a clearer picture what's required and who your customers will be.

Takeaways

- Not all musicians are able to leverage their brand. The common assumption that today's musicians can or should just rely on playing shows and selling t-shirts in lieu of other forms of compensation ignores the fact that there's an army of musicians – from composers, to salaried orchestra players, to session musicians – that have career structures that doesn't make it possible to build a monetizable brand. This should in no way diminish their value or importance; we simply need to remember that the community of creators is large, diverse, and specialized, and does not lend itself to "one size fits all" solutions.

- For musicians and bands who are in a position to leverage their brand, the key for them is to be flexible and open minded and, above all, strategic. Our interviewees not only knew that their brand is valuable, they also recognized that decisions about everything from merchandising deals to corporate support have an impact on their artistic reputation.

- Good music and top notch performances are what makes these artists desirable in the first place so artistic integrity must always take precedence, but faced with diminishing label support and less money from recorded music sales, the smart artists are figuring out ways to leverage their brands, broaden their fan bases, and earn more money.

- Most artists-musicians are earning money from multiple "roles"

- When looking about the activities that generated income, more than half of the musicians surveyed earned their income from activity in three roles or more in the past 12 months. Some are composers+performers+teachers.

- Others are performers-recording artists, but also making a bit of money off their brand.

- Live performance was the most likely source of income, followed by being a salaried player.

- The estimated music income of $34,455, and role data above suggest two findings.

- The majority of artists and music creators are wearing many hats. Many are earning money from three or more distinct roles in the music business.

- The majority of artists and music creators are part of the working middle class. Yes, there are some musicians who make much, much more than the survey's aggregate earned music income of $34,455, and congratulations to them. There are very few musicians who break through to those upper echelons. Think about the artist and music creator landscape as large, diverse, and specialized. There's an army of working class musicians, performers and composers who are working multiple roles to create a career as an artist.

To Do

Notes:

_____

_____

_____

_____

Artist Development in the Music Business
Chapter 13 – Trademarks

Trademarks: A trademark is a symbol and is generally used to identify a particular product, which indicates its source. A trademark can be a combination of words, phrases, symbols, logos, designs, images, or devices. It is used by an individual, legal entity or business organization to distinguish their products from others. For example, fans and customers may be able to identify the products of many musical artists from their logo, which may be embossed on their products. Once registered, trademarks are protected legally and the owners can sue persons for unauthorized use of their trademarks.

Trademarks prevent counterfeit products through registration with the U.S. Trademark Office. Once registered, a business can prevent the import of counterfeit products by registering the mark with the U.S. Customs Department.

Another crucial step in Artist Development is securing a Trademark with the United States Patent and Trademark Office (USPTO). Other than equipment and gear, securing a Trademark is probably the most expensive item that an artist will have to spend for their Artist Development. The good news: A Trademark is valid for 10 years before it must be renewed. As explained in the Image section of the Artist Development Plan, the name of the artist is of upmost importance in establishing a brand.

In starting as a musical band or artist, choosing a good name may be a difficult task. Along with a name that will highlight the artist's unique identity, consider some of the legal aspects that relate to the name. If the artist is attempting to make it big in the music business, by writing songs, making recordings and selling merchandise; it becomes necessary have to trademark of the artist's name. This is applicable to both if you are a solo musician or a band, or both.

A trademark is an Intellectual Property and it can assume the form of a word, a phrase, a logo, or a combination of them all. As discussed in a separate section of the Artist Development Plan, Intellectual Property is a creation that has commercial value, and can be protected by patents, copyrights and trademarks. The United States Patent and Trademark Office (USPTO) accepts online applications for trademark registration through the Trademark Electronic Application System (TEAS). Before choosing a particular word, phrase or logo as a trademark, an artist should go through the USPTO database in order to ensure that the mark is not already in use. A detailed description of the goods and services provided by the artist's business should accompany the application, since the mark is intended for use or is already being used with those goods or services.

Online applicants receive a serial number immediately after applying for registration. The entire process of registering the trademark can take anywhere between 6 months and 1 year, depending on the complexity of the situation and the legal issues involved. If the artist is uncomfortable filing their own trademark, trademark lawyers are available to help with the process of registering a trademark. The details on the fee for registering the mark can be obtained from the USPTO website. The application for a trademark has to be filed by the person who controls the use of the mark.

What is a Trademark?

According to the United States trademark office, a trademark can be defined as a distinct name, sign or any type of indicator (logo, slogan, word, symbol, design or a combination of all) that is used by an individual, legal entity or business organization, such as a singer-songwriter or band, to distinguish and identify their goods or services from that of others. In other words, trademarks of the artist, or the artist's products, shows their source of origin and helps the fans and customers in identifying them as well as their particular product.

A trademark is used by companies or business organizations in order to associate their name or logo as a unique brand. The existence of a trademark on any product plays an excellent psychological effect on fans and consumers. The trademark basically helps the fan to identify the artist's product. The logic behind the use of trademark is extremely simple. It's easy for humans to remember graphics and pictures as opposed to plain written language or text. The logos and symbols that are used for the trademark to make it is easy to identify, and get registered into the minds of fans and potential customers.

Trademarks are another way of branding for an artist.

Trademark Types

1. Non-Registered Trademark
2. Service Trademark
3. Registered Trademark

Trademark Types

There are three (3) types of trademarks that are currently in use in the United States.

1. Non-Registered Trademark
   The first one is the unregistered trademark, represented by letters TM. Violation of this trademark is not legally enforceable. A non-registered trademark is a logo and name that is not registered in accordance with the trademark office. In case of violation of such a trademark, the case that is filed often remains undecided. In a trademark infringement law suit, if the claimant is able to produce a record that proves that he was the first person to use the logo/name/symbol, then the accused usually has to compensate for damages.

2. Service Trademark

This type of mark is represented by letters 'SM,' and is commonly used by the service sector brands.

3. Registered Trademark
The registered trademark is the most commonly used trademark, and is legally enforceable, and is represented by an 'R,' enclosed in a circle ®. A registered trademark is recorded in accordance with the trademark office. Violating a registered trademark is an offense and the accused may have to pay heavy fines and compensations.

Trademark Symbols

Generally, two symbols are used to denote a trademark. One is '™,' which represents a trademark symbol and the other is '®,' which is used to denote an application for registered trademark. These symbols are displayed immediately after the trademark, in a superscript style. If the product carries the symbol '™,' then the trademark may have never been registered or may be in the process of registration. If the symbol is '®,' then, it denotes a trademark that is registered with the United States Trademark Office.

In the United States, the government authority to issue and validate a Trademark is the U.S. Patent and Trademark Office (USPTO or PTO). The proprietary rights of the trademark can be established with its first date of commercial use or by registration with the trademark office. In cases of infringement, registered trademarks enjoy a higher level of legal protection, as compared to non-registered ones.

The United States Patent and Trademark Office may be accessed online at www.USPTO.gov. This is a great place to start to discover if the desired trademark is available, and then to actually register the mark.

Reasons to Trademark

There are numerous reasons why an artist needs to trademark and register their name. First of all, a trademark plays a central role in preventing the use of the artist's name by another artist or other musical groups. Trademark law states that an artist or band with a registered trademark cannot use a name that is similar to another artist or band. There have been many cases where bands have ended up changing their names just because they used a name similar to another group. That's why it's important to create a unique name of the artist or band name in the first place.

It is recommended to come up with a unique name that does not sound or seem similar to another group, and trademark it as soon as possible to preclude other groups from using it. Trademarking a band name also allows an artist to legally distribute merchandise, sell records, and carry out music business dealings with the trademarked logo on it.

Advantages of a Trademark

1. Proof of Use and Ownership
   In case a common law trademark is registered by a person who is not the first user of the mark, that person gets the right to use it and the original user of the common law mark loses all rights. Hence it is best if the trademark is registered.
2. Right to Use it Nationwide
   The trademark can accompany goods or services distributed throughout the nation where it is registered.
3. Preventing Counterfeit Products
   A business can prevent the import of counterfeit products by registering the mark with the U.S. Customs department.
4. Trademarks in Foreign Countries
   A Federally registered trademark can be used in order to expedite the process of obtaining a trademark from a foreign government. This is necessary in case the products of the artist are exported, because a trademark only has national validity.
5. Settling of Disputes
   A registered trademark is helpful in settling any disputes in a federal court of law, regarding the use of the trademark by others.
6. Selling the Business
   In case of selling the business, it would be helpful if the owner has registered trademarks.
   Trademarks result in increasing the worth of a business by helping to distinguish the products of a particular artist or business from others. This is important if an artist owns their recordings and releases them on their own record label, may eventually sell their record label to another person or business.
7. Showing Legitimacy
   Every music business professional such as record label executives and publishers will want to know that the artist that they are about to collaborate with has a trademark on their name. Can you imagine a record label signing an artist to the label and then put in lots of time and money to make the product: the recording, the mixing, the mastering and the CDs, then the record company releases the product, and three days later, they get a cease and desist letter from someone who has trademarked that artist's name? The record label will demand that the artist's name is trademarked before they ink a deal.

> ## Trademark Advantages
>
> - Proof of Use and Ownership
>
> - Right to Use it Nationwide
>
> - Preventing Counterfeit Products
>
> - Trademarks in Foreign Countries
>
> - Settling of Disputes
>
> - Selling the Business
>
> - Showing Legitimacy

According to legal provisions, the product engraved with a trademark cannot be imitated. A fake product of the same quality cannot be produced and sold under the same name and logo. If done, it is considered to be a violation of trademark rights. Those rights are held by the producer of original product.

It is evident that registering a trademark is a necessity rather than a convention. The benefits of registering clearly outweigh the cost involved in registering the mark. Every business, however small, should protect its right to use its mark by registering it.

++++++++++++++++++++++++++++

Trademark Categories & Classes

Class 35 is for Advertising and Business because you must identify a category for the mark. For example, you could have a soft drink come out and you could call it Toyota because it's a soft drink and not a car. So you have to have a category of where you're going to go. So, if you're an advertising a business, you're category 35.

Class 41 is Education and Entertainment. So a lot of artists use this category because Class 41 includes singers, dancers and musicians.

Now, you don't have to trademark your own name. I don't need to trademark John Latimer, I am John Latimer. If you want to confuse me with other John Latimer's that are out there, I can't help that. Now, a lot of times, I've used the name Latimer and there are 3 or 4 bands out there with the same name in the world and none of them are trademarked. So, if I wanted to trademark the name Latimer, as an artist, I would use Class 41 and spend the 400 dollars.

A mark is a graphic image. It's not a name. Now that graphic image may have letters in it that spell something but it's the image that you're marking. It's not the name.

I recommend that artists file for trademark to protect against others from using their chosen name. The only time you don't really need it is when you're using your own name. So if I was using John Latimer, I don't need to trademark that. It's me.

The basic intention of a business, whether artistic or otherwise, is to distinguish their product from others in the market.

On comparing the trademark vs. copyright protection, one thing is clear. Today, such protection is considered to be an important asset, especially by corporations. Both trademark and copyright, though different, have helped many people and organizations, protect their intellectual properties and financial interests.

How to Trademark a Logo

If an artist wants to protect a logo from infringements, they can register it as a trademark.

Trademarking a logo is very much important, many artists spend a lot of time and money in developing an appropriate logo to represent their brand. Protection of the logo can be done by trademarking, which refers to the registration of the logo with the concerned authority.

Most of us identify the golden 'M' logo on the products of McDonald's and know that it is the registered trademark of the fast food giant. Likewise names like The Beatles and Jay-Z are also trademarks. Logos have emerged as an integral part of business, as products with logos imprinted are viewed as the authentic ones. Unique and innovative logos play an important role in the promotional campaigns and advertising of every artist and their products. Logos are often used in online promotion of products, on flyers, posters, CD covers, and on websites.

Do Trademarks Need Registration?
According to the Federal law, registering the trademark is not mandatory. As per common law, any person who uses the mark first has the authority to continue using it. Whether common law or registered, a trademark is necessary to protect the reputation of an artist's business by conveying to the public that its products are original, and helping them distinguish between counterfeits and originals. This in turn will help the artist build a solid reputation for quality and reliability with its customers, thus increasing its customer base.

The first step is to visit the United States Patent and Trademark Office (USPTO) website and obtain the necessary forms. Applications may be filed electronically or they may be printed and then sent to the appropriate mailing address. Complete the form; such as name, contact details, kind of entity to be trademarked, trademark name, and similar information. File the application online itself and pay the amount using the artist's debit/credit card.

If submitting the applications by mail, a check is required. A temporary serial number will be sent via email or mail, according to how the request was sent. After the submittal is done, the trademark office examiner will review all aspects of the application. They will check to see whether there are any possible discrepancies, any symbols or marks that do not stand as trademarks, and other details.

Once the application has been filed, it will take a few months for the authorities to verify and grant registration for this intellectual property. If there are any doubts regarding the process of trademarking a logo, then, it will be better to consult a trademark lawyer and then proceed with the application. Consider hiring an intellectual property attorney for this purpose.

The trademark examiner checks the availability of the trademark requested. He or she will post the trademark in the official gazette, a weekly publication referring to which another party has an opportunity to oppose the approval of the trademark. Once all detailed verifications are completed, the band or artist name or log is trademarked. A notice will then be issued. A notice is also sent in case the application is disapproved. Renewal of the trademarked name must occur after the fifth year and before the tenth year of formal registration.

To trademark a band or artist name, it usually takes between six months to a year or even more. When it comes to this process, it is recommended to take legal advice from an attorney.

Step 1: The first step in registering an artist's trademark is to determine if the artist or artist's product qualifies for the trademark application. Usually, any non-trademarked product, goods, or service, that has a commercial value, can qualify for an application of trademark. It is common practice in the United States that any product or service that is developed, innovated or invented for a use in commerce, is good enough to qualify for trademark. If the product is not for sale to the public or has no commercial value, then it does not qualify for trademark. Obviously, an artist and the artist's art may become commercially available and therefore qualifies for registration. In addition, if the artist is planning on releasing their own recordings, they may want to consider a trademark for their record label (yet, another business for the artist).

Step 2: The second step for the artist to secure a trademark is to ensure they have a unique name and/or logo. (The name of the artist was addressed in the section about Image.) One way to do this is to go through the government's database of trademark applications. It is also necessary to confirm whether the trademark resembles some other trademark or not. In the United States, this may be accomplished by visiting the U.S. Trademark office online and then use the Trademark Electronic Search System (TESS) database in order to verify if the trademark is unique or not.

You may also conduct a trademark search by visiting the Trademark Public Search Library, between 8:00 a.m. and 5:30 p.m. at the Public Search Facility - Madison East, 1st Floor; 600 Dulany St.; Alexandria, VA 22313. Use of the Public Search Library is free to the public. These libraries have CD-ROMS containing the database of registered and pending marks. (However, the CD-ROMS do not contain images of the design marks.)

If the logo is already trademarked by someone else, then, there is no point in proceeding with the application for trademark registration. If this step is skipped and the artist's logo is found to be similar to another artist or band then the application fees will be forfeited. If there is no existing trademarked logo similar to the one filed, then perhaps all the requirements for trade marking an artist's logo may be met.

> **Advice: Consult an attorney who specializes in trademarks or intellectual property.**

Identification of Goods and Services
Now that you have chosen your mark and conducted a trademark search, you will need to draft a description of goods and/or services. A trademark application is incomplete without a statement identifying the goods and/or services with which the mark is used or will be used. The identification of goods and/or services must be specific enough to identify the nature of the goods and/or services. The level of specificity depends on the type of goods and/or services. For examples of acceptable identifications, please consult the Acceptable Identification of Goods and Services Manual.

++++++++++++++++++++++++++++

Logo Designs

A professional logo design is a matter of good planning, thinking and using your creativity in the best way possible. Here are some tips to ensure you come up with the best possible design.

As discussed in the image section of the Artist Development Plan, artists need to establish an identity and one good way is through the use of a logo. Believe it or not, a logo is a big part of an artist's image. This image has to portray the artist is a positive way. It should be very attractive and appealing and can make use of graphic, text, symbols, and calligraphy to project the business of the artist. The logo should represent the artist in the best way possible.

Tips for Logo Design
There are many things designers have to keep in mind when it comes to company logo design.

• You must take into account the business of the company to come up with a good logo design. This should say either in a direct manner or through a symbolic way, what the company stands for. The design must be able to connect to the audience about the company so that the product is associated with the logo very easily. It is not compulsory to convey the business of the company, but this would also depend largely on the client. There are times when you may have the freedom to experiment.

• Avoid complicated graphical forms. Many times, if the design is simple, it helps in connecting with the audience rather than complicated forms.

• You have to plan the colors and the fonts with utmost care. Remember the company logo design needs to appear on the letterhead or even a poster on the sidewalk. The colors should merge easily and be easy to reproduce in the print and web media of advertising. The colors you choose can also help one to establish the identity of the brand. The fonts used should be readable and should have a connection with the concept. You cannot use highly decorative fonts for a brand that sells clothes for children. In such cases, the designer can design a font that looks like a child's scrawl. This would help establish a connection of the product and the logo for the reader.

- The contours of the design should be such that it can look good in color as well as in black and white. Remember, the advertising concepts may require the logo design to be flexible enough to blend with the color schemes used for the press advertisement.

- Look at the successful logos around you. Try to know the concept behind the design and the reason it has been universally accepted. Is it the font or is it the color? Does it have a graphic that is symbolic or is it very simple in its appearance? Most logo designers need to keep their minds open and analyze and evaluate the reasons of the most popular logos in the market. Refer to the latest entertainment magazines, check out the advertising gimmicks and how the logos are used to enhance the advertisements at times. This can help you evaluate and be inspired to create something new.

- Break all rules! When starting off on a logo design, pick up your pencil and paper and let your mind wander. Forget all the tips above and try to unearth new concepts and new ideas. This will help you arrive to a design that is really unique and outstanding in its appearance.

- You must also think about the proportions of the logo. The design should be well-balanced and should look attractive in whatever size it may be used. The logo you design may look good on the computer, but the proportions you use, may not be very attractive once you blow up the design.

- You must make a careful study of the competitor's logo. Know the popularity of the products, the image the company portrays, the logo used and the various segments it caters to. Try to do a complete brand study of the competitors. This will help you plan a very attractive design and also maintain its exclusivity.

- Always bear in mind that the custom logo would be used for many years as most brands shy away from changing their logos very frequently. These establish the face of the company and most companies would prefer to avoid changes as it may cause the company to lose the identity of the brand. The company can suffer from brand recognition if it does not maintain the identity of the logo. Therefore, whatever you may design, you must be confident about the concept and the graphics. Try to think from an average person's point of view as well. This would help you to come up with a professional and attractive design that will appeal to the classes as well as the masses, which will help in the popularity of the logo design.

Your logo design should be such that every time you launch a new brand, you should be able to attract new clients who would want to seek your professional help. That would be the basic reward for a successful logo design!

In addition to securing a trademark as a part of the Artist Development Plan, it's also part of the Business Plan of the artist. To organize and develop an artist's career properly, make sure that the trademark process is completed properly and a trademark is secured for the artist.

To Do:

Artist Development in the Music Business
Chapter 14 – Publishing Preparation

In addition to live performances and sales of recordings, one of the main sources of income for artists in the music business is that of licensing songs, i.e., publishing. If the artist is a songwriter, the consideration of preparing to publish is an important part of the Artist Development Plan.

Songwriters are their own publishers until they enter into an agreement to license their songs to a third party; preferably a qualified, connected and respected music publisher. This includes the songwriter-artist asking the band to consider using the songwriter's next big hit. Publishing is the pitching of the song. That's a different "hat" to wear than that of a songwriter. It's also a different hat than that of a performer or musician. As soon as the songwriter takes that song to someone to perform it… maybe it's the artist's band, or maybe it's the songwriter themselves, that songwriter is now wearing the publisher's hat. A publisher's job is finding commercial uses for a song. Publishers try to convince others to use the song for such things as performances and recordings as well as use in film and television or the gaming industry. Do you see how that's a completely different "hat" than that of a songwriter? A publisher has to make a sale and find a commercial use for the song. That's how they get paid. That's how they make money. Publishing is indeed another income source for the artist who is a songwriter. This is the songwriter-artist.

But to get to that, the songwriter must pitch the song to the rest of the band and say, "Hey, I just wrote a new song. Let's try it out."

The band, at that point may say, "We're not interested in any of your stuff," or "Yeah, you always come up with good quality stuff, let's try it again." At that moment, the songwriter has taken off the "songwriting hat," and put on the "song plugging hat" to pitch the song to the band to perform or record. Whether the songwriter is in the band or not, it doesn't matter. They're still pitching it to the band. That's the job of a publisher. That "song plugging hat" is the publishing hat. Many songwriters are publishers and don't even know it. They are in the publishing business whenever they pitch a song that they own and/or control.

By law, until and unless a songwriter assigns the publishing rights of their songs to someone else (i.e., a music publisher), that songwriter is his or her own music publisher. However, that does not mean that a songwriter is necessarily an effective music publisher.

Music publishing is hard, time-consuming work and not every songwriter wants to spend their creative energy chasing the pennies, as publishing is sometimes called. Just remember, these pennies turn into dollars in the long run.

A Music Publisher's Job

Publishers need to create a demand for their songs. In other words, the publisher needs to have songs in their catalog of such quality that demand is unavoidable. If the songwriter-artist is in a band, they may be pitching their song(s) to the band. They want them to play their song and to record their song. When doing this, the songwriter-artist is acting as a song-plugger. A song-plugger works for or with a publishing company. Perhaps, it the artist's publishing company.

The copyrights owned and administered by publishing companies are one of the most important forms of intellectual property in the music business. (The other valuable Intellectual Properties are the copyright on a master recording of the song which is typically owned by a record company, and the trademark which is owned by the artist.) Publishing companies play a central role in managing this vital asset.

Working with a Publisher

Content (songs) is the most valuable asset that a songwriter-artist owns, yet making money with songs, via publishing, may be the least understood. The moment an artist creates lyrics or melodies and writes down the music, the artist owns that composition--as soon as the pen writes a lyric or a note is played next to another to make a song. Many songwriters underestimate the value of their creative content and too often give away their publishing or license it too cheaply because they need money.

Music publishing is all you need to say to inspire groans of confusion or knowing smiles. Music publishing is tedious, detail oriented, and (some would say) boring; but it also happens to be the single most enduring source of income in this ever-changing entertainment industry.

Why is publishing considered the holy grail of income streams for a creator of songs?

A song copyright doesn't just sit there and generate income - it needs to be promoted so that it will be used. Further, it must be protected against misuse. This is what music publishing is all about: The promotion and protection of - and if it's done well - the profiting from copyrights. As previously discussed, content creation is the first part of Artist Development. Content protection is the second part.

So, if the artist-songwriter is the publisher or if the songs are licensed from the songwriter to a music publishing company, steps can be taken to ensure that copyrights are properly administered and exploited. This information is vital to everyone working in the music business - after all, music publishing deals with the very basics of the music business: the songs. Without the songs, we might as well be selling shoes or shampoo. It is only by knowing exactly how music publishing works that a songwriter can become an effective publisher.

Speaking of which, who are these music publishers?

If the songwriter-artist is not prepared to make the investment of creating a staffed and fully-functional publishing branch, they will only do their song(s) a disservice. Music publishing requires expertise and extra amounts of patience. It's also a whole different industry than that of writing, producing or promoting recordings. Prepare to hire the staff, do the legwork, and the complete all additional work. It essentially is a whole new business. Music publishing can be a great way to make a lot of money... after a while. If the artist is not willing, or wanting, to do their own publishing they should consider working with an established, reputable music publisher who they will work with the songwriter-artist to promote their copyrights. This may mean that the publisher will also promote the recordings those copyrights appear on and ultimately the artists themselves.

In the music business, a music publisher (or publishing company) is responsible for ensuring the songwriters and composers receive payment when their compositions are used. Through an agreement called a publishing contract, a songwriter or composer "assigns" the copyright of their composition to a publishing company. In return, the company licenses compositions, helps monitor where compositions are used, collects royalties and distributes them to the composers. They also secure commissions for music and promote existing compositions to recording artists, record producers as well as music supervisors of film and television companies.

Whether the artist is a writer, a publisher or owns a record label - or all three - they should be aware of music publishing basics, and exactly how music publishing generates income. A dedicated songwriter should focus on the love of one's craft, but there is no denying the income potential from publishing and songwriting is one of the highest in the music business. Just because a songwriter can be their own publisher does not mean they are good at being a publisher. It's a different "hat." It is like starting a whole new business. Hey songwriters… are you ready to start working a new part-time job?

If the songwriter-artist wrote the songs and also does the pitching of those songs, then perhaps, they are also the publisher. If they signed a publishing deal, they are not the publisher. The party to whom they assigned the songs is now the publisher. Songwriting is competitive and signing a publishing contract could be a major deal. Songwriters who assign their music publishing to a music publisher might be giving up 50% of the total royalties, but in return may be getting a stable lifestyle as well as valuable experience with other staff writers. Collaborating on a song can be very educational. Some of the best songs ever written were done with other songwriters who bounced ideas around until something stuck. Publishers should encourage this because it affects their financial bottom line. Publishers pitch songs (as part of their catalog) to artists, producers, collaborators and companies. They ensure that all their songs have a registered copyright.

If you are a performer and wrote your single and have no publisher, THEN YOU ARE THE PUBLISHER! Yes, another "hat." 100% of the royalties are 100% yours. To be fair, 50% of the total royalties is owned by the songwriter and 50% of the total royalties are owned by the publishing company. In the publishing industry this translates to: 100% of the songwriting royalties are owned by the songwriter and 100% of the publishing royalties are owned by the music publisher.

> **100% = 50% + 50%**

Some songwriter-publishers setup an administration deal with a publisher. The artist-publisher still does the song-plugging but, 5% to 25% of the royalties are paid to administer the royalties and payments.

In addition, there are co-publishing deals where the songwriter-publisher collaborates with a music publisher and publishing royalties are split 50/50 (but can vary). If this turns out to be the case, the songwriter royalties are still 100% but the publishing royalties are split leaving you (the songwriter and the owner of your publishing company) with roughly 75% of total royalties.

> **100% = 50% + (25% + 25%)**

+++++++++++++++++++++++++++++++

Publishing Royalties

(See the Chap. on Finance & Funding)

Mechanical - income from the duplication of phonorecords (physical copies) of recorded music.

Performance - income from the performance of music.

Synchronization (or synch) - income from granting rights to use music in TV, movies, and commercials.

Print - income from the sale of music in print (i.e. sheet music).

Grand (dramatic performance) rights - income from granting rights to perform music compositions publicly in a dramatic setting like a play, Broadway musical, or ballet.

Foreign sources - self-explanatory -- can be a godsend if for some reason you don't do well on home soil.

> **Publishing Royalties**
>
> Mechanical Royalties
>
> Performance Royalties
>
> Synchronization Royalties
>
> Print Royalties
>
> Grand Rights Royalties
>
> Foreign Royalties

+++++++++++++++++++++++++++++++

Mechanical Royalties

Record companies pay the publisher mechanical royalties based on a license fee determined by the number of phonorecords manufactured. The publisher then pays the songwriter(s) their portion of the fee.

For example: A record company estimates that they will sell 1,000,000 units of a single song sound recording. These sales may come in the form of recordings on a compact disc, vinyl record or MP3 download. Using the current statutory rate of 9.1 cents for the mechanical royalty rate of a 5 minute song, the record company would pay the publisher $91,000 for a license to manufacture, duplicate or replicate 1,000,000 units of the song.

If the record company sells no recordings, the publisher owes them nothing. The song was recorded and the recording was mechanically duplicated.

The $91,000 received by the publisher for the mechanical royalty is 100% of the total royalty. The publisher will keep the publishing royalty and pay the songwriter(s) the songwriting royalty.

9.1 cents X 1,000,000 units = $91,000

50% for the publisher(s) = $45,500
50% for the songwriter(s) = $45,500

If the recording of the song is also a part of a record album, the record company would still pay 9.1 cents per duplication.

+++++++++++++++++++++++++++++

Harry Fox Agency

Let's not forget Harry Fox Agency. For a fee, they administer much of the mechanical rights business. Record companies can license the music from the Harry Fox Organization who, in turn forwards the money to the publisher. A huge plus with these guys is that they will audit record companies for suspicious bookkeeping. They take their fee from whatever they recover from the record company.

+++++++++++++++++++++++++++++

Performance Royalties

When a songwriter's song is performed on a stage or performed as a recording in a restaurant or radio station or any other business, a royalty is paid to the songwriter for the use of that song. This is called a Performance Royalty.

Performance royalties are paid via licenses that are granted by Performance Rights Organizations (PRO) such as ASCAP (American Society of Composers, Authors and Publishers), BMI (Broadcast Music, Inc), and/or SESAC. These three organizations issue licenses for a fee to any person or business that uses music; either live or recorded. (More about PROs in a separate section of the Artist Development Plan).

This is how it works. A songwriter and a publisher join a Performing Rights Organization to avoid the problem of contacting every business who uses their song. Nightclubs, radio stations, restaurants and many other businesses pay a fee to a Performing Rights Organization for a license and permission to use songs in the course of doing their business. The fee varies by PRO, the size of the venue and by the amount of music the business uses.

These PROs track their members song's on radio, TV, and other public places in the U.S. to determine how much to pay individual songwriters and publishers. Performing Rights Organizations are businesses designed to represent songwriters and publishers and their right to be compensated for having their music performed in public. Songwriters and Publishers are paid a performance royalty for the right to use their song IF they (and the song) are registered with PRO. This means that if you, your publisher and your song are not registered with a Performance Rights Organization, YOU WON'T GET PAID ANY PERFORMANCE ROYALTIES!

Each Performing Rights Organization uses their own "mysterious" formula to come up with the payout to their members. Again, this gets paid as a 50/50 split to publisher/writer (unless some deal was made and publisher gets more).

++++++++++++++++++++++++++++++

Synchronization Royalties

A music synchronization license, or "synch" for short, is a license granted by the holder of the copyright of a particular composition allowing the licensee to "synch" music with some kind of visual media output (film, television shows, advertisements, video games, accompanying website music, movie trailers, etc.).

The rights to a composition or the "song," which is different from the studio sound recording, are most often administered by the publishing company that represents the songwriter.

The value in the copyright of a song recording is divided into two pieces:

1. the composition, which is the underlying lyrics and melody written by the songwriter and administered by the music publisher, and

2. the "master" sound recording, which is the actual studio recording of the song and most often owned by a record label.

When an audio/visual project producer wants to use a recording of a song in their work, they must contact both the owner of the composition (songwriter via publishing company) as well as the owner of the sound recording (record label). In many cases, video producers choose to use their own audio recording version of a particular song. In this case they would only pay the publisher for the use of the song and not the record company because they are not using the recording owned by the record company.

Once the producer has made an inquiry with the copyright administrator (and additionally the record label, if they choose to use their recording, the rights holder/administrator issues a quote, usually for a one-time fee. This can initiate negotiations, whose points of interest usually include things like how the work is being used, the length of the segment, the prominence of the cue (is it background music? or used as the title track during the credits), and the overall popularity and importance of the song/recording. Sync licensing fees can range anywhere from free, to a few hundred dollars, to tens of thousands of dollars for popular recordings of songs.

+++++++++++++++++++++++++++++

Print Royalties

Print Royalties are paid from a music publisher to a songwriter for printing a song, or its download, (a song sheet, fake sheet, lyrics or music).

The royalty payment is made by the publisher and corresponds to the agreement (license) between the songwriter and the music publisher as with other music royalties.

If the writer's work is only part of a publication, then the royalty paid is pro-rata, a facet which is more often met in a book of lyrics or in a book of hymns and sometimes in an anthology.

Church music – that is, music that is based on written work – is important particularly in the Americas and in some other countries of Europe. Examples are hymns, anthems and songbooks. Unlike novels and plays, hymns are sung with regularity. Very often, the hymns and songs are sung from lyrics in a book, or more common nowadays, from the work projected on computer screen. In the U.S., the Christian Copyright Licensing Incorporated is the collection agency for royalties but song or hymn writers have to be registered with them and the songs identified.

+++++++++++++++++++++++++++++

Grand Rights Royalties

If a song is used is a theatrical play, it might be dramatized. The right to dramatize is a separate right – known as a grand right. This income is once again shared by the publisher and the songwriter(s). There is no convention to the amount of royalties paid for grand rights and it is freely negotiated between the publisher and the director of the play.

+++++++++++++++++++++++++++++

Foreign Royalties

Viewed from a U.S. perspective, foreign publishing involves two basic types of publishing 1) sub-publishing and 2) co-publishing occurrences in one or more territories outside that of basic origin. Sub-publishing, itself, is one of two forms: sub-publishers who merely license out the original work or those which make and sell the products which are the subject of the license, such as print books and records (with local artists performing the work).

Sub-publishers who produce and market a product retain 10–15% of the marked retail price and remit the balance to the main publisher with whom they have the copyright license. Those sub-publishers who merely license out the work earn between 15–25%. [26]

+++++++++++++++++++++++++++++

SoundExchange

SoundExchange is a non-profit company and functions very much like a Performance Rights Organization in that it collects royalties on the behalf of sound recording copyright owners and featured artists for non-interactive digital transmissions, including satellite and Internet radio.

++++++++++++++++++++++++++++++

About Licensing

As a part of the Artist Development Plan, prepare for licensing of songs and licensing of recordings of songs. Licenses are legal agreements between two or more parties expressly giving permission to use a song (or recording of a song) on a compact disc, television program, theatrical play, nightclub, ringtone, computer game or even music-on-hold while on the telephone.

All the terms and conditions for use (especially how much is paid) are spelled out when a license is issued.

(Sample publishing contracts and agreements are located in the forms section of this book.)

++++++++++++++++++++++++++++++

Pitching to Music Publishers

1. Do not flood a publisher with songs. Sending a CD or ten-song tape, without suggesting one or two specific tracks, will probably result in getting none of your tunes heard. Forget sending reviews, pictures, or other promotional materials.

Send a professionally mastered, high bias or chrome tape (or CD), with a typewritten lyric sheet, and ALL your information on the tape and the lyric sheet. Do yourself a favor and send no more than two songs at a time. If a publisher sees a tape with 8 songs, and a tape with 2 songs, chances are the 2-song tape gets listened to first. (It's off the desk more quickly that way.) The longer the pitch is, the longer it takes to get around to plowing through it.

2. TARGET!! The most difficult part of Publishing is finding the perfect place to pitch a song. When you send a song for publishing consideration, try to name a few acts or artists who you feel the song fits. Be sure that these artists do NOT write their own material, and that the song fits musically, subject-wise, stance wise with the latest work by the Artist. You can write a GREAT song...but if it is not in the style being used today, your chances of a cut are slim. If you are pitching for TV or film usage, try to remember that 90% of those songs are genre specific! I.e., if it's a Country Song, they usually would like to hear fiddles or steel or both, so there is no doubt about the feel of the scene.

In a biker bar, they might want songs with heavy guitar leads- but when pitching material for records, it is the quality of the WRITING more than the flavor or production.

3. Be educated. Make sure you know what you are trying to do. Are you a songwriter? Are you a singer? Are you a singer who writes? Are you a songwriter who is also a performing artist? All these paths are different. Most publishers work with dedicated songwriters as a first choice, simply because it is not a publisher's job to find a home for an artist... their job is to find a place for the song.

4. Be educated. Find out how you collect money earned from writing.

(Royalties.) You must know the common terms to communicate intelligently. Use the Web. The Performing Rights Organizations (such as ASCAP and BMI) collect your Performance Royalties (basically, in the U.S., money earned from airplay,) and Harry Fox Agency sets the Standard Rate for record royalty payments. You also need to know about ppls, Synch Rights, Master Use Licenses, etc. There are excellent resource materials in book form and on the web, and most cities have great songwriting organizations to guide you (Songwriters Guild of America, National Academy of Songwriters, etc.).

5. Be educated. Songwriting is like any other skilled profession. There are rules and tools. It's always ok to challenge or break the rules... as long as it is by choice, and not by ignorance. Study the craft of songwriting. Use tight rhyming where you can. Make your form consistent. Be creative. Be familiar with the work of who it is you are trying to pitch. Why should anyone cut your song if you don't even know his or her work? Listen to the radio for what's happening in your genre NOW!

HINT: A songwriter's competition is not the bad stuff you hear... it is the BEST of the BEST.

++++++++++++++++++++++++++++

Publishing Tips

Other than talent, songs are the most valuable assets that songwriter-artists own.

Publishing is probably the least understood area of the music business.

To Do

Notes:

Artist Development in the Music Business
Chapter 15 – Performing Rights Organizations

The Copyright Law of the United States, Section 101 defines a Performing Rights Organization as "an association, corporation, or other entity that licenses the public performance of non-dramatic musical works on behalf of copyright owners of such works.

The Performing Rights Organizations, (also known as PROs) in the United States are ASCAP, BMI and SESAC.

ASCAP is the American Society of Composers, Authors and Publishers (ASCAP). BMI is Broadcast Music, Inc. SESAC is SESAC, Inc."

These associations or companies team up with songwriters and publishers to collect money when a song is used in a performance; either live or recorded. On behalf of the member songwriters and publishers, these P.R.O.s issue performing rights licenses. They track public performances. They collect performing license revenues and then distribute those revenues to songwriters and music publishers.

The Performing Rights Organizations in the United States are ASCAP, BMI and SESAC.

A Performing Rights Organization collects money owed to songwriter-artists for the public performance of their songs. Some examples would be radio airplay, concerts, "elevator music," and even music on hold for phone systems. These are all uses of the song that the writer(s) gets paid a "performance royalty." It is the P.R.O.'s job to collect that royalty and distribute it to the appropriate songwriter-artists and/or publishers.

> **Bands don't join P.R.O.s; songwriters and publishers do.**
>
> **Bands don't pay P.R.O.s; promoters who hire bands do.**

In order to comply with the U.S. copyright law, any venue such as a nightclub or performance establishment that plays copyrighted music is legally required to secure permission to use that copyrighted music. It doesn't matter if the playing of these songs are performed in a live performance, such as a performer on a stage, or by mechanical means, such as a DJ spinning records. This user of songs can secure licenses from the three Performing Rights Organizations recognized by the U.S. Copyright Act of 1976. Since venues do not know which songs will be used during the course of the year, they purchase blanket licenses from all three P.R.O.s that cover them for the whole year.

When a concert promoter is preparing the details of promoting a musical event, they may be thinking that paying the performers and their entourages covers them for the music that's being played. However, the promoter may be overlooking an important aspect of promoting their event. The detail they may be missing is that many times, the artist performing the work is not the songwriter or composer of the work. This means that the promoter must obtain permission to use that copyrighted work before their event occurs. This is true of all types of music - classical, jazz, country, rock, rap, hip-hop, dance and any other style of music that they may be presenting. However, if all the music performed during a promoter's event is considered public domain, the promoter does not pay any money for the use of those songs.

Public performances of music is one way that songwriters and composers earn their living. Users of songwriter's songs need to obtain permission to use that work as stated in the U.S. copyright law, which was written to protect musical works. Rather than have businesses, promoters, nightclubs, etc. have to contact every songwriter or composer to obtain permission to use the music that they want to present, Performing Rights Organizations handle the details of licensing the musical works and then pay the owner of the copyrights.

Music speaks to the heart and that's one reason businesses use music as a means to attract customers and hence, income. Music also plays an important role in thousands of businesses; from radio, television and cable broadcasts, to streaming music over the internet, to live and recorded music used in restaurants, hotels and retail stores. If they are using music as a part of their daily business activities, they will need to purchase a license to do so. Paying is PRO is much easier for the licensee as well as the licensor.

Copyright owners give P.R.O.'s permission to license performances of their works, and P.R.O.'s generate fees on their behalf from businesses which use their music. This permits thousands of music users to work with thousands of music creators from around the world.

As a part of Artist Development, it is important that if the artist is a songwriter or content creator, they should belong to a Performing Rights Organization. Study ASCAP, BMI and SESAC and see which one is best for the artist.

If a songwriter-artist is not a member of a PRO, they won't get paid if their song is getting played on the radio. They won't get paid if their song gets played at a football game. So, it's real important for songwriters, and their publishing companies, to get involved with a Performing Rights Organization.

License fees are based on a series of determinants, depending on the type of establishment.

**Songwriters: Join a right P.R.O.
ASCAP, BMI or SESAC**

Types of Companies Licensing Music from P.R.O.s

- Airlines
- Auto Racing Tracks
- Background/Foreground Music Service
- Baseball - Leagues and Teams
- Basketball - Leagues and Teams
- Body Building Contests
- Bowling Centers
- Boxing
- Business Meetings
- Buses
- Campgrounds
- Carnivals
- Circuses
- Clogging
- Colleges and Universities
- Concerts and Recitals
- Conventions
- Dance Clubs and Associations
- Dancing Schools
- Direct Marketing
- Distribution Companies
- Dog Racing Tracks
- Dog Shows and Competitions
- Drive-In Theatres - Recorded Music
- Elevators
- Expositions
- Fairs
- Family Shows
- Festivals
- Football - Leagues and Teams
- Football Games
- Funeral Establishments
- Gymnastic Competitions
- Halls of Fame, Wax Museums, etc
- Helicopters
- Hockey - Leagues and Teams
- Horse and Harness Racing Tracks
- Hotels
- Ice Skating Rinks
- Industrial Shows
- Jukeboxes
- Lacrosse - Indoor and Outdoor
- Laser Shows
- Local Government Entities
- Lounges
- Motels
- Motion Picture Theatres
- Multi-Media Film Program
- Municipalities
- Museums
- Music-In-Business
- Music-On-Hold
- Music Equipment Retailers
- Nightclubs
- Playgrounds (Indoor)
- Polo Matches (Horses)
- Professional Speakers
- Private Clubs
- Radio-Over-Speaker Music Supplier
- Radio Stations
- Restaurants, Taverns & Nightclubs
- Retail Stores - Individual and Chain
- Rodeos
- Roller Skating Rinks
- Roller Games / Roller Derby
- Shopping Centers and Shopping Malls
- Skating Competitions
- Skating Rinks - Ice or Roller
- Soccer - Teams and Leagues
- Speakers, Professional
- Square/Round Dancing
- Symphony Orchestras
- Telephone Music Service
- Television Stations
- Theme and Amusement Parks
- Tournaments
- Tractor Pulls
- Trade Shows
- Train Cars
- Training Sessions
- Video Services
- Volleyball - Indoor and Outdoor
- Web Sites
- Wrestling
- YMCA / YMHA / YWHA / YWCA
- Zoos and Aquariums

Performing Rights Organizations

```
A.S.C.A.P.

B.M.I

S.E.S.A.C.
```

ASCAP - American Society of Composers, Authors and Publishers

Established in 1914, ASCAP is the first and leading Performing Rights Organization in the U.S., representing the world's largest repertory which totals over 8 million copyrighted musical works of every style and genre from more than 220,000 composers, lyricists and music publisher members. Additionally, ASCAP represents the works in the repertories of 70 affiliated foreign performing rights organizations created by many thousand affiliated international members. ASCAP is committed to protecting the rights of its members by licensing and collecting royalties for the public performance of their copyrighted works, and then distributing these fees to the Society's members based on performances. Unlike the other American Performing Rights Organizations, ASCAP's Board of Directors is made up solely of writers and publishers, elected by the membership every two years. www.ascap.com

BMI – Broadcast Music Incorporated

BMI is an American performing rights organization that represents more than 300,000 songwriters, composers and music publishers in all genres of music. The non-profit-making company, founded in 1939, collects license fees on behalf of those American creators it represents, as well as thousands of creators from around the world who chose BMI for representation in the United States. The license fees BMI collects for the "public performances" of its repertoire of more than 6.5 million compositions - including radio airplay, broadcast and cable television carriage, Internet and live and recorded performances by all other users of music - are then distributed as royalties to the writers, composers and copyright holders it represents. www.bmi.com

SESAC – Society of European Stage Authors and Composers

SESAC was founded in 1930 as to serve European composers not adequately represented in the United States. Though the company name was once an acronym, today it is simply SESAC and not an abbreviation of anything. Since that time SESAC has significantly expanded the number of songwriters and publishers represented and its repertory now includes all music genres. As a reflection of this change, S.E.S.A.C. became SESAC, Inc. www.sesac.com

SOCAN - Society of Composers, Authors and Music Publishers of Canada. www.socan.ca

SoundExchange

Okay, so songwriters have a source to help them collect fees owed to them when their song is performed publicly, either live or on the radio. But what if their song is streamed on an internet radio station? That's not the same as being played on terrestrial radio. Enter SoundExchange.

In addition to traditional Performing Rights Organizations, there's a new service which performs a similar function but for non-interactive digital downloads and streaming on the worldwide web. It's called SoundExchange.

SoundExchange collects fees for non-interactive digital downloads and streaming. This is another way for musicians-artists to get paid, but more importantly, this is your record label; now you can make money, because it's your P circle copyright.

When a song is broadcast on terrestrial radio, how much money does the band make? Does anybody know? That's right... Nothing! The band makes nothing when the song that they performed or possibly recorded gets played on the radio. So, who makes money when the song is played on the radio? Yes, the songwriter and the songwriter's publisher. Both make money, theoretically, every single time it's played on the radio; not the band who performed the song.

SoundExchange is for non-interactive performances of a song on the Internet, such as Pandora or Sirius/XM. You may be able to pick a genre but you can't pick the artists. You may be able to pick the artist, but you can't pick the song. It's non-interactive. You can't pick what song that you want to listen to.

However, on web sites such as YouTube or MySpace, it may list five (5) recordings of the same song. You can pick the song and you can play the song. This is considered interactive and not an area for SoundExchange.

Sound Exchange is non-interactive and it doesn't pay the songwriter. It pays the P Circle copyright, which is usually owned by a record label. The record label has an agreement with the artist for royalties and, so now the musician-artist has a chance to make some money.

But so do the record labels. This is an income source for the artist who owns their own record label. If the writer is a performer, they're wearing a different hat. Perhaps the writer, as a performer, plays in a band, and the band produces a recording and releases it on their own record label. The record label posts it on the web and it's gets played, now the record label's going to get paid, which pays their artists / performers. The songwriter gets paid from ASCAP, BMI. So, more money can be made.

To Do

Notes:

Artist Development in the Music Business
Chapter 16 – Gear, Equipment & Instruments

Gear, equipment, instruments, amps, microphones and, yes, transportation are all important considerations for an artist. Procuring and preparing the proper instruments and gear prior to Product Development is another part of the Artist Development Plan. Unless an artist is going solo and always, sings a-cappella, it is assumed there must be some sort of musical accompaniment such as a guitar or a piano or other instrument accompanying them.

Artists should invest in the best instruments and musical equipment that they can afford. No artist can perform their best work using mediocre equipment. Artists shouldn't go with just name brands, they should listen to the quality of the instrument before they purchase it.

Part of putting together an Artist Development Plan is to identify the gear and equipment that the artist currently owns, and then to project the instruments, equipment or gear that will be needed for future projects in development. This part of the Artist Development Plan must be a part of and follow the Finance Plan of artist's Business Plan, especially due to the expenses incurred. Sometimes, as a business decision, it may be more prudent for an artist to invest in the promotion of a new recording instead of purchasing a new amp, for example.

Equipment List

What equipment does the artist currently own? Write it down. If the artist is a partnership or has more than one owner, perhaps the equipment is actually owned by one participant or by the entire group. If the artist's company owns any gear or equipment, it should be identified. It is a good idea, to separate whether the gear is owned by the company (band) or by an individual involved with the company. If the company decides to purchase a van, for example, to assist the artist with getting from gig to gig, then all of the owners of the company now own part of a new asset. However, the artist's guitarist, who may also be one of the owners of the artist's company, contributes the use of their guitar for performances, then the company does not own that piece of equipment; the guitarist does.

In addition to the gear, equipment and instruments that are a part of the artist's gear-list, this is a good time to overview the inventory and determine if any new gear is needed. If so, plan to put this item into the Finance Plan and then begin putting money aside in order to eventually purchase the asset.

Endorsements

As an artist becomes more successful, product endorsements may play an important role to their financial bottom-line. (See more about Endorsements in the Finance section of the Artist Development Plan.) Many musical instrument manufacturers provide artists with free (or discounted) instruments in the hopes that the artist will be seen using that particular instrument by other artists, who then may then go and purchase the instrument.

Artists who accept endorsement deals should not do it just to get free gear. If the artist doesn't believe in the product, they are not going to talk about it in a good, positive way. The manufacturer of the instrument would suffer and, ultimately, so would the artist.

Once the artist gear-list is compiled, potential instrument manufacturers may be identified for future endorsements. Artists would be wise to gather the names and contacts for each instrument or equipment manufacturer. Some artists begin the branding by adding these music equipment manufacturer contacts to their promotion list database.

Funds for Instruments

Sometimes it tears me up to see a good, quality, talented band and the lead guitar player cannot afford new strings: constantly re-tuning all night long. Swearing at the guitar because it's not responding as expected. The guitarist can't or won't invest the money for upkeep. It's expensive to keep an instrument in good shape. Look at price of bass strings for example.

In addition and more importantly, the cost of a new axe can be astronomical. The artist will have to account for use of funds to allocate for new equipment. This should be well-defined in the Finance Plan section.

++++++++++++++++++++++++++++

Artists have got to have good gear to perform well. If an artist uses mediocre gear, they're going to get mediocre sound. Good gear doesn't mean expensive gear. It just means good gear. And as a quality musician, you'll know what's good and what's not so good for you.

In addition, while working with collaborators such as band members, agents or record labels, they will want to make sure that, since the artist is representing them, they will want the artist to have good quality equipment to use.

> **Music expresses that which cannot be said and on which it is impossible to be silent.**
> **~ Victor Hugo**

Types of Musical Instruments

Every single musical instrument, right from the African djembe to the Indonesian gamelan angklung, and the Arabic shababa to the Indian sitar, is a testament to the fact that music is a universal language having multiple dialects.

In today's world, artists are privileged to have a long list of different musical instruments to create their art. Here are various types of musical instruments available in the modern world.

The sheer magnitude of the different musical instruments from all over the world can be mesmerizing.

Wind Instruments

Wind instruments require a person to blow into the instrument in order to produce a sound. They work on the principle of sound waves, frequencies, resonance, harmonics, and acoustics. When an artist blows into the instrument, the pitch of the sound note produced varies depending on the length of the internal air column in which the sound waves vibrate. The shorter the air column, the higher is the pitch of the note produced, and vice versa. Some popular wind instruments include: flutes, piccolos, clarinets, bassoons, English horns, oboes, accordions, saxophones, bagpipes, pianicas and harmonicas.

Percussion Instruments

Percussion instruments require a person to strike or beat the instrument surface in order to generate vibrations, which then produce the desired sound note. Depending on the type of surface, one can use one's hands, fingers, sticks, or other similar objects for striking the instrument surface as well as the force of the strike. A characteristic feature of percussion instruments is that the type of sound produced varies depending on the spot that is struck on the instrument surface. For example: in case of the djembe, striking it at the center produces a deep and muffled sort of thump, whereas striking it at the edges produces a sharp and crisp sound, which is totally different from the earlier one. Some of the well-known percussion instruments are: drums, congas, djembes, duffs, tables, dhols, nagaras, cymbals, bells, xylophones, marimbas, triangles, and tambourines.

Brass Instruments

All those shiny trumpets and trombones that are featured so prominently in jazz, Dixieland, and blues' music are classic examples of brass instruments. Not all brass instruments are made from brass, but are named "brass" due to the nature and texture of their sound that they produce. They work on pretty much the same principle as wind instruments, with a few modifications here and there. In case of brass instruments, the length of the air column can be changed using press valves or through a slide mechanism. Some of the popular ones are: trumpets, trombones, bugles, French horns, conchs, tubas, alto horns, bazookas, and cimbassos.

String Instruments

All guitars, violins and pianos fall under the category of string instruments. String instruments work on the basis of sound wave vibrations that are created with the help of strings. The pitch of the sound note produced depends on the length of the air column as well as the type and thickness of the string involved. Some of the famous string instruments are: guitars, pianos (also considered a percussion instrument because of the striking of the keys), violins, violas, sitars, cellos, double basses, mandolins, banjos and harps.

Electronic Instruments

These are some of the newer musical instruments that have been produced in recent years with the advent of technology. Most of them are designed to reproduce the sounds of existing musical instruments in a simple and user-friendly way. Some of the common electronic instruments include: piano keyboards, octopads, rhythm machines, samplers, synthesizers, synclaviers, Theremins, mellotrons and omnichords.

Despite different areas of the world being associated with different musical instruments, all of them ultimately unite in contributing towards the common language of music. Therefore, one can safely say that music's universal appeal is clearly visible in the many types of musical instruments that one gets to see all over the world.

Care of Musical Instruments

A musical instrument is considered as a musician's best friend. Instruments need consistent attention and care to help them last longer. Taking care of a musical instrument is considered an essential part of learning to play that instrument. Proper care of musical instruments helps to consistently maintain the quality of its musical output. Musical instruments vary in their size, usability and manufacturing material. Depending upon these characteristics, the methods applied to take care of different instruments are not the same.

> **Advice: When caring for an instrument never try to become your musical instrument's 'doctor.'**
>
> **If you don't know what you're doing, you may create more damage to the instrument.**
>
> **It is always a safe bet to visit a specialist in musical instrument repairs.**

Here are some suggestions applicable to all types of instruments. If followed, they will help to maintain the monetary value and quality of the musical instrument.

- It is advisable to protect your musical instruments from extreme temperatures such as excessive cold air, direct sunlight and artificial heat. Make sure to store the instrument in a cool, dry and safe place when not in use. During winters, let the instrument acclimatize to a warmer temperature before it is played. This helps to maintain its performance standard in any weather.
- Do not delay repair work when required. A neglected instrument gives a degraded emission of sound or a buzzing sound.
- It is advisable to invest in a superior quality cover or protective box for the instrument. Avoid using bags for covering the instruments.
- After every practice or performance, clean the

instrument and replace it back in its box for its safety.
- Musical instruments are very costly. Ensure not to leave them unattended at any new place or with strangers. If left out in the open, they might get damaged, stolen or get lost.
- Never leave the instrument in a closed vehicle or a humid place.
- When traveling, avoid loading the instrument in the cargo compartment. There is a high chance of instrument damage due to mishandling.
- Since musical instruments are precious to artists, the artist, and many times, instruments, appreciate in value. It is advisable to insure the instrument in case of any losses or damage.

Caring for Wind Instruments

- Never pick up the musical instrument by the keys. Ensure to hold the instrument at the two ends when removing it. The same care needs to be taken when replacing the instrument back after its use.
- The channels of wind instruments tend to catch moisture due to the air blown through them when they are being played. This moisture can affect the internal surface of the instrument and create cracks in them, thus affecting the quality of the music emitted. Similarly, internal moisture may lead to fungal growth in the channels of the instrument.
- Always use a clean cloth to clean your instrument. Usage of damp wiping material in any way should be avoided.
- If the instrument is supposed to be assembled before its usage, then ensure that all joints are cleaned before they are assembled. The musician may also apply grease in very small proportions on corks if required.
- Avoid consuming food before playing a wind instrument as there is a high chance of food particles being blown inside the instrument when playing it. This not only affects the quality of music emitted but makes the instrument unhygienic.
- If there are any joints in the instruments held together with screws, ensure that they are adequately tightened.
- Every once in a while, take your instruments to the repair workshop to ensure that the instrument is perfect. You may opt for some professional help in getting your instrument cleaned.
- It is recommended that you clean and wipe the mouth piece of these instruments just before and immediately after using them.

Caring for Brass Instruments

- Brass instruments are generally easily dismantled. However, if a certain cork is tight do not force the screws of the cork to open. Always opt for professional help.
- These instruments once dismantled can be washed with some warm water to remove dust particles inside the instrument. Use a soft cloth to dry the instrument. You may dry the instrument thoroughly in a cool

dry place without direct exposure to sunlight.
- Take care to grease all valves of the instrument with a special valve oil before reassembling the instrument.
- Avoid usage of chemicals such as a brass cleaner to shine your instrument as these chemicals tend to leave a sticky feel on the instrument's surface.

Caring for Key Instruments

- These instruments are primarily played with the help of the black and white keys and foot pedals.
- It is essential to protect the keys by covering them carefully whenever the instrument is not in use. Use protective plastic coated pads as instrument covers.
- The musical keys tend to accumulate dust over a period of time with usage. This dust can be wiped clean with a soft dry cloth.
- There might be instances of sticky and jammed keys. It is recommended that the musician should seek professional help in this case.

Caring for String Instruments

- Always use a clean dry cloth to cleanse your instruments. Ensure that the instruments are devoid of any dust particles.
- For wooden surfaced instruments, a coat of fresh varnish and wood polish is highly essential once in a while.
- Do not replace all the strings at one go. Replace them gradually so as not to reduce the strain on the strings. Ensure your hands are clean when using the strings as they tend to accumulate a lot of dry skin and body oil.
- When hanging an instrument with 2 bow strings, ensure to use the one opposite to the chin-rest.
- Always follow the user guide issued along with the instrument.

To Do

Notes:
_____
_____
_____
_____
_____
_____

Artist Development in the Music Business
Chapter 17 - Teams & Collaborators

There is no shame in taking pride in achievements or position. Remember, nobody gets to the top alone. It's only lonely at the top if an artist forgets all the people they met along the way and fail to acknowledge their contributions to their success.

The most successful artists have one thing in common: a great team. No artist can make it alone. The development of an artist's team is another important step in the Artist Development Plan. This team may include other musicians, singers, songwriters or arrangers. The team may also include managers, agents, lawyers and publicists. No matter how the artist's team is structured, a great team makes it much easier for the artist to succeed. Remember this: friends and family don't always make a great team. It's nice that they may have helped the artist in the past, but do they have the where-with-all, knowledge and connections for continued help in the hardest industry in the world?

There are two types of teams that an artist will work with: Creative Teams and Business Teams.

The Creative Team

Musicians
If the artist is a solo act, perhaps a musical accompanist or backup vocalist will never be needed. However, most artists will find it necessary to involve other musicians at some time in their career to collaborate for either performing or recording, or both.

All people are different. This means that all musicians are different. Some have chops and others have feel. The perfect situation for an artist is when a collaborator-musician has both chops and feel.

Songwriters and Co-Songwriters
Many artists are also songwriters. However, many artists team up with songwriters to perform and/or record their songs.

The Music Business Team

There are many individuals who may comprise an artist's team and here are a few of the main ones. Many of these team members also have teams that will also contribute to an artist's career such as a record label may have a team of producers who may then have a team of engineers, or a booking agency who may have a team of agents.

Talent Managers

Although many artists begin their career by managing it themselves, they have to recognize that it is a totally different role than that of an artist. An artist wears many "hats" and management is just one of them. With that in mind, an Artist Development Plan should consider if the artist is the Manager or the artist has collaborated with a professional to assist with the BIG picture. Of all of the team members, this one could be the most important. The talent manager is to the artist's business, what the artist is to the creative side of the endeavor. The manager is the artist's quarterback. They run the plays. An artist must have absolute trust in the Manager. The manager is essentially another member of the band. Artists should look for a manager who understands what the artist is trying to accomplish and also that they share the same goals and objectives. It won't help an artist to sign with a manager who wants the artist to self-release their album if the artist is really interested in a major label deal. For most musicians, the manager is the first team member to enter the picture.

Attorney

An artist with a quality music attorney has a definite advantage over other artists. Quality music attorneys not only help an artist with advice and counsel or with entertainment contracts but also with the connections they have within the industry. A good attorney may be the most important person on an artist's team.

Booking Agent

Live performances are another major of income for an artist. Although a Product development issue, obtaining gigs for an artist is what a booking agent does. A good agent is an important member of the artist's team. Booking a single show isn't really that big a deal. Booking a tour, on the other hand, is a lot of work. Without the right contacts, not to mention the time and knowledge, many musicians have a difficult time booking tours on their own. An agent may be able to help. Successful booking agents have contacts with talent buyers and promoters. They know venues and have a good feel for the kinds of places that the artist should and could be playing. Agents book shows, negotiate deals, and schedule tours for an artist.

> **Tip: When beginning to work with a potential nightclub promoter, the artist should evaluate if the "promoter" is really a saloon keeper or someone truly interested in Artist Development. There is a difference.**

Concert Promoter / Talent Buyer

Also, as a part of Artist Development, many artists collaborate with talent buyers and promoters for events, shows and concerts. Hopefully, an artist will collaborate with many concert promoters during their career to help build their fan base and potential customers. Talent buyers are the people the artist's booking agent convinces to take a chance on the artist for bookings. The promoter will secure a venue and promote the performance. Hopefully the concert or event has a great attendance and the promoter / talent buyer is ready for re-bookings of the artist. These promoters are a part of the artist's team indirectly, but not as an owner of the artist's company.

Record Label
Artists may have a record label, or they may produce and release their own recordings. Although another part of Product development, an artist must look forward with their planning. If an artist is signed to a major or an indie record label, an artist must add them to their "team." artists don't necessarily have to have a label on their team, but quality labels can certainly help an artist. Many record labels have promotion departments, sales departments, distribution channels as well as connections with other music business professionals. In order for a record label to survive, it is imperative that they team up with quality artists.

Publicist
An artist's publicist convinces print and web media to write about the artist. Many times the publicist also tries to convince radio stations to play the artist's music. Having a professional publicist is another key player on the artist's team. Like promoters, artists probably won't have just one publicist. Artists are more likely to have different publicists for different kinds of media. Artists may even work with different publicists from release to release or tour to tour. Publicists can be very helpful to an artist because publicists have contacts. If an artist calls a writer at a newspaper or magazine and asks for a review, they may be politely refused. However, when an artist's publicist calls, that magazine usually listens…and the artists wins. This is because publicists have the know-how and finesse to get the job done.

Building a Positive Team

Many teams often are positive because they have a positive leader. To create a good positive team, the artist should focus on their own happiness, well-being, and emotional intelligence. This is the first step. Enthusiasm is contagious.

There are many ways to build a positive team.

• Teams that fully understand the purpose of what they do are usually more engaged than teams without this focus. This is why it's important for artists to create mission and vision statements for their team. These statements are inspiring messages that express the deeper purpose of the work and goals stated in the Artist's Business Plan.

• Create a team organizational chart to define each person's role, the group's projected outcome, and the artist's expectations. Team charts are useful because they provide focus and direction. After all, when an artist's team know what they're doing (and why), they can all move forward together, instead of pulling in different directions. For example, an artist may be able to coordinate with all team members to organize and set logistics for an upcoming release and/or tour. In addition, when a team sees the BIG picture, they may be better able to offer ideas to enhance the artist's career.

- Next, look at the objectives that have been set for the team. Make sure that the team members' goals align with those of the artist's organization. Without this framework in place, the team members might feel unmotivated, simply because they're not sure what they should be doing, or because they don't understand how their role benefits the artist or the artist's goals.

- Artists should keep in mind that they play an enormous part in how their team feel and respond day-to-day, as well as in their long-term success. Communicate regularly. Keep the team informed about what's happening in the organization, as well as within the team. The more open and transparent the artist is, the easier it will be to build trust and create good relationships. Schedule regular meetings to discuss important updates or changes to the objectives and goals. This also gives team members a chance to voice any concerns or issues that they're having with their work.

- Research shows that autonomy plays a significant role in how satisfied people are in their jobs, so it may be important for an artist to give more power to everyone on their team. This might mean delegating important tasks, or simply stepping back and letting their team show that they're going to complete a project. An added benefit of encouraging autonomy is that people's work often improves when they have the power to choose when and how they complete it.

- The artist's team members can't be positive and focused if they don't have the resources they need to do their jobs. So, support the team. Ask them how they can do their jobs better, and then help them.

Positivity is a habit, and the only way that an artist can cultivate long-term positivity with their team is to reinforce it daily. This takes focus and self-discipline, but the benefits can be huge!

Above all, artists should be thankful and grateful to their team.

++++++++++++++++++++++++++++

Collaborators & Partners

You can't do it yourself. So, who's on your team?

Usually there are a multitude of participants involved with an artist's career depending, of course, on the artist. An orchestra with formal attire has far more participants than a solo performer on the street corner. Usually, the bigger the artist or band is, then the more people who may participate with them. These individuals may be part of a larger company or they may be in a work-for-hire situation.

Potential Music Business Collaborators

- A&R Manager
- A&R Scout
- Accompanist
- Account Executive
- Account Manager
- Accountant (Qualified)
- Acoustical Consultant
- Acting coach/teacher
- Actor
- Actress
- Administrative Assistant
- Administrator
- Advertising Sales
- Agent
- Arranger
- Artist Liaison
- Talent Manager
- Band Member
- Artist Relations Representative
- Audio Contractor
- Audio Engineer
- Audio for Forensic Sciences
- Audio for Gaming Production
- Audio Post Production to Picture
- Audio Programmer
- Audio Research / Development
- Audio Sales
- Audio Software Engineer
- Audio Technician
- Audio Video Network Engineer
- Audio Video System Designer
- Backing Singer
- Bar Manager
- Bar Staff
- Board Operator
- Booker
- Booking Agent
- Booking Manager
- Box Office Assistant
- Box Office Manager
- Brand/Product Management, Mgr
- Business Affairs Assistant
- Business Consultant
- Business Development, Manager
- Business Manager
- Camera Operator
- Carpenter
- Catalog Manager
- Catalog Marketing Manager
- Choreographer
- Club DJ
- Club Manager
- Coach – Vocal, Dance, etc
- Community Music Worker
- Composer
- Concert Manager
- Concert Promoter
- Conductor
- Consultant
- Controller
- Copyist
- Copyright Assistant
- Copywriter
- Corporate Audio Video Mixer
- Creative Services, Manager
- Crew
- Customer Support Representative
- Dance Instructor
- Dancer
- Database Management
- Director, Music Video
- Disc Jockey
- Distribution, Management
- Distribution, Sales Reps
- Distributor
- DJ
- Driver
- Duo
- Duplicator / Replicator
- Editor
- Education / Development Officer
- Educator / Instructor
- Engineer
- Engineer, Front of House Sound

Engineer, Monitor
Engineer, Recording
Engraver
Events, Management
Executive Assistant
Executive Director
Facilities Manager
Festival Organizer
Financial, Executive
Financial, Staff
General Manager
Grant Writer
Graphic Artist / Designer
House Manager
House of Worship Audio Mixer
Human Resources Manager
Impersonator, Musician
Impersonator, Vocals
Independent Radio Promoter
Intern
Internet Promotion
IT Programmer
Record Label, Manager
Legal Counsel
Librarian
Licensing, Assistant
Licensing, Manager
Lighting Director
Lighting Technician
Make-up Artist
Manager
Manufacturer
Marketing Analyst
Marketing, Manager
Mastering Engineer
MC – Master of Ceremonies
Media Manager
Media Relations / PR, Manager
Membership Representative
Merchandiser
Music Attorney
Music Attorney Paralegal
Music Director
Music Editor
Music Ensemble / Band
Music Journalist

Music Log In Clerk
Music Publishing, Manager
Music Software Engineer
Music Supervisor
Music Teacher
Music Technologist
Music Therapist
Musician
Musicologist
New Media Manager
Office Manager
Operations Manager
Orchestra, Manager
Personal Assistant
Personal Manager
Photographer
Piano Tuner
Presenter
Press Office Director
Producer
Production Assistant
Production Coordinator
Production Director
Program Director
Project Manager
Promoter
Promotion
Promotion Director
Public Relations Specialist
Publicist
Publisher
Radio Management
Radio Producer
Radio Programmer
Radio Promotion
Radio Talent
Receptionist / Front Desk
Recording Engineer
Recruiter
Rehearsal Pianist
Remixer
Remote Broadcast Audio Mixer
Repairer
Researcher
Retail Sales
Retail Sales Manager

Reviewer Writer
Road / Tour Manager
Road Manager
Royalty Accounts, Director
Sales Executive
Sales Representative
Sales, Director
Scenographer
Security
Session Musician
Singer
Singer / Songwriter
Social Media Specialist
Software Engineer
Song-Plugger
Songwriter
Sound Designer
Sound Engineer
Sound Reinforcement Engineer
Sound Technician
Sponsor Manager
Spot Operator
Stage Hand
Stage Manager
Steward/Hostess
Street Team
Studio Manager
Studio Manager, Assistant
Stylist
Subscription Sales

Supply Chain Analyst
Supply Chain Manager
Supply Chain Planner
Syndicator
Talent Buyer
Talent Scout
Technical Director
Technical Writer
Technician
Technician, Backline
Technician, Instrument
Technician, Lighting
Technician, Sound
Technician, Studio
Technician, Wiring
Theatre Manager
Theatrical Sound Designer
Ticket Seller
Ticket Taker
Tour, Manager
Venue, Assistant
Venue, Director
Videographer
Vocalist
Voice-Over artist
Web Engineer
Web Producer
Website Designer
Writer

+++

Team Building

Who's on the team? In the music business, solo singer-songwriters are the only potential entity that does not need a team. However, even for the solo-artist, it's a much tougher road without a good team. A band needs a team of good quality musicians. A recording session might need a team consisting of an engineer, producer, and/or side-musicians. A performance tour may need a bus driver, an agent and a sound engineer.

Few people in the entertainment industry understand how to create an effective team. Many bands form because the members all share a common bond such as attending the same school, living in the same neighborhood or through networking in their respective area of the country. Belonging to a team, in the broadest sense, is a result of feeling part of something larger than yourself. It has a lot to do with the understanding of the mission or objectives of the art and the artist. Hopefully the mission is well defined in the Artist Business Plan.

In a team-oriented environment, contributions are made by individuals to the overall success of the organization. The organization may be the band, the record label working with the artist or the team of members working together on one gig. Artists work with fellow members of the organization to produce these results. Even though an artist may have a specific job function, they are unified with other members to accomplish the overall objectives. The bigger picture drives their actions; their function exists to serve the bigger picture.

In the music business, the talent manager or producer is usually in charge of helping the artist find and secure effective team members and are always exploring ways to improve business results and profitability. Many view team-based, horizontal, organization structures as the best design for each project of an artist's career. These team members can be partners, collaborators or independent contractors.

No matter what an artist calls their team-based improvement effort: continuous improvement, total quality, lean project budgets or self-directed work teams, they are striving to improve results for their fans and customers.

Successful team building, that creates effective, focused work teams, requires attention to each of the following.

- Clear Expectations: Has the leadership clearly communicated its expectations for the team's performance and expected outcomes? Is the artist or artist manager demonstrating constancy of purpose in supporting the team with resources of people, time and money? Does the work of the team receive sufficient emphasis as a priority in terms of the time, discussion, attention and interest directed its way by management?

- Context: Do team members understand why they are participating on the team? Do they understand how the strategy of using teams will help the artist attain its communicated business goals? Can team members define their team's importance to the accomplishment of corporate goals? Does the team understand where its work fits in the total context of the artist's goals, principles, vision and values?

- Commitment: Do team members want to participate on the team? Are members committed to accomplishing the mission and expected outcomes? Do team members perceive their service as valuable to the artist and to their own careers? Do team members anticipate recognition for their contributions? Do team members expect their skills to grow and develop on the team? Are team members excited and challenged by the team's opportunity?

- The depth of the commitment of team members to work together effectively to accomplish the goals of the team is a critical factor in team success. The relationships team members develop out of this commitment are all important in team building and team success. The artist should only want to work with committed team members who believe in the artist as well as the artist's work.

- Competence: Does the team feel that it has the appropriate people participating? (As an example, in process of booking a tour, is each step or team member of the process on board, such as the agent and the publicist?) Does the team feel that its members have the knowledge, skill and capability to address the issues for which the team was formed? If not, does the team have access to the help it needs? Does the team feel it has the resources, strategies and support needed to accomplish its mission? If a member of the team feels as though the artist will never be successful, their attitude will reflect with the team and with the other members.

- Charter: Has the team taken its assigned area of responsibility and designed its own mission, vision and strategies to accomplish the mission? Has the team defined and communicated its goals; its anticipated outcomes and contributions; its timelines; and how it will measure both the outcomes of its work and the process the team followed to accomplish their task? Does the leadership team or other coordinating group support what the team has designed?

- Control: Does the team have enough freedom and empowerment to feel the ownership necessary to accomplish its goals? At the same time, do team members clearly understand their boundaries? How far may members go in pursuit of solutions? Are limitations (i.e. monetary and time resources) defined at the beginning of the project before the team experiences barriers and rework?

- Is the team's reporting relationship and accountability understood by all members of the organization? Has the organization defined the team's authority? To make recommendations? To implement its plan? Is there a defined review process so both the team and the organization are consistently aligned in direction and purpose? Do team members hold each other accountable for project timelines, commitments and results? Does the organization have a plan to increase opportunities for self-management among organization members?

- Collaboration: Does the team understand team and group process? Do members understand the stages of group development? Are team members working together effectively interpersonally? Do all team members understand the roles and responsibilities of team members? Team leaders? Team recorders? Can the team approach problem solving, process improvement, goal setting and measurement jointly? Do team members cooperate to accomplish the team charter? Has the team established group norms or rules of conduct in areas such as conflict resolution, consensus decision making and meeting management? Is the team using an appropriate strategy to accomplish its action plan?

- Communication: Are team members clear about the priority of their tasks? Is there an established method for the teams to give feedback and receive honest performance feedback? Does the organization provide important business information regularly? Do the teams understand the complete context for their existence? Do team members communicate clearly and honestly with each other? Do team members bring diverse opinions to the table? Are necessary conflicts raised and addressed?

- Creative Innovation: Is the organization really interested in change? Does it value creative thinking, unique solutions, and new ideas? Does it reward people who take reasonable risks to make improvements? Or does it reward the people who fit in and maintain the status quo? Does it provide the training, education, access to books and films, and field trips necessary to stimulate new thinking?

- Consequences: Do team members feel responsible and accountable for team achievements? Are rewards and recognition supplied when teams are successful? Is reasonable risk respected and encouraged in the organization? Do team members fear reprisal? Do team members spend their time finger pointing rather than resolving problems? Is the organization designing reward systems that recognize both team and individual performance? Is the organization planning to share gains and increased profitability with team and individual contributors? Can contributors see their impact on increased organization success?

- Coordination: Are teams coordinated by a central leadership team that assists the groups to obtain what they need for success? Have priorities and resource allocation been planned across departments? Do teams understand the concept of the internal customer—the next process, anyone to whom they provide a product or a service? Are cross-functional and multi-department teams common and working together effectively? Is the organization developing a customer-focused process-focused orientation and moving away from traditional departmental thinking?

- Cultural Change: Does the organization recognize that the team-based, collaborative, empowering, enabling organizational culture of the future is different than the traditional, hierarchical organization it may currently be? Is the organization planning to, or in the process of, changing how it rewards, recognizes, appraises, hires, develops, plans with, motivates and manages the people it employs?

Attracting Collaborators

The best way to get noticed is to be great, or potentially great. This is not always so easy. However, it's the job of music business executives to be aware of what new acts are causing a stir in their own backyard. It's also their job to listen to the demos that come in the mail or e-mail by the dozens every week. This brings up the issue of protocol. Yes, there is etiquette for all areas of music marketing, and the artist protocol for dealing with music business professional is to 1.) get permission to submit material, 2.) wait a week to ten days, and 3.) call to inquire about a response. Believe it or not, politeness and respect are fairly uncommon virtues in the music business. Make sure not to interrupt meetings. Ask the person if now is a good time for them to talk.

Referrals

This business is all about relationships and networking. Yes, it's also about talent, but look at the top charted songs this week. There is plenty of room at the top. Many of the charted artists are there because they have made the right connections. If the artist does not have qualified referrals, perhaps someone on the team does. Artists with a connected manager, lawyer or agent may have a better chance of success than one who does not.

Launching an image is one of the biggest time commitments and personal investments an artist will undertake in their career. It may become easy to unknowingly let certain details slip through the cracks.

Eighty percent (80%) of building an image relies heavily on how an artist markets and promotes themselves. Only 20% is about execution. Therefore in order to set an artist up for success, it's important for them to understand the fundamentals of building an image to accomplish all tasks.

Step 1 – The Business Brand Identity

In addition to establishing, securing and registering a good name, artists will need to start their business brand identity. This includes business cards, logos, and a website. Start here because every opportunity you get to meet someone new is an opportunity for you to convert someone into a new fan or customer. If you do not have these standard marketing materials, how will anyone have confidence in your company?

Step 2 – The Business Plan

Now begin working on your business plan. It is very important to have a clear vision of your company and who your target audience is. Writing a business plan from A to Z will help you understand how much money you'd like to make and how to plan accordingly to put the steps into place so that you can make your desired image.

Step 3 – The Marketing Plan

A marketing plan will help you define who your target demographic is and what steps you will need to take to reach your target demographic. It will also help you further define which services you intend to offer and enable you to later define your niche as you grow your business as well as help you define your fee structure. A marketing plan is part of the business plan.

Step 4 – The Sales Pitch

Once you have a better idea of the products and services you intend to offer, you need to sound like an expert. Therefore it is essential that you master your sales pitch to turn every social opportunity into a business opportunity.

Step 5 – Delivering Messages to the Press

Building your credibility starts by developing a press kit. Press kits include many things such as, professional photos, your biography, and press releases.

++++++++++++++++++++++++++++

Finding Quality Team Members

There are a lot of people in the music business who want to help artists reach their music goals - even people who make sacrifices themselves to work in music just because they love it. Unfortunately, to find these people, artists have to navigate a minefield of people who see their dreams as their personal goldmine. Artists should learn to spot the red flags of potential problems so they don't end up on the losing end of a bad deal.

1. **Paying for a Deal** - A manager, agent or publicist should never ask the artist to pay a fee upfront for representation. That doesn't mean these people don't get paid - they do; either according to a set schedule arranged between the artist or on a per campaign basis. Artists should never pay someone who charges them a fee to "get on their books." If someone says they can "make an artist a star" write them a big

check, the artist should avoid them all together.

2. **Found Online** - A lot of artists have established legitimate connections via Facebook or MySpace and other websites, but artists should know that these are exceptions and not the rule. There are countless numbers of movies in which some small town kid heads to Hollywood with nothing but "a dollar and dream," and then someone rolls up to offer them a hot meal and a great way to make some cash. It never ends well, and online, artists are that virtual kid. Artists should consider people who want to make an online deal with them like that shady character until they have good proof otherwise.

3. **You Can't Get Any Advice** - If someone comes at the artist with a legal contract but doesn't want the artist to seek an outside opinion about what that contract means for them, they should be very concerned.

4. **Pay to Play** - Artists may not always get paid to play a gig, and they may end up out of pocket after they compute their travel costs, but that doesn't mean they should ever pay a promoter for a chance to take the stage. It's bad form (and illegal in many areas).

There are exceptions - for example, some bands "buy on" to major stadium/arena tours, in essence, paying money for the chance to open for a top selling band. For smaller shows, if an artist is booking and promoting the show them self, they may have to meet a bar minimum or pay a venue rental fee. However, they should never directly pay to play. And no, it doesn't matter how many clubs in the area operate under that shady procedure.

5. **Bad Percentages** - There are many people who might get a cut of an artist's earnings for their work for the artist, but artists should never be handing out a larger percentage of their earnings to any one person than they are keeping them self. Does that management deal give the manager 70% and the artist 30%? Don't sign.

6. **No Way Out of the Deal** - Options to renew contracts are a normal part of many deals - they are a safety net to prevent someone from putting in all of the hard work and someone else reaping all of the benefits. But if the options give potential collaborators with the power to renew the deal again and again AND the option to leave the deal at any time, beware.

7. **It Just Doesn't Make Sense** - If someone guarantees the artist they can take them from playing music in their bedroom to a major label contract in a month, get their lottery numbers, because they are clearly the luckiest person in the world. (OK, unless they work for a major label, in which case the artist is pretty lucky them self.) Having big goals

and going for them is important, but in music, slow and steady generally wins the race. Artists want to work with someone who believes the artist can make it all the way and tries to make it happen, but be wary of the person who thinks they can help the artist skip steps.

Firing a Collaborator

Depending on where an artist is in their career, dropping a collaborator for someone new could cause a significant amount of professional upheaval - not to mention the personal toll and the bad blood that could result. With so much on the line, it's important to differentiate between an artist and their collaborator relationship. It may need some fine tuning and one that an artist really needs to draw a line under. If an artist sees any of the following signs, it may be time to pull the trigger and move on from the collaboration relationship. If not, the artist may need to sit down with their collaborator and work on getting back on the same page about their goals and career.

1. The Collaborator Can't Be Reached

Some music collaborators work exclusively with one artist, while others have their own roster. Whichever situation describes the artist's collaborator, they should be a priority for them. Even if they collaborate with other artists that are more established and successful, artist shouldn't feel like they have to play second class citizen to the stars. No collaborator should work with an artist if they're not committed to the artist's success and seeing them reach their musical goals. Part of that is being available to the artist. If they can't take calls from the artist, are they really taking any calls on the artist's behalf?

Even if an artist is very inexperienced in the music business, they don't have to settle for blind allegiance and waiting around for an exasperated return call from a collaborator who is annoyed they have to explain everything to them. They should be willing to discuss the whats and whys of their work with the artist – after all, this is the artist's life and music they're working on. If they're going to be out of touch for a period of time, for reasons personal or professional, fine - all they need to do is let the artist know when they will be available again and what they will be doing to keep the ball rolling on the artist's career in the meantime.

A good collaborator is part of the artist's team, not someone who treats the artist like an annoyance.

2. Visions Vary

An artist collaborator wouldn't be doing their job if they didn't reign in some of the artists ideas and didn't give them a realistic outlook on what they can accomplish at each stage of their career. A collaborator is the one who tells the artist what they should focus on, say, getting small market commercial radio plays instead of trying to hire a radio promoter to get the artist into the top 30 markets when they haven't had so much of a college spin yet. In other words, a good collaborator isn't a yes man/woman – a good collaborator instead helps an artist funnel their energies into the work from which they're likely to get the best results.

However, while saying "no" to some of an artist's ideas is not unusual for a collaborator, but completely dismissing the artist's ambitions for their music is another thing entirely. If an artist wants to stay indie and the collaborator is pitching the artist to majors exclusively, the artist has got a problem. If the artist loves their sound and their collaborator wants them to go more (insert musical direction here), the artist has got a problem. Bands and collaborators should share a general philosophy and vision about the music business and what success looks like for them as an artist. If an artist doesn't, they'll end up at cross purposes, even if their collaborator actually does get some results for them.

3. Your Collaborator Doesn't Consult

There are some things in an artist's music career that their collaborator will usually have the ability to decide for them - things that an artist's trust them to do on their behalf and that they're happy to let them handle so the artist can focus on other things.

On the other hand, an artist's collaborator shouldn't commit the artist to big deals and contracts without consulting them at all. The collaborator makes money when the artist makes money, so it may be tempting for them to grab a well paying deal, but they still need to run it by the artist. Imagine a collaborator agreeing to allow one of an artist's songs to be used in a commercial campaign without asking the artist first and so on and so forth - if the collaborator jumps the gun and signs deals on the artist's behalf that the artist doesn't want, it's a problem.

4. They Don't Love The Music

A collaborator should be excited about an artist's music - period. Artists don't have to settle for anything less. Although their constructive feedback should be welcome - this kind of feedback is critical in creative industries - they should first and foremost be a fan of the artist's work. Nothing is more demoralizing than having this person who is the artist's representative in the industry be under-enthusiastic about the artist's music. Collaborators who love the artist's music will be more inclined to work it hard - they'll be motivated because they'll think it's so good that they want everyone to hear it.

5. No Results

This is probably the number one reason musicians consider firing their collaborator, but it's not so cut and dry. Before an artist gives their collaborator the boot for not coming back with the results they want, they should take a good, hard look at the overall picture. WHY isn't the collaborator getting any results? Or - are they getting results, but they're not getting the results that the artist had in mind?

Collaborators sometimes do everything they're supposed to do and still find themselves facing their ire of their artist because the musicians underestimate how slowly some things can move in the music business or because the musicians have an unrealistic picture of about the kinds of opportunities that are really available to them at the stage they are at in their music careers. If everything an artist's collaborator says makes sense, and they're working hard for the artist, the artist shouldn't automatically assume they're doing something wrong. The artist may simply need to sit down and find out from the collaborator what kind of obstacles they are facing so the artist may get a better understanding of why things may be moving slowly.

On the other hand, if your collaborator can't get anything done for an artist because they're not working hard on the artist's behalf or because they don't really know what they're doing, then the artist probably have a good reason for wanting to get someone else on board.

To Do

Notes:

_____
_____
_____
_____
_____
_____
_____
_____
_____
_____
_____
_____
_____
_____

Artist Development in the Music Business
Chapter 18 - Preparing for Product Development

Product Development Overview
Making and Selling Music

Product Development for an artist focuses on all the business arrangements after the Artist Development details have been completed. Product Development is all about recording, performing, marketing and selling products. Once the Artist Development Plan has been completed, Product Development is them implemented. This includes the recording and performing of the songs and persona.

Promotion Preparation

Before moving into Product Development, prepare some promotional items that may be needed as projects are planned an implemented. This preparation makes it easier when the time comes to release new products or performances. While the product is being developed, the promotional aspects can start coming alive. Envision how the music will be promoted and sold by the time the act enters the recording studio. Envision how the artist will look and sound when the stage lights go on while performing.

Image and Brand Promotion

The varied methods that are used for the promotion of a brand have a direct impact on the sales of a product. In that sense, an understanding of the varied brand promotion strategies is necessary for the success of any artist and/or business of an artist.

An artist might have the best product in the market. They may have the best songs, or the best performance, or the best recordings. However, without people being aware of that product, there are going to be no sales. Having a quality product is an important factor but only one component to success. The ways in which the artist promotes the product is just as important. Along with the regular factors that are used in the promotion of any product, one very crucial factor is that of brand promotion as a means of product promotion. In other words, the artist's image and brand is the promotion of the product. The brand forms the identity of a product or service. It is classified as having a distinct name, symbol, logo and a distinct sound as discussed in the Image section of the Artist Development Plan.

The sale of products largely depends on the brand sound and brand name, and the brand influences the sales of a product. Therefore, it becomes important for artists to learn varied brand promotion strategies that can be applied to promote the artist as well as to create a name for them in the market.

Brand Promotion Objectives

It is not merely with an objective of increasing sales that strategies for brand promotion are brought into play; there are varied other factors and objectives that also drive the brand. Brand promotion will lead to awareness about the varied products of the artist that fall under their brand as well as ensuring fans and customer loyalty.

A promotion of the artist's brand leads to a direct promotion of the varied products as well. In that way, artists do not necessarily have to advertise and promote each individual product, but an overall promotion of the brand will lead to a promotion of the products automatically. This is why it is seen that famous brands are more popular and ensure more sales than lesser known brands. Customers and fans who become loyal to a particular brand will generally opt for the same brand and the products that they produce.

Thus the main objectives of brand promotion are as follows:
- Dispelling information about the varied products and performances of the artist
- Making the public aware of the factors that differentiate the brand from others
- Strategies to increase the demand of the brand
- Establishing brand equity (The power of the brand adds to the product)
- To stabilize sales to survive market fluctuations
- Eliminate competitive artists' marketing strategies
- To build a good image in the market

Brand Promotion Methods

While there are several direct, 'above the line' advertising strategies that are used, which bring about positive results; there is also the emergence of 'below the line' advertising that has become an important factor in the marketing circuit.

Direct Brand Promotion

Direct brand promotion includes factors like advertising on TV, radio, newspapers, through pamphlets and similar. Of these, we are aware.

In-Direct Brand Promotion

There are methods that make use of an indirect way of advertising and brand promotion - that being the usage of certain brand promotion activities and techniques. These are the following:

1. Sponsoring Events: Sponsoring social events is a great way to promote a brand. Equating brands with a good cause, automatically lends a positive vibe to the brand.

2. Associating with a Good Cause: Associating with a good cause creates a positive image in the eyes of the society. This positive image then carries forth to lend the brand a good name.

3. Coupons and Contests: Giving out free coupons and holding contests works in the same manner as that of spreading goodwill.

4. High Quality Products: Another way in which you can ensure brand promotion is to have only high quality products as a part of the brand. High quality products ensure that there is mouth publicity. This form of publicity makes a maximum impact in the general public, and that's why it's called "word of mouth."

Visuals

Whilst people may be aware of the many months it can take to write and record music, or to organize and go out on tours, visuals are often taken very much for granted. And yet, as we have seen, they are vitally important to a band's success. From the smallest badge or flyer to the tour poster and the T-shirt design to the album cover and the publicity shots to the stage set. All of these need to be carefully thought out and will take a tremendous amount of creativity and imagination. Not only can they be a sure-fire way of bringing a band to the public's attention, they can also give off messages on many different levels about a band's musical style.

Promotion:
What has or has not been accomplished in the areas of Artist Development and Product Development will make or break the chances of success with the artist's music. The label will promote and publicize the music and artist to maximize the prospect of sales, and ultimately, income. Promotion should involve offline as well as online exposure for the artist and the artist's music.

Publicity:
Publicity is the deliberate attempt to manage the public's perception of a product. The subjects of publicity include people (for example, politicians and performing artists), goods and services, organizations of all kinds, and works of art or entertainment.

Branding:
A brand is a name, logo, slogan, and/or design scheme associated with a product or service.

Branding is the process of creating a relationship or a connection between a company's product and emotional perception of the customer for the purpose of generation segregation among competition and building loyalty among customers.

Web:
The use of the World Wide Web in Product Development includes promotion and marketing, as well as distribution and sales. A quality web presence is essential to the success of any product.

++++++++++++++++++++++++++++

Product Development Tips

1.) Focus on the active and passive income streams – publishing, live performances, recordings, merchandise, royalties.

2.) Identify projects – gigs, recordings, tours, special events, etc.

3.) Begin assembling your promo ammo for each project

4.) Plan your work and work your plan

5.) Utilize project management techniques for maximum productivity

6.) Communicate regularly with your team on short / long term objectives

7.) Keep accurate records to insure goals are being achieved

8.) Review, evaluate and learn from each project

9.) Set calendars and agendas for future recordings and performances

10.) Prepare for each gig – set list, announcements, and logistics

11.) Remember the importance of pre-production before you enter the studio

12.) Determine and communicate goals prior to recording

13.) If your recording is not a demo, don't forget Mastering.

14.) Packaging includes how your song is visually represented online

15.) Determine the format for physical recordings – CD, vinyl

16.) Sales and licensing includes publishing, merchandise and live appearances

17.) Consider both online distribution as well as physical distribution

18.) Plan your publicity campaign in the early stages of a new project / product

19.) The front door to today's artist is their web presence

20.) Promote, promote, promote… and then promote some more

++++++++++++++++++++++++++++

Promoting Your Image and Brand

Here are some ideas that may be helpful in promoting an artist's brand:

- Train your collaborators to be champions of your brand. Explain the relevance of your image and brand to the success of your business. Explain how their roles impact the business' image and brand, both positively and negatively.
- Make word of mouth easy. Provide incentives for your staff and customers to tell friends and relatives about your business.
- Communicate your values to your customers. You could do this by displaying your mission statement, customer service standards and policies, using slogans, signage and store design.
- Lead by example. How you act towards your customers and the public; both on a day-to-day basis and during extraordinary circumstances, helps to cement your business image and brand into the customer's mind.
- Business history. Where did your business start? If you are a local, family-owned business competing with the large multi-national giants, make sure people know that.

++++++++++++++++++++++++++++

Branding And Company Promotions

- Sales Creators develop programs to build branding.
- Name recognition
- Display advertisements
- Company promotional materials
- Direct mail
- Internet and e-mail

Name Recognition and 'Slogos'
The creation of your company logo and its symbolism is very important.

Display Advertisements
Your company's message to be heard and seen by the buying public.

Company Promotional Materials
There are several creative and effective ways to promote your company.

Direct Mail Promotions
There are several creative and effective ways to reach your customers by direct mail.

Interactive Web Site
Utilize the power of the Internet for your type of business.

Musician's Press Kit
Once a CD launch date is established, it is customary for the manager to prepare a press kit (also known as a media kit). The press kit is a professional package of materials used to contact record label executives, radio stations, newspapers and A&R reps as a way of generating interest in the artist and their music. Additionally, many managers prefer using an electronic press kit (EPK), which is the same as a conventional press kit, except it is downloadable as an electronic file instead of a hard copy form which must be mailed.

By this stage in the artist's career, their manager should possess an adequate grasp of their level of talent. Expense is not important in the press kit, but flash is. It should catch the eye and interest of those to whom it is directed. A press kit normally consists of the following:

- Pamphlet with artist(s) biography, career highlights and promotional photos.
- Quotes and/or press clippings on the artist including Band Show Reviews and CD Demo Reviews that the press can easily edit and submit into their publication. A good quote from a reputable source adds credibility and lets the reader know the artist has already been reviewed and their material is worth listening to.
- Gig sheet containing recent, current, and future gigs. The gig sheet shows the artist is growing in popularity with the community.
- A Demo CD featuring the artist's latest music release. A minimum of three songs is recommended. In some cases the entire CD is sent so the publication or radio station can review the entire CD.
- Complimentary tickets to the CD launch event (if there is one).
- Contact Information.

++++++++++++++++++++++++++++++

Artists Promotion Packages

The press kit, similar to a personal resume, is often the first impression of your band (or product). It is imperative that a band with professional aspirations invest adequate time and money into making the best presentation possible. Each band's press kit will be different, and kits can be modified to fit an individual situation. Here are a few items which will likely be included in any press kit.

Your press/promo kit is a very important addition to your demo CD, or record. Sometimes, for getting gigs, it's THE most important part of getting the buyer's attention. Honestly, many talent buyers don't listen to the CD unless the press/promo kit indicates that the band has some sort of credibility. This is the presentation side of who and what your band is like and what others are saying about your act. It completes the picture (somewhat) for people to learn more about you or your band.

There are THREE basic types of basically the same kit!!

- THE PRESS KIT (analog – paper)
- THE PROMO KIT (analog – paper)
- And, the new hybrid – THE ELECTRONIC PRESS KIT (EPK)

All three of them have a lot of the same materials in them. However, it's important to keep in mind WHO you are sending to. The PRESS KIT is the industry standard, because it contains press clippings written about you or your band. The PROMO KIT is what you put together to promote your band until you have some press, then it becomes a PRESS KIT.

The object is to portray yourself as a professional artist, moving up, making strides, and developing your fan base. Industry types that receive press kits on a regular basis are looking for substantial, legitimate press and promotional materials - resources that reflect your band's progress - NOT FLUFF! Fluff only serves to show that you don't have genuine credentials. THIS DOES NOT WORK! Industry people know in an instant what credible press is and can spot fluff a mile away.

- Recorded material, live or studio recordings
- A concise biography or history of the band
- Any positive press, include the date/publication
- Photograph -- a good live photo will work in a pinch
- A listing or reference from venues already played

The best advice we can give is to keep your kits efficient and as inexpensive as possible.

++++++++++++++++++++++++++++++

Promo Kits

What to put in a Promo Kit:

1 - **Official Band Photo (or PROMO SHOT)**. This needs to be a GOOD professional photograph that shows you in the best possible light. Don't use dark or complex backgrounds. Do NOT take your band's photo against the backdrop of any of the following: Railroad tracks, brick walls, staircases or bridges. It's

OLD!! You can get bulk copies made up that have the photo, the name of the band (artist), the contact information and, of course, your website.

A good publicity photo will get a lot of mileage. And similar to the logo it pays to research publicity photographs of other musicians. Check the advertisements in any music magazine or look at the ads for upcoming performances in your area. Whatever creative notions come to mind you will have to seriously consider your budget. Getting your photo taken is an area where you can't afford to skimp and let a family member take the photo, unless they happen to be a professional photographer. Otherwise you will need to shop around and once again keep the photography students in mind. When it comes to getting the prints made, glossy black and whites are required for reproduction in newspapers. Inexpensive bulk-duplicated prints are suitable for distribution to other industry contacts.

Make SURE the photo is in focus and you can see the bands faces well. Artsy photos are rarely ever re-printed in newspapers or other periodicals.

It's ok to include a color shot, but be sure and include the black and white shot also. (It saves them one step if they AREN'T going to use color.)

2 - **Your CD** - I can't tell you how important it is to have a professional sounding recording in there. Also, be sure to highlight a couple of tracks to listen to, particularly if you are getting any attention and/or airplay on that track. When you don't have a lot of PRESS, let your music do the talking.

My trash can gets full from all of the CRAP I immediately throw away out of the PROMO kit. I really only want to SEE what you look like, HEAR what you sound like and see what OTHERS are saying (writing) about you.

3 – **Press**
* Articles written about you, or that include you in a positive light. Talent buyers, promoters, and booking agents are looking for an indication that you are doing business in other markets and that you stand a chance to catch on and do business in a NEW market. Specialty buyers are looking for things that will indicate that YOU are the perfect fit for whatever special project they are buying for. Record companies are looking for bands on the rise that have a good professional image without the use of fluff!

* Reviews! (Positive of course) Live or of your CD.

* PRE-views (They are coming to town and we hear they are pretty good.)

4 - **Bio**
* The first portion of this is the bio which is a short biography of the musicians involved in the project. The bio is a SHORT account (one page or less) of concise information that will give the reader a brief OVERVIEW of who you are - the members? Names? The geographical location of where you're from, and some influences and the demographic of which you are trying to reach. All pertinent information regarding your musical history should be included. It includes A FEW words about how long you've been together and

maybe a few accolades you've received and a couple of places and/or MAJOR artists you've done support slots for. CAUTION: Don't over hype how many openers you've done in local clubs. It points out that you are always the opener, never the headliner.

5 - **Stickers** - (a few) and any SMALL promotional device that you don't feel shat upon if it were to immediately find its way into the garbage.

6 – **Poster** - A nice poster - not a flyer - a NICE POSTER - and just ONE! Do not send a whole stack of them. If you are sending it to a club and you get the gig, he's got one to put up until you can SERVICE THE DATE with a bunch of posters.

7 – **Fact Sheet** - Separate from the bio are the fact sheet and quote sheet. If you are just starting out you may not have enough of either to make separate sheets and that is okay. After all, shorter is better because people don't want to spend a lot of time reading it. In the event that you do have enough history for separate sheets, the one page rule also applies here. The fact sheet should deal with any favorable sales figures, big shows played such as festivals, air play, big bands you've opened for, past tours, and so on. Being the fact sheet, it should also stick to the facts.

*****Make SURE that you have your WEB SITE ADDRESS and a WORKING CONTACT PHONE NUMBER on EVERY page, the CD and the Photograph. ****

Packaging
DO send it in a nice little report cover, utilizing your logo/graphics on the front if possible. DON'T spend an arm and a leg going out of your way to make some incredibly fancy carrying device. It's wasted. I received a promo kit one time that came in a plastic thermo-formed specialty box and it included a cigar, a mini-bottle of brandy, a compact disc and NO bio. I smoked the Cigar, drank the brandy, listened to about 30 seconds of their terrible CD and can't remember their name.

What to leave out (a/k/a fluff)
1. Flyers from some other gig - especially if you were only the support act. All this shows is that you've done this other gig.
2. Copies of ads for a show that you were on. This doesn't mean anything.
3. Copies of news articles or reviews that only mention that you were part of the bill.
4. Bad reviews.
5. Artsy fartsy photos other than your official band photo.
6. Any kind of scent such as patchouli on the mailing envelope.
7. If you don't have anything other than "fluff," maybe you should just send in a photo and a tape (or CD or whatever). Try to have a photo that will print well in the newspaper types.

Using the Promo Kit
Now that the package is complete, the next step is putting it to use. Radio stations, agents, clubs/promoters, managers, record companies, and newspapers are all possible destinations. But before you put your promotional materials in the mail, be sure to at least consider a few facts. As mentioned earlier, those who receive promotional materials, get it by the ton. They won't be pleased if you waste their

time with something that they are already known to be uninterested in. The recipient of your package should also be clearly indicated on the outside as well as the letter within. If not, it will get thrown in with all of the other unsolicited material, even if it was requested by a contact at the company. This is something that only takes a few seconds but, if you don't address it to someone in particular, then no one in particular will bother to look at it. You may find out who to address your material to through industry publications, company web sites, or by contacting the company by phone. If you contact the company directly, this is a chance to make a first impression before even making your "real" first impression. Always remember to conduct yourself with the utmost courtesy when dealing with anyone employed at companies you hope to deal with, no matter what level they are at.

Once you have established what companies are interested in your style and who the proper contact person in the organization is, you are ready to mail your promo package. Before you take this final step, it is advisable to review the promotional materials one last time for any errors or necessary updates. Another thing to consider when looking things over is whether or not your contact information is included on each individual item. If not, this needs to be corrected because no matter how much they like you they can't do anything about it if the one sheet with your name, e-mail, etc., is lost. Again, anything can happen once the package is out of your hands, so be sure your contact info is complete, legible, and plastered on every item you send off.

In the long run, it pays to take your time, be thorough, and hire professionals whenever possible to avoid any mistakes that give an amateurish impression. Whoever receives your package, no matter how overloaded with promo material they are, cannot be given an excuse to blow you off.

To Do

Notes:

Artist Development in the Music Business
Chapter 19 - Project Management

The entertainment business is full of projects and almost all about project management. Projects such as writing a song, recording a song, performing a song, performing a set of songs, producing an album or producing a video are all examples projects in the music business. The discipline of planning, organizing, securing and managing resources are essential to bring about the successful completion of specific project goals and objectives of an artist.

Who:
Who is the sponsor of the project?
Who cares about the project?
Who is on the project team?
Who is affected?
Who knows most about the situation?
Who can help with the solution?
Who needs to be informed?

What:
What (exactly) do I want to achieve?
What really matters to me?
What are the objectives and outcomes of the project?
What issue/problem or opportunity is the project addressing?
What resources have been allocated to the project?
What are the risks involved in the project?
What assumptions do you need to test?
What is the budget for the project?

Where:
Where are the resources for the project?
Where will the project team be based?
Where is the project plan?

When:
When does the project start?
When is the planned finish date?

Why:
Why is the organization investing in the project?
Why have I been asked to manage the project?

How:
How will the situation be different when the project is successfully completed?
How do I contribute to the organization?
How will changes to the project be reported and approved?
How was the project plan created (or the timescale for the project determined)?

How much:
How was the budget created?
How much will the project cost?
How much financial return is expected?

++++++++++++++++++++++++++++

50 Project Management Checkpoints

1. Confirm the Project Management Plan is in place and up-to-date?
2. Confirm the Project Management Worksheet is in place and up-to-date?
3. Confirm the Project Progress meeting as scheduled been conducted and MOM maintained?
4. Confirm all the intended stakeholders participated in the meeting (including project support and other affected groups)?
5. Confirm all the inter-group issues been discussed?
6. Confirm all issues been recorded in the MOM for tracking purpose?
7. Confirm all the actions been identified and recorded in the MOM?
8. Confirm all the issues been assigned with appropriate owners?
9. Confirm the Metrics Planning details been entered into the Project Management Worksheet?
10. Confirm all the review and testing metrics been collected and entered in the Project Management Worksheet?
11. Confirm the resource detail sheet of the Project Management Worksheet been completely filled-in and updated with the current information?
12. Confirm the Project Management Worksheet – Planning sheet been filled in with all the milestone delivery details?
13. Confirm the Project Management Worksheet - Training sheet been filled in with the entire training plan details?
14. Confirm all the appropriate details been filled into the size, schedule and effort details?
15. Confirm the quality of work sheet been filled with relevant data and up-to-date?
16. Confirm the verification data sheet been filled with relevant data and up-to-date?
17. Confirm the accomplishments and incidents been filled with relevant data and up-to-date?
18. Confirm Corrective action sheet been filled with all the project assumptions, corrective action and the current status?
19. Confirm all the identified risks been entered in the Risk Management Sheet?
20. Confirm corrective action been planned for any prediction on Schedule and Effort variations?
21. Confirm Project Schedule is up-to-date?
22. Confirm Traceability Matrix is up-to-date?
23. Confirm all the sections of the Project Plan been updated to reflect the current status of the project?
24. Confirm defect tracking & analysis are done for defects detected in the work package?
25. Changes requests are tracked to closure
26. Confirm all the planning documents been baselined and being controlled?
27. Confirm all the change requests been documented and available in the Project repository?
28. Confirm all change requests been analyzed for the impact on the project schedule, size and efforts?
29. Confirm all the impacts of changes been communicated to the customer and his approval been obtained for the revised schedule, effort & size estimates?
30. Confirm Configuration Management tool identified in Project Management Plan been used?
31. Confirm all the identified High risk contractual terms monitored and

controlled, mitigated if occurred as per the plan?
32. Confirm all the identified risks monitored, controlled, mitigated if occurred as per the plan?
33. Confirm the effectiveness of the Risk Mitigation been assessed?
34. Confirm the Risk status been updated in the Project Management Worksheet?
35. Confirm any new risks identified during the execution of project been added to the Project Management Worksheet?
36. Confirm reviews for the designated work package executed as mentioned in Project Management Plan?
37. Confirm reviews findings tracked to closure?
38. Confirm process and guidelines stated in Project Management Plan are implemented?
39. Confirm reviewed and approved test plan exist?
40. Confirm test coverage criteria as mentioned in Project Management Plan?
41. Confirm reviewed and approved test procedure exists for all identified phases of testing (unit, integration, system and acceptance testing) as defined in the QA section of Project Management Plan?
42. Confirm Test Specifications exist?
43. Confirm Test Summary Reports exists?
44. Confirm Reviews and Testing Metrics been collected?
45. Confirm Project Specific Trainings are conducted as per Project Management Plan?
46. Confirm Training Records (including feedback) are available?
47. Confirm the Project status report been made and shared with the customer at the agreed frequency identified in Project Management Plan?
48. Confirm all the issues identified in the status report been tracked to closure or the status is up-to-date?
49. Confirm all the appropriate project information been updated in Project repository?
50. Confirm the Learning in the project been captured?

++++++++++++++++++++++++++++++

Gantt Charts

A Gantt chart is a type of bar chart that illustrates a schedule of a proposed project. Gantt charts illustrate the start and finish dates of the terminal elements and summary elements of a project. Terminal elements and summary elements comprise the work breakdown structure of the project. For an artist, booking a new performance may be a terminal on one end and "getting paid at the end of a gig" might be a terminal on the other end, for example. Some Gantt charts also show the dependency relationships between activities. Gantt charts of a project show current schedule status using percent-complete shadings and a vertical "TODAY" line.

Gantt charts have become a common technique for representing the phases and activities of a project work breakdown structure, so they can be understood by the whole team of an artist.

Gantt charts only represent part of the triple constraints (cost, time and scope) of projects, because they focus primarily on schedule management.

++++++++++++++++++++++++++++++

Project Plan

Writing a project plan forces you to think about the potential for achieving the goals and objectives. The project plan shows how to make it happen. Your project plan should include:

- Overview of the project
- Details of market & consumers
- Costs
- Projected returns (including how long it will take to see returns)
- Marketing plans
- Your qualifications (info about career, education, etc.)

++++++++++++++++++++++++++++++

Project Control

Project control is that element of a project that keeps it on-track, on-time and within budget. Every project that an artist plans, with the exception of songwriting, should have some type of control in place. Project control begins early in the development of a project with planning. It ends late in the project cycle by reviewing each step in the process. Each project, whether a recording or performance, CD release or tour, should be assessed for the appropriate level of control. Too much control is too time consuming and too little control is very risky. If project control is not implemented correctly, the cost to the artist in terms of errors, fixes, and additional fees, might sink the project.

Project controlling should be established as an independent function in project management. The tasks of project controlling are:

- Creating and maintaining a system of finding and securing opportunities. This might be accomplished through music placement tip-sheets, securing choice gigs well in advance or following what certain Music Supervisors are currently working on.
- Establishment of a way to communicate potential problems of project parameters.
- Development of project steps.
- Establishing methods to accomplish an appropriate project structure, project workflow, project control and governance.

Fulfillment and implementation of these tasks can be achieved by applying specific methods of project control. The following methods of project controlling can be applied:

- Investment analysis
- Cost-benefit analyses
- Value benefit analysis
- Expert surveys
- Simulation calculations
- Risk profile analyses
- Milestone trend analysis
- Cost trend analysis
- Target/actual-comparison

Control systems are needed for cost, risk, quality, communication, time, change, procurement, and human resources. In addition, auditors should consider how important the projects are to the financial statements, how reliant the stakeholders are on controls, and how many controls exist. Artists should review the development process and procedures for how they are implemented. The process of development and the quality of the final product may also be assessed if needed. An artist may want the auditing firm to be involved throughout the process to catch problems earlier so that they can be fixed more easily. An auditor can serve as a controls consultant as part of the development team or as an independent auditor as part of an audit.

++++++++++++++++++++++++++++++

Project Managers

There are plenty of projects in the entertainment industry and each project should have someone who is in charge. Project managers can have the responsibility of the planning, execution, and closing of any project, typically relating to recording, tours, performances, merchandising, etc.

A project manager is the person accountable for accomplishing the stated project objectives. For example, an agent is the project manager for securing bookings for a tour. The tour manager is the project manager for ensuring that the tour runs smoothly. A producer is the project manager for sound recordings of the artist. Key project management responsibilities include creating clear and attainable project objectives, building the project requirements, and managing the triple constraint for projects, which is cost, time, and scope.

Project Management Triangle

* Cost
* Time
* Scope

A project manager has to determine and implement the exact needs of the artist and/or artist's project. The ability to adapt to the various internal procedures is essential in ensuring that the key issues of cost, time, quality and above all, artist satisfaction, can be realized.

Project Management Triangle
Like any human undertaking, projects need to be performed and delivered under certain constraints. Traditionally, these constraints have been listed as "cost," "time," and "scope." These are also referred to as the "project management triangle," where each side represents a constraint. One side of the triangle cannot be changed without affecting the others. A further refinement of the constraints separates product "quality" or "performance" from scope, and turns quality into a fourth constraint.

The time constraint refers to the amount of time available to complete a project. The cost constraint refers to the budgeted amount available for the project. The scope constraint refers to what must be done to produce the project's end result. These three constraints are often competing constraints: increased scope typically means increased time and increased cost, a tight time constraint could mean increased costs and reduced scope, and a tight budget could mean increased time and reduced scope.

The discipline of project management is about providing the tools and techniques that enable the project team (not just the project manager) to organize their work to meet these constraints.

+++++++++++++++++++++++++++++

Stages of Project Management

After the who, what, when, where, why and how much for a specific project have been answered, the focus turns to the various stages of project management.

A project is a temporary endeavor and has a defined beginning and end (usually constrained by date, but can be by funding or deliverables). Each project is designed to meet unique goals and objectives, usually to bring about beneficial change or added value. The temporary nature of projects stands in contrast to business as usual for an artist. Most activities of an artist involve projects. In practice, the management of these two systems is often found to be quite different such as, the role of a songwriter and the role of a performer. Each requires the development of distinct skills and the adoption of separate focus.

The primary challenge of project management is to achieve all of the project goals and objectives while honoring the preconceived project constraints. Typical constraints are time, scope, and budget. The secondary, and more ambitious, challenge is to meet pre-defined objectives of the artist and/or artist's company.

+++++++++++++++++++++++++++++

Project Management Steps
- Project Initiation
- Defining the Project
- Executing the Plan
- Monitoring the Project
- Closing Down the Project

Project Management Processes

Traditionally, project management includes a number of key elements: five (5) process groups, and a control system.

Key Elements of Project Management
- Project Initiation
- Defining the Project
- Executing the Plan
- Monitoring the Project
- Closing Down the Project

Project Initiation

Initiating Process Group Processes
The project initiation processes determine the nature and scope of the project while developing a business case for the project. If this stage is not performed well, it is unlikely that the project will be successful in meeting the artist's business needs. The key project controls needed here are an understanding of the business environment and making sure that all necessary controls are incorporated into the project.

The initiating stage should include a plan that encompasses the following areas:

- Developing a business case for the project
- Analyzing the business needs
- Determining the nature and scope of the project
- Making sure the project fits the artist's agenda
- Reviewing all key risks and possible deficiencies
- Identifying stakeholders and all concerned with the project
- Consulting a finance expert
- Getting the business case approved by collaborators and /or senior managers
- Projecting the costs
- Projecting the tasks
- Projecting the deliverables
- Projecting the schedule

Defining the Project

After the initiation stage, the project is planned to an appropriate level of detail. The main purpose is to adequately plan time, budget and resources to estimate the work needed, and to manage the risk during project execution. As with the Project Initiation process, a failure to adequately plan will greatly reduce the project's chances of success.

Project planning generally consists of determining how to plan:

- Developing the scope statement;
- selecting the planning team;
- identifying deliverables and creating the work breakdown structure;
- identifying the activities needed to complete those deliverables and networking the activities in their logical sequence;
- estimating the resource requirements for the activities;
- estimating time and cost for activities;
- developing the schedule;
- developing the budget;
- risk planning;
- gaining formal approval to begin work.

In addition, processes such as planning for communications, identifying roles and responsibilities, determining purchases for the project and holding a kick-off meeting are also advisable.

Executing the Project Plan

Executing the project's plan consists of the processes used to complete the work and involves coordinating people and resources, as well as integrating and performing the activities of the project in accordance with the project management plan. The deliverables, whether a recording, a re-write of a song, album design, etc. are produced from the processes performed as defined in the Project Management Plan.

Executing the plan involves:

* Making a project planning checklist

- Listing all the activities and work to be completed
- Grouping tasks under different category headings
- Writing down the dependencies of all activities
- Estimating how much time each activity will take to complete
- Identifying activities that have to be completed by the date it is due

- Prioritizing the planned activities
- Making a communication plan and communicate it with all concerned
- Completing a full risk analysis
- Appointing a team member to manage each risk
- Filtering your project for slipping tasks
- Making a Gantt chart to monitor the project's progress
- Establishing a milestone plan for each stage of the project
- Checking the project by the milestone dates
- Setting a realistic deadline for the project

Monitoring the Project

Monitoring and controlling consists of those processes performed to observe project execution so that potential problems can be identified in a timely manner and corrective action can be taken, when necessary, to control the execution of the project. The key benefit is that project performance is observed and measured regularly to identify variances from the project management plan.

Monitoring and Controlling includes:
- Measuring the ongoing project activities ('where we are');
- Monitoring the project variables (cost, effort, scope, etc.) against the Project Management Plan and the project performance baseline ('where we should be');
- Identify corrective actions to address issues and risks properly ('how can we get on track again'); and
- Influencing the factors that could circumvent integrated change control so only approved changes are implemented.

In multi-phase projects, the monitoring and control process also provides feedback between project phases in order to implement corrective or preventive actions, and to bring the project into compliance with the project management plan.

Monitoring and Controlling Cycle
In this stage, auditors should pay attention to how effectively and quickly user problems are resolved.

Over the course of any project, the work scope may change. Change is a normal and expected part of the process. If the project is writing a song, changes are almost inevitable. Many times, songs must be re-written until perfect. If the project is preparing a recording, it may be necessary to modify the song's arrangement. Depending on the studio utilized for a recording, other problems such as site conditions, material availability, engineer or producer changes, and impacts from third parties, to name a few, may impact the project.

When changes are introduced to the project, the viability of the project has to be re-assessed. It is important not to lose sight of the initial goals and targets of the project. When the changes accumulate, the forecasted result may not justify the original proposed investment of time and money into the project.

Closing the Project

Every project has a beginning, a middle and an end. Closing down a project includes the formal acceptance of the project collaborators and the ending thereof. Administrative activities include the archiving of the files and documenting lessons learned.

This phase consists of:
- Project closure: Finalize all activities across all of the process groups to formally close the project or a project phase
- Contract closure: Complete and settle each contract (including the resolution of any open items) and close each contract applicable to the project or project phase
- Setting a date for a post project review
- Inviting collaborators, senior managers and project team
- Debriefing the project team at the meeting
- Checking whether results matched the original plan
- Checking the budget, quality and deadlines
- Making a list of unfinished tasks
- Writing a final project report and sharing it with all concerned
- Informing all involved in the project about its close down
- Writing personal thank you notes to project contributors
- Celebrate the close down within your team.

To Do

Notes:

Artist Development in the Music Business
Chapter 20 – Preparing to License

One of the last parts of putting together an Artist Development Plan is preparing for product development. One of the primary areas of product development is that of licensing. In addition, there's preparing for recording, preparing for performing and preparing for merchandising. This section is about preparing for licensing. Artist should not attempt to complete any product development issues prior to completing all of their Artist Development.

When an artist reviews the Artist Development Plan, it becomes apparent that all the details of preparing for licensing has been identified. For example:

Music Supervision

Placing Music in a Movie or TV Show

Music supervision is primarily concerned with connecting the right song with the right moving image; be that a TV commercial, a movie, or a TV show. The more accurate term for "connecting" is "synchronizing." So, a "synch" or "synchronization," is the act of taking a piece of music and connecting it with a moving image in a movie or TV show/ad.

You may quickly realize that music supervision has a lot to do with music publishing. You can't simply grab any piece of music you want and throw it in a film. There are a host of copyright issues surrounding synchronizations that, in large part, define the role of the music supervisor.

First the cool/glamorous part. A music supervisor gets to work with the director of the visual content (movie, TV show, Ad, etc.), and help this person realize their vision by the addition of music. If you've ever seen a film where you have the option to turn the music off, you've seen just how important music is to making a film successful.

Music supervision really came of age in the mid sixties, and it came from a surprising place. The creators of the television show The Monkees, Bob Rafelson and Bert Schnieder, were young and idealistic, and recently flush with money and influence from the unexpected phenomenon that was The Monkees. Being young and idealistic, the pair decided to use their money and influence to make what they deemed an important movie. Their attempt to catch the cultural zeitgeist of the late 60s resulted in Easy Rider.

Certainly Easy Rider wasn't the first film to use popular music to make a point— The Graduate, featuring the songs of Simon and Garfunkel, came out a year prior to Easy Rider—but it did it in such an emphatic way that it opened the flood gates. Directors like Scorsese (Taxi

Driver, Mean Streets), Coppola (Apocalypse Now), Schlesinger (Midnight Cowboy), Ashby (Harold and Maude), and many others redefined how music and images could be used together to create a meaningful experience. In the process, the role of the music supervisor emerged.

Role of the Music Supervisor
It's important to realize from the examples above, that while in theory the music supervisor is responsible for choosing the music to synchronize with the images, it's really the director (particularly the auteur of the 70s, the last great era of American cinema*) who controls the vision. Often the director will "comp" (i.e. temporarily place) the music in a film, fall in love with the way this music compliments the images, and then task the music supervisor with "clearing" the music. Of course, on the other hand, there may be a relationship of trust between the director and the music supervisor, where the director sort of hands over the film to the music supervisor in order to fill it with music. At that point, the music supervisor comps music in that she feels completes the vision of the director, and—once decided upon by the director— goes out and clears this music.

You note that irrespective of who chooses the music, the music supervisor has to go clear it. Clearing music is typically a two-step process (at least). In order for a piece of music to be used in a film, the music supervisor must get approval from, typically, two parties.

++++++++++++++++++++++++++++

Music Clearance

First, the music supervisor must negotiate with the publisher who controls the rights to the song itself. Of course, if you're an artist who has not assigned any of your songs over to a publisher, you are the de facto publisher, and the music supervisor must negotiate with you directly. The music supervisor is trying to convince the publisher to grant him a "synch" license. Synch is short for synchronization, and this license gives the music supervisor the right to synchronize your music with the director's moving images.

There is not a set fee for this, it's completely negotiable. If you're an unknown artist who likely will benefit from the exposure of having your music used in a film, the music supervisor is unlikely to offer you anything more than a very nominal sum. Of course, if you're a popular artist, and your music is in large demand, the music supervisor is going to have to pay up to get you to agree to the synch license. Also, it's important to note that a publisher can flatly deny this request; irrespective of how much money is offered. Some artists (believe it or not) don't want their music used in films or TV, and their publishers will simply turn down a request.

The second party the music supervisor must get approval from is the "master holder." The master holder is the company or person who controls the recording/download on which the song appears. This is typically the record label, but it can be the artist herself if she has self-released a record. Like the publisher, the master holder can negotiate whatever rate the market will bear, and, again like the publisher, the master holder can simply refuse any request.

So, if you're a music supervisor, your ideal scenario is what is called a "one-stop" license, where you can "clear" both the publishing and the master rights in one fell swoop. Typically this occurs when artists self release or when the label and the publisher are the same person.

I said above that you typically have to clear both the publishing rights and the master-holder rights, but not always. The exception is when you can clear the publishing rights, but not the master rights. At this point, you can choose to have someone re-record the songs so that you don't have to deal with the master holder. This occurred on the soundtrack to the movie I am Sam, in which the entire soundtrack is comprised of covers of Beatles songs. In this case, the publisher had to agree to allow the copyright of the songs to be used in the film, but the music supervisor did not have to deal with the master holder (The Beatles' label, EMI) at all.

Part of the negotiating process of clearing the songs is the extent of use. You may, for example as a music supervisor, only be able to clear the song for use in the film. On the other hand, you might also get rights to the song for a soundtrack album, or to be aired in the trailer or as part of the commercial. Home video is a whole other set of negotiations that the music supervisor must contend with as well. This is all, of course, great for the content holders (publishers and master holders), as it represents potential income and exposure. For the music supervisor, it represents work…and a lot of it. This is why they get their names listed pretty early on in the credits.

A Note on Score

There is a difference between synchronization—taking a pre-existing piece of music and connecting it with a moving image—and score. Score is music that is specifically composed for a movie. It doesn't have to be symphonic or classical. Randy Newman, for example, has scored numerous movies, such as the Pixar films, and his work is largely piano and vocal based. As many scores are commissioned by the director/music supervisor, they are typically what is referred to as "works made for hire." This means that the composer is paid a fee for his work, which then becomes the property of the director (or the production company), as opposed to a synch license, in which the ownership of the piece of music never transfers.

Clearly music used in movies and TV shows is one of the most effective ways for musicians to gain an audience. Bands' careers are often massively accelerated by a well-placed synch. This relationship between success and synch has of course made the process of getting music into a film or TV show a very competitive one. Music supervisors are the new gatekeepers of popularity in some ways. They are courted by countless artists and labels in the hopes that they will give them a spot on the OC or the new Tarantino movie. Conversely, the music supervisor is attempting to walk the delicate line of honoring the creative vision of the director while still bringing in music that might compel people to be interested in the film. It truly is the nexus of art and commerce. As we stir newer mediums, like video games, into the mix this line gets all the more blurry.

As a musician you first have to determine your stance on whether or not you want your music used in movies or commercials. While we've quickly moved from an ethos in which using your music to sell beer (or anything else) was considered "selling out," to a place where you're viewed as out of time should you not leap at any opportunity that might generate exposure and cash, the long-term effects of using music in this manner (particularly ads) is not yet known.

Once you have decided that you're OK with allowing your music to be used, it's a matter of getting directors and music supervisors interested in your music. Like anything else in the record industry, there are no short cuts. While there are services out there that claim they can put your music in front of music supervisors, think about that for a second. Do you really think paying someone $100 a month to get your music in front of some music supervisor is really going to give you a leg up over the intense competition coming from people who are out there selling records, and touring, and getting their music written about and played on the radio (particularly getting their music played on KCRW in Santa Monica, which many, many music supervisors listen to…hint, hint)? Of course not. Don't do it. Instead, get out there. Get your music heard and written about. Also, try to connect with some local filmmakers and allow them to comp your music in to their films. Who knows where the next Tarantino is coming from. Bring attention to your music in as many ways as possible, and you will soon get attention from music supervisors. Remember, these people view themselves as cutting-edge taste-makers, therefore, they like to feel they are discovering things on their own; thus pitching them ain't going to work.

If you're thinking that music supervision might be a cool gig, go west, young man. Start connecting with people in the film community. Start getting to know young and upcoming directors (film schools would be a good place to start), and — all the while — cultivate a unique knowledge and point of view with music. A great music supervisor has an expansive understanding of music; both current and past. They can as effortlessly pull from their mental library some obscure track from a 50s rockabilly band as they can draw on the most contemporary electronica. So, get out there and absorb, and then start showing your knowledge. This can be done via blogging, writing in a more traditional manner, and, of course, DJing. All the while, make those connections.

Music and film are so deeply intertwined that we can't imagine one without the other. However, as with all things in this business of music, there is a process that must be understood in order to operate at the high level efficiency needed to compete.

Supervision
The process of placing music in a movie or TV show, and a description of the relevant licenses and parties involved in this process. It is relevant to anyone

interested in having their music used in movies, as well as those considering a career as a music supervisor.

Overview

First off, music supervision is primarily concerned with connecting the right song with the right moving image; be that a TV commercial, a movie, or a TV show. The more accurate term for "connecting" is "synchronizing." So, a "synch" or "synchronization," is the act of taking a piece of music and connecting it with a moving image in a movie or TV show/ad. You should quickly realize that music supervision has a lot to do with music publishing. Music Supervisors can't simply grab any piece of music and throw it in a film. There are a host of copyright issues surrounding synchronizations that, in large part, define the role of the music supervisor.

A music supervisor works with the director of the visual content (movie, TV show, Ad, etc.), and help this person realize their vision by the addition of music. Watch a film where you have the option to turn the music off. You'll see just how important music is to making a film successful. Think, for example, what Goodfellas, would have been like without the coda to "Layla" coming in just at the right moment; consider any of the Tarantino films devoid of music; imagine any of the Hitchcock films without the phenomenal contribution of Bernard Herrmann. The music augments and often completes the vision the director had.

History

Music supervision really came of age in the mid sixties, and it came from a surprising place. The creators of the television show The Monkees, Bob Rafelson and Bert Schnieder, were young and idealistic, and recently flush with money and influence from the unexpected phenomenon that was The Monkees. Being young and idealistic, the pair decided to use their money and influence to make what they deemed an important movie. Their attempt to catch the cultural zeitgeist of the late 60s resulted in Easy Rider.* Notable for many reasons—Jack Nicholson's stand-out support performance, a pre-"Hey Mickey" Toni Basil, and a drug buyer played by Phil Spector, among other curiosities—it's most enduring legacy is, I believe, its brilliant use of music to fully flesh out the visual elements. While most people associate the movie with Steppenwolf's "Born to Be Wild," the music in the movie is fairly diverse. It includes songs from The Byrds, The Jimi Hendrix Experience, The Band, The Holy Modal Rounders, and others.

Certainly Easy Rider wasn't the first film to use popular music to make a point—The Graduate, featuring the songs of Simon and Garfunkel, came out a year prior to Easy Rider—but it did it in such an emphatic way that it opened the flood gates. Directors like Scorsese (Taxi Driver, Mean Streets), Coppola (Apocalypse Now), Schlesinger (Midnight Cowboy), Ashby (Harold and Maude), and many others redefined how music and images could be used together to create a meaningful experience. In the process, the role of the music supervisor emerged.

Role of the Music Supervisor

It's important to realize from the examples above, that while in theory the music supervisor is responsible for choosing the music to synchronize with the images, it's really the director who controls the vision. Often the director will "comp" (i.e. temporarily place) the music in a film, fall in love with the way this music compliments the images, and then task the music supervisor with "clearing" the music. Of course, on the other hand, there may be a relationship of trust between the director and the music supervisor, where the director sort of hands over the film to the music supervisor in order to fill it with music. At that point, the music supervisor comps music in that they feel completes the vision of the director, and—once decided upon by the director— goes out and clears this music.

Irrespective of who chooses the music, the music supervisor has to clear it. Clearing music is typically a two-step process (at least). In order for a piece of music to be used in a film, the music supervisor must get approval from, typically, two parties: the songwriter / publisher and the owner of the recording of the song such as a record label.

Music Clearance
First, the music supervisor must negotiate with the publisher who controls the rights to the song itself. Of course, if you're an artist who has not assigned any of your songs over to a publisher, you are the de facto publisher, and the music supervisor must negotiate with you directly. The music supervisor is trying to convince the publisher to grant him a "synch" license. Synch is short for synchronization, and this license gives the music supervisor the right to synchronize the songwriter's music with the director's moving images.

There is no set fee for this, it's completely negotiable. If you're an unknown songwriter-artist who likely benefit from the exposure of having your music used in a film, the music supervisor is unlikely to offer you anything more than a very nominal sum. Of course, if you're a popular artist, and your music is in large demand, the music supervisor is going to have to pay up to get you to agree to the synch license. Also, it's important to note that a publisher can flatly deny this request; irrespective of how much money is offered. Some artists (believe it or not) don't want their music used in films or TV (Neil Young and Radiohead come to mind*), and their publishers will simply turn down a request.

The second party the music supervisor must get approval from is the "master holder." The master holder is the company or person who controls the recording/download on which the song appears. This is typically the record label, but it can be the artist if the artist has self-released a recording. Like the publisher, the master holder can negotiate whatever rate the market will bear, and, again like the publisher, the master holder can simply refuse any request.

The ideal scenario for a music supervisor is what is called a "all-in" license, where they can "clear" both the publishing and the master rights in one fell swoop. Typically this occurs when artists self release or when the label and the publisher are the same person/company.

Typically music supervisors have to clear both the publishing rights and the master-holder rights, but not always.

The exception is when they can clear the publishing rights, but not the master rights. At this point, music supervisors can choose to have someone re-record the songs so that they don't have to deal with the master holder. This occurred on the soundtrack to the movie I am Sam, in which the entire soundtrack is comprised of covers of Beatles songs. In this case, the publisher had to agree to allow the copyright of the songs to be used in the film, but the music supervisor did not have to deal with the master holder (The Beatles' label, EMI) at all.

Part of the negotiating process of clearing the songs is the extent of use. For example, a music supervisor may only be able to clear the song for use in the film. On the other hand, they might also get rights to the song for a soundtrack album, or to be aired in the trailer or as part of the commercial. Home video is a whole other set of negotiations that the music supervisor must contend with as well. This is all, of course, great for the content holders (publishers and master holders), as it represents potential income and exposure. For the music supervisor, it represents work…and a lot of it. This is why they get their names listed pretty early on in the credits.

There is a difference between synchronization—taking a pre-existing piece of music and connecting it with a moving image—and score. Score is music that is specifically composed for a movie. Bernard Herrmann and his work for Hitchcock is an example of score. It doesn't have to be symphonic or classical. Randy Newman, for example, has scored numerous movies, such as the Pixar films, and his work is largely piano and vocal based. As these scores are commissioned by the director/music supervisor, they are typically what is referred to as "works made for hire." This means that the composer is paid a fee for his work, which then becomes the property of the director (or the production company), as opposed to a synch license, in which the ownership of the piece of music never transfers.

Summary and Strategy

Clearly music used in movies and TV shows is one of the most effective ways for musicians to gain an audience. Bands' careers are often massively accelerated by a well-placed synchronization of one of their songs and/or recordings. This has made the process of getting music into a film or TV show a very competitive one. Music supervisors are the new gatekeepers of popularity in some ways. They are courted by countless artists, publishers and record labels in the hopes that they will give them a spot in their new video project. Conversely, the music supervisor is attempting to walk the delicate line of honoring the creative vision of the director while still bringing in music that might compel people to be interested in the film. It truly is the nexus of art and commerce. As we stir newer mediums, like video games, into the mix this line gets all the more blurry.

Artists have to determine their stance on whether or not they want their music used in movies or commercials. While we've quickly moved from an ethos in which using your music to sell beer (or anything else) was considered "selling out," to a place where you're viewed as out of time should you not leap at any opportunity that might generate exposure and cash, the long-term effects of using music in this manner (particularly ads) is not yet known.

Once an artist have decided that they're OK with allowing their music to be used, it's a matter of getting directors and music supervisors interested in the music. Like anything else in the record industry, there are not short cuts. While there are services out there that claim they can put your music in front of music supervisors, think about that for a second given everything that's been discussed in this article. Do you really think paying someone $100 a month to get your music in front of some music supervisor is really going to give you a leg up over the intense competition coming from people who are out there selling records, and touring, and getting their music written about and played on the radio (particularly getting their music played on KCRW in Santa Monica, which many, many music supervisors listen to…hint, hint)? Of course not. Don't do it. Instead, get out there. Get your music heard and written about. Also, try to connect with some local filmmakers and allow them to comp your music in to their films. Who knows where the next Tarantino is coming from. Bring attention to your music in as many ways as possible, and you will soon get attention from music supervisors. Remember, these people view themselves as cutting-edge taste-makers, therefore, they like to feel they are discovering things on their own; thus pitching them ain't going to work.

If you're thinking that music supervision might be a cool gig, go west, young man. Start connecting with people in the film community. Start getting to know young and upcoming directors (film schools would be a good place to start), and — all the while — cultivate a unique knowledge and point of view with music. A great music supervisor has an expansive understanding of music; both current and past. They can as effortlessly pull from their mental library some obscure track from a 50s rockabilly band as they can draw on the most contemporary electronica. So, get out there and absorb, and then start showing your knowledge. This can be done via blogging, writing in a more traditional manner, and, of course, DJing. All the while, make those connections.

Music and film are so deeply intertwined that we can't imagine one without the other. However, as with all things in this business of music, there is a process that must be understood in order to operate at the high level efficiency needed to compete. This article hopefully gives you a starting point.

Pitching Music Publishers

1. Do not flood a Publisher with songs. Sending a CD or ten-song tape, without suggesting one or two specific tracks will probably result in getting none of your tunes heard. Forget sending reviews, pictures, or other promotional materials. Send a professionally mastered, high bias or chrome tape (or CD), with a typewritten lyric sheet, and ALL your information on the tape and the lyric sheet. Do yourself a favor and send no more than two songs at a time. If a Publisher sees a tape with 8 songs, and a tape with 2 songs, chances are the 2-song tape gets listened to first. (It's off the desk more quickly that way.) The

longer the pitch is, the longer it takes to get around to plowing through it.

2. TARGET!! The most difficult part of Publishing is finding the perfect place to pitch a song. When you send a song for Publishing consideration, try to name a few acts or artists who you feel the song fits. Be sure that these artists do NOT write their own material, and that the song fits musically, subject-wise, stance wise with the latest work by the Artist. You can write a GREAT song...but if it is not in the style being used today, your chances of a cut are slim. If you are pitching for TV or Film usage, try to remember that 90% of those songs are genre specific! I.E., if it's a Country Song, they usually would like to hear fiddles or steel or both, so there is no doubt about the feel of the scene. In a Biker Bar, they might want songs with heavy guitar leads- but when pitching material for records, it is the quality of the WRITING more than the flavor or production.

3. Be educated. Make sure you know what you are trying to do. Are you a writer? Are you a winger? Are you a singer who writes? Are you a writer who is also an artist? All these paths are different. Most Publishers work with dedicated Writers as a first choice, simply because it is not a Publisher's job to find a home for an Artist... their job is to find a place for the Song.

4. Be educated. Find out how you collect money earned from writing. (Royalties.) You must know the common terms to communicate intelligently. Use the Web. The Performing Rights Organizations (such as ASCAP and BMI) collect your Performance Royalties (basically, in the U.S., money earned from airplay,) and Harry Fox Agency sets the Standard Rate for record royalty payments. You also need to know about ppls, Synch Rights, Master Use Licenses, etc. There are excellent resource materials in book form and on the Web, and most cities have great songwriting organizations to guide you (Songwriters Guild of America, National Academy of Songwriters, etc.) Check your city guide.

- 5. Be educated. Songwriting is like any other skilled profession. There are rules and tools. It's always ok to challenge or break the rules... as long as it is by choice, and not by ignorance. Study the craft of songwriting. Use tight rhyming where you can. Make your form consistent. Be creative. Be familiar with the work of who it is you are trying to pitch. Why should anyone cut your song if you don't even know his or her work? Listen to the radio for what's happening in your genre NOW. Remember- Your competition is not the bad stuff you hear... it is the BEST of the BEST.

To Do

Notes:

Artist Development in the Music Business
Chapter 21
Preparing for Product Development - Performances

The last two parts of putting together an Artist Development Plan is preparing for product development. One of the primary areas of product development is that of performing. Another is recording. In addition, there's preparing for merchandising and licensing. This section is about preparing to perform. Artists should not attempt to complete any product development issues prior to completing all of their Artist Development.

When an Artist reviews the Artist Development Plan, it becomes apparent that all the detail of preparing to perform or record has been identified. For example, look at the catalog of songs that the Artist has. These are the only possible songs for an Artist to perform or record. If an Artist adds another song to the catalog, that part of the Artist Development Plan should be updated.

Preparation is the most crucial step in live performances, and it all happens prior to the Artist entering the stage.

The trick: Be prepared thoroughly. Any musician can be fearless in a performance if they prepare properly.

There are a few ways for Artists to be and feel confident while performing.

1. Artistic
To be artistically prepared for performances, Artists must choose music that fits their style and then learn it so well that they can deliver every phrase with conviction. The chosen songs are listed in the content section of the Artist Development Plan. They are also listed in the section of Products & Services of an artist's Business Plan.

2. Technical
When an Artist is technically prepared, they're in command of their instrument. This is true even in high-pressure settings. In addition, part of being prepared technically, is to know about the equipment being used to present a live performance. In addition to knowing their instrument, this includes a basic knowledge of performance venues, lighting and sound systems.

3. Mental / Emotional
Artists perform best when they are mentally clear and emotionally engaged. Although it may be easy for an Artist to establish clarity and engagement in the practice room, it's a whole new world learning how to remain focused during the buzz of a live show.

4. Physical
Performing live takes strength. So, ahead of a planned performance, Artists need to manage their activities so that they are fresh when the stage door opens. Based on physical demands, Artists should avoid arduous rehearsals on the day of show, plan what and when they eat, and make time for naps when possible.

5. Organizational
Poor planning on the logistics of performing live can cause anxiety and

frustration for the Artist. This may happen when an Artist gets lost when traveling to a venue, brings the wrong stage clothes, or misplaces an instrument. This anxiety will show itself to an audience. Prudent organization may ensure that the Artist arrive early and is fully equipped for all performances.

6. Delivery
Artists should decide how they want to affect the person they are performing to (or singing to). Is the intent to charm the listener, offend them, destroy them, etc.? This is called a delivery objective and may change as the Artist goes through the rehearsal process and discover new things about the piece.

7. Blocking
Blocking is learning where an Artist may be located on stage during a particular musical piece. In any performance, Artists have got to know what's going on around them so they can hear their cues in the next part of their performance.

8. Hydrate
Drink a lot of fluids and most importantly have fun! Performing is work, but you can let loose, and have fun. Have lots and lots of energy. Artists don't want to lose their audience because they're not engaged.

Tips and guidelines to optimize a performance:

1. Warm up thoroughly from lip buzzing, tonguing, flexibility, range and scales. Play from the lowest notes to the highest in your warm up. The idea is: Artists should be able to perform after warming up. Make sure that it's done correctly!
2. Prepare the piece over and over. Practice the hard parts completely until muscle memory can do it automatically.
3. Practice the entire piece and be able to play it to 'performance standards' 3 times in a row.
4. Performance Day - About 1.45 hours before the performance, begin air and breathing exercises. Slowly get the muscles moving and allow for plenty of rest time. Resist the urge to play high notes. By the end of this time, muscles should be pliable mush; completely and totally relaxed. An hour before the concert, begin to play long notes, consciously going for the richest, warmest tone. Next, concentrate on flexibility. Finally, as stated before, Artists need to warm up in the upper register to perform in the upper register. Play various sections to gain confidence, without over practicing.
5. Mental Preparation – If the piece is prepared to perform, here are some quotes that may have a deep mental impact. As you prepare for your performance, say many times to yourself:
   - I will perform and play to the best of my ability
   - I can't wait to show my expertise on this axe
   - I know I play well and now is the time to show it
   - I'm excited about this opportunity to make music and create musical experiences for others
   - I am satisfied with myself and who I am

   Warm up the body and the mind. The performance will shine.

Gigs
It is important for a band to have experience performing in front of crowds. Birthday parties, free shows (like basement shows), and talent shows are good sources of experience and do not require a lot of commitment (in terms of fan pull) on the part of the artist. If an artist wants a gig in a bar or nightclub venue, the manager expects several conditions. The following is a list of some

questions frequently asked by bar owners/managers (in no particular order):
- What genre of music is the artist affiliated with?
- How many people are expected to attend the event?
- Is a door cover required?
- Can a door person be provided?
- Will the band sell their demo cd?

These are some of the main questions. In most cases a demo CD will be requested. This can be any type of recording, featuring any number of songs (preferably the artist's better songs). The primary objective for the bar owner is to fill their floor on any given night. To do this, the band should be as professional and as practiced as possible as to keep the bar patrons and more importantly, the bar owner, interested. This will have a positive effect on their ability to get booked for another show in the future. Another critical factor is maximizing audience attendance by promoting and advertising. Although most bars and other entertainment venues prefer managers bring a good number of attendees to their shows, this is not mandatory to do so every time. In very rare situations for small bands, an entertainment venue could charge the band a fee for a certain number of people 'not' showing up to the show. This is a number of people guaranteed to be present and would have been agreed upon between the owner and band before the show. If those people do not come, the band pays. This fee is to cover bar expenses and loss of money invested in setting up the show for the headlining band, and is usually implemented in larger, more well-known venues.

To Do

Notes:

Artist Development in the Music Business
Chapter 22 - Preparing to Record

The last two parts of putting together an Artist Development Plan is preparing for product development. One of the areas of product development is that of recording. Another is performing. In addition, there's preparing for merchandising and licensing. This section is about preparing to record. Artists should not attempt to complete any Product Development issues prior to completing all of their Artist Development Plan.

When an Artist reviews the Artist Development Plan, it becomes apparent that all the detail of preparing to record or perform has been identified. For example, look at the catalog of songs that the Artist has. These are the only possible songs for an Artist to perform or record. If an Artist adds another song to the catalog, that part of the Artist Development Plan should be updated.

Preparation is the most crucial step in making a recording, and it all goes on before an Artist sets foot into a recording studio. After an Artist has decided to make a recording, they need to sit down and outline the project. Once again: plan the work, and work the plan. List the overall objective for the recording such as making a compact disc to distribute to radio, or to sell at gigs? Or recording a demo to showcase songs for a publishing deal? It's best to have a clear vision for what you are going to do with the recording before starting to record.

Producing a recording is like taking an audio snapshot of an Artist's sound at a given moment in time. Since it can be expensive to make a quality recording, it's important for the Artist to recognize that very likely they will be using these recordings to represent themselves for a long time. The better prepared an Artist is before entering the studio, the more fun they'll have making the recording and the better it will sound. The "fun' attitude will reflect in the musicianship, and ultimately, the recording itself.

When it comes to making a recording, an Artist has a lot of big decisions to make that will influence the way the end product sounds. In other words, the more an Artist does to prepare before the record light comes on, the more enjoyable the process and the more the quality of the product will be.

Pre-Production
Pre-production is everything that is done before an Artist enters the recording studio. This includes song selection, arrangement ideas, rehearsing, scheduling any session musicians, securing a recording studio and engineer. This task should include preparing the artwork as well as a lining up a possible duplication house to mass produce the finished master - if the recording is being released as hard copy on compact disc. The amount of work in pre-production is easily double that of the actual recording session, especially if the Artist has never done this before. However, there is someone who can help make this process much more effective and significantly simpler.
The Producer

If you're wondering whether or not a producer is a good idea for your project, then it's important to understand what a producer offers in the first place. In a word, it's experience. Let's assume the upcoming project is your first, second or even third independently released recording. This means that the Artist's studio experience is comparatively limited next to a producer, who may have completed dozens of projects. In other words, a producer has spent significant time becoming an expert at something that's still relatively new to an Artist. With this production experience comes a variety of skills that the producer will use to help the Artist with a polished, professional-sounding project. This skill set typically includes everything from knowledge of the craft of songwriting (useful in song selection and improvement), relationships with session musicians (which often includes the ability to play instruments at a very high level themselves), the communication skills to explain to the musicians what the overall "vision" of the project is, knowledge (or ownership) of a good recording studio and, last but not least, the ability to work with the Artist and to help bring out the best performances as possible. Finally, the perspective that a producer brings to a project can be extremely useful for an Artist as it's often difficult to make clear judgments about their own vocal or instrumental tracks.

Choosing a producer is another major step, as is choosing not to use a producer. This is best discussed in detail with the members of the band, as well as anyone whose has recorded an album. Producers can be the single-most important person in getting a project in on time and on budget - but they can also sink a project as well if they are poorly suited to the material.

The Recording Studio

With the advent of improved recording technology and affordable, high-quality equipment, great recordings can be made almost anywhere. Recording is no longer the exclusive domain of the big, multi-room complex. That being said, there are a few things an Artist should consider before choosing a studio for their project.

First and foremost is sound quality. Ask the studio owner or engineer for a demo of something that's been recorded in their studio. The Artist should be even more specific with their inquires. For example the Artist should ask that the music on the demo be in the style of the project that they are planning to record. In other words, if the Artist is planning on recording country music, it doesn't matter if the studio has a great-sounding r&b demo. An r&b demo may not necessarily translate into a great-sounding country recording.

Secondly, make sure the space is comfortable where the Artist will be working. Although working in a big, beautiful studio can be inspiring for some, it can be intimidating for others.

Lastly, don't forget to ask about any and all fees. The obvious one would be the hourly rate but it's important to ask the owner or engineer what other charges that may be incurred. This can be everything from a separate engineer charge, cost for burning CDs and even separate charges for certain pieces of studio equipment. A studio ought to be able to give you a decent estimate for what your overall project should cost. Some studios simplify the process even further by providing an all-in project fee that is decided up front. It's always better to know all of this at the beginning of a project so that there are no unpleasant surprises when it comes time to pay.

Preparing to Record Tips

1. Practice the tune(s) to a metronome and note the setting. Remember that in the studio, even if it's an inexpensive one, time is money and the less time spent on cutting the basic tracks provides more time for other parts of the recording process.
2. Put new strings on the guitar. Okay I know this is a no brainer but you would be surprised how many novice musicians are clueless to this. With that in mind, perhaps changing the battery in the pre-amp is prudent.
3. Have a firm idea of how the song is arranged. With today's software, editing is simple and sections can be moved fairly easily. But once again, time editing may eat up the budget.

For the band many of the same rules apply:
1. Make sure the band is well rehearsed or has a firm idea of the song.
2. The band will more then likely have to where headphones while recording – to some musicians, this can be a different experience especially if they've been use to playing live. In addition, musicians might have to record in different rooms and might not be able to have eye contact with each other. Make sure the song endings don't require everyone having to look at each other.
3. Make sure all musical equipment (amps, cords, pedals, guitars, strings, drum heads) are in proper working before the session begins.
4. Make sure the drummer and/or percussionist(s) has no problem playing along with a "click" track. (Sometimes it's not necessary to use a click track but in most cases, it's necessary.)

Funding a Recording

Ahhh, the budget. Recording takes time, and studio time equals money. Most often, Artists get what they pay for, and if real quality is desired, it won't be cheap. A way of thinking about this is to envision a triangle, and at the separate points you have HIGH QUALITY, FAST, and CHEAP. Pick two, any two, but ONLY two! That's a good rule of thumb to go by. Be realistic. Factor in materials as well. Recording a full album on two inch analog tape can get into hundreds and even thousands of dollars quickly. ADAT sessions can stay under $150 with back-ups. There are trade-offs with each medium.

Also in the recording budget, Artists need to factor the expenses such as meals while at the studio, possible rentals needed in the course of a session, repairs, setups, traveling, exotic dancers, and so on. These things add up, and can add up fast if there is no budget.

Additionally, Artists might want to ask if they can help set up and tear down the session – this can be a great learning experience and it will help the Artist get familiar with recording equipment and recording techniques. Plus it might get some free extra recording time!

The Recording Process
In the studio, the first stage is typically recording basic tracks. This is when drums and bass are recorded, usually to a scratch guitar and vocals, and a click track. After all the drums and bass are completed (sometimes in two separate stages), Artists typically move on to the other rhythm instruments. It makes the most sense to build from the foundation up, laying down the strong timekeeping elements first, and then progressing on to melodic instruments. Usually, little filler parts such as percussion and key parts are added last to help fill in any unwanted space.

This type of session might be for a typical rock band. For singer-songwriters, the entire process might be recording the guitar and voice live, or whatever combination of instruments performed. The best method, regardless of instrumentation, is to lay the strong timekeeping elements first, and then move on. In today's drum-machine perfect world, a click track makes a lot of sense. It is often recommended to record with one. It keeps time as well as allowing more options later during the recording process.

Once basic tracks are recorded, additional parts are overdubbed, meaning they are played to the existing tracks. Again, progressing from the strong time keeping parts to the more melodic parts is always best. Recording the main melody line, often a lead vocal, is best done with the tracks completed as much as possible. This gives a singer the best possible chance of developing the emotion everyone has worked into the track.

After all the tracks are recorded, a cursory check should be done on a rough mix to make sure everything is complete and correct. Often, engineers and producers will perform a few final edits, create composite tracks of vocals and leads, and then prep for editing and mixing.

Mixing is the stage where all the elements are combined to deliver the final track. Mixing can be very straightforward, almost pushing up the faders and printing, to very complex mixes taking a few days per song. It's really dependant on the nature of the production. Something with more tracks takes longer to weed through. Keep in mind that every time during tracking someone says "we'll just take out whatever we don't want in the mix," just added at least an hour to the mix time, and budget.

After all the songs are mixed, typically the mixes get tweaked, or little revisions, perhaps a word is too low here or maybe the solo should be a little louder there. Also, spend one last day running all the mixes in the sequence of the album to a final master, and then listen to the whole print start to finish.

Every project should have the material mastered at a competent facility. Often times, this last step is the biggest difference between albums of similar scope and budget. By not skimping on this crucial final step, you can present your material at its very best.

Finally, keep distractions to a minimum.
1. Shut off the cell phones
2. Don't bring any unnecessary people to the studio
3. Don't bring in drinks/food into the control room or studio
4. Keep the band chit-chat down while in the control room. It makes it tough to hear.

Artist Development in the Music Business
Chapter 23 - Quick Tips

Artist Development

1.) Be professional at all times and expect others to be professional.
2.) Be prepared mentally, physically, musically and creatively
3.) Prepare and follow a plan and schedule
4.) Identify your team and collaborators
5.) Communicate with your team, band and fans
6.) Create constant flow of new quality content
7.) Accept and delegate responsibilities
8.) Provide incentives for delegated jobs
9.) Hone chops, tighten songs and sets
10.) Practice – instrument, vocals, song parts and breaks
11.) Respect others on the team and their time, contributions & commitment
12.) Be prepared for rehearsals
13.) Chart your goals and your success
14.) Review, evaluate and set new improvement levels constantly
15.) Demand quality from yourself and your team
16.) Complete team agreements
17.) Separate, if only mentally, you, your partners, your companies, etc
18.) Register name and trademark
19.) Secure image and crossover
20.) This is your career, treat it like one

To Do

Notes:

Artist Development in the Music Business
Chapter 24 – Glossary of Terms

Terms
Sample Publishing Contract Terms

The main terms:

1. The amount of songs/compositions the writer is expected to deliver during a specific period and that the writer is signed exclusively to the publisher. This is usually tied to a specific product i.e., an album of X songs written by the composer, and/or co-writers.

2. An Initial Period - usually 1 year with options to extend if the songs have not been delivered, recorded or released, depending on the wording of the contract.

3. Exclusive Extensions and Options - which will include further minimum commitments and time periods. If signing to the publishing arm of a record company these terms may reflect those in the deal and both may co-terminate at the same time.

4. The territories and period during which the Publisher may control and exploit the songs delivered in the agreement. 10 - 15 years or shorter for successful writers is pretty standard, the shorter the better as at the end of term the songs are
returned to the writer who can then choose to exploit the songs themselves or assign them to a new publisher.

5. A retention period for songs delivered to the publisher and not exploited during a reasonable period of time should be included which then allows these particular works copyrights to be returned to the writer.

6. Territories is the term for the right to publish in various countries. Assuming negotiation is possible the writer may wish to sign agreements with other publishers or set up their own publishing operation in certain countries.

7. Royalties to be paid to the writer and the basis that these are calculated. This can be either a percentage of 'gross' or 'net' receipts. If the publisher will only agree to pay on the 'net' receipts received in the UK it is usually possible to negotiate a percentage of the gross retained by sub-publishers will be set at a reasonable level, otherwise the writer who shares the income will not receive very much!

8. Percentage of Royalties - for most writers this ranges between 60% and 80% of gross income which also applies to the publishers' share of performance income. 50% of gross performance income is also paid direct from PRS if the songwriting performer is a member. These figures are reduced in the case of 'cover' versions (songs not recorded by the writer as an artist), although there are exceptions to this.

9. Advances - this is an income paid to the writer, sometimes in installments, in advance of receiving royalties on songs written. These reflect delivery and release of a product similar to a record deal although there are other alternatives, i.e., installments linked to signing a publishing deal and/or record deal. The publishers advance is repaid only when royalties are received from exploitation of the product, if it doesn't sell the writer will often be expected to repay the advance at the termination of contract depending on the terms of agreement.

10. The definition of an acceptable record deal should make provision for signing with alternative companies other than the five majors.

11. The waiving of moral rights and full assignment of the copyright in the songs subject to the agreement by the writer to the publisher. Clauses should be included to prevent usage of work which has been detrimentally and materially changed, i.e., the addition of parodic, lewd or derogatory words to the original lyrics.

12. Publishers Obligations - Vague wording to the effect that the publisher will use reasonable endeavors to exploit the songs delivered by the writer are pretty standard as most publishers like to keep their contractual obligations to a minimum! Occasionally a publisher will agree to provide home studio equipment, demo facilities, tour support or large equipment costs but any expenses like these are expected to be recoupable.   a) Registration of works to worldwide collecting societies to ensure collection of income should be undertaken by the publisher on behalf

Music Business Definitions

You gotta know what you're talking about.

360 Deals - An increasingly common major label deal structure in which the label not only earns income from the sale of recorded music of their artists but also gets a cut of other artist income, including money generated by touring and merchandise sales.

7" / 10" / 12": The diameter of vinyl records. 7" items are usually singles that play at 45 rpm, 10" items could be a single or an EP, and 12" items could be a single (45 rpm) or an album (33 1/3 rpm

A&R is the person or group of people who sign new acts to a record label. (They used to select material from publishers for artists signed to their label, hence Artists and Repertoire.)

Acetate In sound recording an acetate disc is a reference audio disc used during production of a gramophone record (e.g. an LP record). The acetate disc is created as one of the initial stages of record production and used to determine how a given recording will transfer to disc.

Advance – In the field of intellectual property licensing, an advance against royalties is a payment made by the licensee to the licensor at the start of the period of licensing (usually immediately upon contract, or on delivery of the property being licensed) which is to be offset against future royalty payments.

Advance the Show – A telephone call to a promoter from a road manager to go over specifics of an upcoming performance.

Aftermarket: For the purposes of the discography, this term describes any item that contains material being resold in a secondary fashion, usually by a company not normally associated with the artist or the record label. The best examples are box sets; most of the time the CDs are regular copies of albums or singles that are easy to find, but have been repackaged with miscellaneous trinkets (e.g., a book, poster, postcard, shirt, or button). Even though some of a box's contents may be official, the box itself is not.

AFM - (AF of M) American Federation of Musicians. The musicians' union sets minimum wages and working conditions for American artists. The majority of performance contracts are drawn up using the AF of M standard contract format. The AF of M also provides a variety of services to its members, including health insurance, legal aid, etc.

Agent - A person who seeks employment for artists, actors, musicians, actors and other people in the entertainment business and negotiates performance contracts. An Agent gets the artist the gig. Agents make their money by making a percentage of the money that their client is paid. There are different regulations that govern different types of agents that are established by artist's unions and the legal jurisdiction in which the agent operates. There are also professional organizations that license talent agencies.

Aggregator - A digital music aggregator collects music from a number of different sources such as musicians and labels and then distributes them to online music distributors. By doing so, iTunes and Amazon don't need to worry about dealing with the time consuming job of getting content to populate their music store. Music aggregators can offer additional services such reconciliation on behalf of the artist from the store, making the process very easy for any unsigned or indie label.

Album - A collection of songs, regardless of format.

All In - the total licensing price of a song and master use combined - OR the two licensing rights- both combined--(as in " is the total fee --ALL IN -for both rights").

Area of Dominant Influence ADI - ADI or Area of Dominant Influence is the geographic area or market reached by a radio or television station. It is used by advertisers and rating companies to determine the potential audience of a station.

Artist - Music industry contract term for musician or performer.

ASCAP - American Society of Composers, Authors, and Publishers. One of three organizations that grants licenses for performances of a given songwriter or publisher's music.

Assignment - Copyright can be assigned to a label or publisher, or a third party such as a royalty collection society. This allows them to act on behalf the copyright owner to issue licenses and collect royalties within the terms of the assignment.

Avails or Availabilities – Term used to identify the availability of artists for performances or appearances.

Axe – a musician's instrument

Backline - Instruments and everything needed onstage to put on a concert, with the exception of some sound and lights. This includes drum kits, base rigs, amps, etc.

Bar Code - A bar-code is a machine readable number (e.g. UPC code) used for various purposes in manufacture, retail and commercial use of a CD. Bar-codes don't just identify CDs at the sales counter, they are also used for chart returns. Some distributors and retailers insist on bar-coding.

Bean Counters - Slang for those who count the money and keep track of sales.

Bill – A list of performers on a show

Blister pack: A Blister Pack is s stiff plastic molding surrounding the case of a CD. The term is borrowed from the marketers who originally made the packaging. Blister Packs were mainly used on 3" CDs so that they could be hung on shop displays. 3" CDs with the original Blister Packs have a slightly higher value than those without; however there is no accurate record as to which releases had this packaging and which did not.

Blanket License - "Blanket license" is a license which allows the music user to perform any or all songs in the Performing Rights Organization's repertory as much or as little as they like. Licensees pay an annual fee for the license. The blanket license saves music users the paperwork, trouble and expense of finding and negotiating licenses with all of the copyright owners of the works that might be used during a year and helps prevent the user from even inadvertently infringing on the copyrights of the P.R.O's members and the many foreign writers whose music is licensed in the U.S.

BMI - Broadcast Music Incorporated. One of three organizations that grants licenses for performances of a given songwriter or publisher's music.

Bogart-Bacall Syndrome - (Also called Lauren Bacall Syndrome) Condition in which improper vocal technique while speaking results in a gravelly-sounding voice. Common in women.

Book – A band is "booked" at a club if they are scheduled to play there.

Booking Agent – A person who solicits work and schedules performances for entertainers.

Bootleg: these are the unauthorized recordings of live or broadcast performances. They are duplicated and sold - often at a premium price - without the permission of the artist, composer or record company.

Box Set: - A set of items that are packaged together.

Break – An artist is about to "break" when he or she is on the verge of becoming very well known - this usually happens after some serious radio airplay or publicity is taking place and the expectations are high for great sales and visibility.

Bridge - In a song, a bridge is usually of different length than the verse or chorus and usually has different music accompaniment. A bridge usually will "sum up" a songs message, or flash forward or backwards in time or often give a different perspective or surprise twist to a song.

Broadcast - the replaying of pre-recorded works to multiple listeners through various media or in a 'semi-live' setting such as a bar or bookstore, and including radio, TV, webcasting, podcasting, etc.

Business Manager - Keeps track of an artist's finances and is usually a CPA who specializes in the entertainment industry.

Buzz - There is a "buzz" about a particular band if people are talking about them and saying positive things.

Buyer - (Talent Buyer, Purchaser, Concert Promoter, Promoter) Makes offers of employment to artist through the artist's agent.

Cap – slang for capacity

Capacity - The number of audience members a concert venue will legally hold.

Card Price – The Card Price is the cost of a CD for a retailer. Often, major labels give a retailer 5 percent discount of the Card Price.

Cassette - A sealed plastic unit containing a length of audio or video tape wound on a pair of spools, for insertion into a recorder or playback device.

Catalog Number - Also known as order number or issue number. 1. The number(s), letter(s), and/or other symbols assigned to a publication by the publisher to establish a unique control of a particular publication. 2. The number, usually different from the matrix- or master-number(s), assigned by the publisher under which an item appears listed in catalogues, leaflets, and other publicity material issued by the company owning the rights to the recording. Usually common to all parts of the published item, appearing generally on each part of a multipart package as well as on the container for the multiple parts. This number may change when, or if, one or more of the parts are re-published again at a later date. Recordings have from time to time been published with the same catalogue number, both inadvertently and deliberately. Dubbings are sometimes assigned the original catalogue number, but frequently with a variant prefix or suffix

Chorus – The chorus is a section of lines that generally contain the catchiest part of the song. Usually the chorus contains a songs hook.

CO Copyright Form - This is the registration form from the Library of Congress that you use to register a song online. It protects the copyright in and to the words and music of the song.

Collective Work - A work, such as a periodical issue, anthology or encyclopedia, in which the Work in its entirety in unmodified form, along with a number of other contributions, constituting separate and independent works in themselves, are assembled into a collective whole. A work that constitutes a Collective Work will not be considered a Derivative Work (as defined below) for the purposes of this License.

Composite Card - An 8x10 photograph containing images of artists in varied "looks" or angles. These are used to obtain modeling, television ad, and acting gigs, but having one doesn't hurt for live tour auditions.

Comps – slang for complimentary tickets

Concert Promoter - Makes offers of employment to artist through the artist's agent.

Copy Protection - Record labels use a number of different (so-called) copy-protection techniques for certain releases. These are formatted in a non-standard way to stop them playing normally in PCs.

Copyright - the exclusive rights granted to the author or creator of an original work, including the right to copy, distribute and adapt the work. Copyright lasts for a certain time period after which the work is said to enter the public domain. Copyright applies to a wide range of works that are substantive and fixed in a medium. Some jurisdictions also recognize "moral rights" of the creator of a work, such as the right to be credited for the work. Copyright is described under the umbrella term intellectual property along with patents and trademarks.

Copyright Exemption and/or Exceptions - A provision in the *Copyright Act* which permits the use of a copyright-protected work, without the payment of license fees, by religious, educational or charitable organizations, when the use of such work is in furtherance of a religious, educational or charitable object.

Copyright infringement - Violation of the exclusive rights of a copyright owner (e.g., publicly performing a copyright-protected musical work without the copyright owner's consent).

Corporate Date - A private show an artist plays for a corporation's convention, party, or retreat.

Cover - (Cover Tune, Cover Song) A song that has been released before by another artist.

Cover Band - A band that plays only cover songs. Sometimes a band chooses to cover only one artist. In this case, a band that only performs songs written by the Grateful Dead would be considered a Grateful Dead cover band.

Cut Outs - Product titles discontinued by the record label, usually due to lack of sales. Often purchased in large amounts by another company and sold dirt-cheap in discount bins.

DAT Master - means to have a DAT master mixed down recording -for dubbing into the film/ or tv production

Deadwood - Unsold tickets at a concert.

Demo - A recording made to demonstrate how a song should sound. Could be done by a songwriter to pitch a song to a recording artist, by an artist to work out the arrangement and production of a song before entering the studio for final recording, or by an artist for use in a promo package to attract labels and Talent Buyers.

Derivative Work - A work based upon the Work or upon the Work and other pre-existing works, such as a translation, musical arrangement, dramatization, fictionalization, motion picture version, sound recording, art reproduction, abridgment, condensation, or any other form in which the Work may be recast, transformed, or adapted, except that a work that constitutes a Collective Work will not be considered a Derivative Work for the purpose of this License. For the avoidance of doubt, where the Work is a musical composition or sound recording, the synchronization of the Work in timed-relation with a moving image ("synching") will be considered a Derivative Work for the purpose of this License.

Diamond Record – Units Shipped of over 10 Million units

Digipak - Digipak is a proprietary range of CD (and DVD) packaging.

Digital Distribution means "moving music files electronically". It normally refers to the online equivalent of traditional distribution (shifting downloads instead of CDs).

Distribution - Traditional distribution is about moving CDs (or other physical recordings) from record labels to retailers. Distributors do more than carry boxes of CDs, they also promote and invest in releases.

Distribution Deal - to obtain a record distributor - to manufacture and mass reproduce stock, sell and distribute a CD or film to the public throughout the retail commercial marketplace. Some record distribution companies may also be record companies as well that commercially distribute other record label's product.

Door Deal – A financial arrangement to pay an artist from the proceeds generated by sales at the door. The artist typically would not receive a guarantee. A door deal may be structured as a percentage of the admission charge before or after expenses such as production, security or certain staff such as a sound technician.

Downstage - The part of the stage closest to the audience.

DRM - Digital Rights Management is a kind of copy-protection. It is a hardware or software device that forces users to comply with copyright owners' conditions.

Dramatic Rights - While the line between dramatic and non dramatic is not clear and depends on the facts, a dramatic performance usually involves using the work to tell a story or as part of a story or plot. Dramatic performances, among others, include:

(I) performance of an entire "dramatic-musical work." For example a performance of the musical play Oklahoma would be a dramatic performance.

(II) performance of one or more musical compositions from a "dramatic-musical work" accompanied by dialogue, pantomime, dance, stage action, or visual representation of the work from which the music is taken. For example a performance of "People Will Say We're In Love" from Oklahoma with costumes, sets or props or dialogue from the show would be dramatic.

(III) performance of one or more musical compositions as part of a story or plot, whether accompanied or unaccompanied by dialogue, pantomime, dance, stage action or visual representation. For example, incorporating a performance of "If I Loved You" into a story or plot would be a dramatic performance of the song.

(IV) performance of a concert version of a "dramatic-musical work." For example, a performance of all the songs in Oklahoma even without costumes or sets would be a dramatic performances.

The term "dramatic-musical work" includes, but is not limited to, a musical comedy, opera, play with music, revue or ballet.

Performing Right's Organizations have the right to license "non-dramatic" public performances of its members' works - for example, recordings broadcast on radio, songs or background music performed as part of a movie or other television program, or live or recorded performances in a bar or restaurant.

Dramatic and grand rights are licensed by the composer or the publisher of the work.

Draw - A band has a "draw" if they can generate a live audience at a live concert. On the flipside, a band that doesn't attract an audience has "no draw."

Emancipated Minor - Person under the age of 18 who has been legally declared an adult and is no longer under his or her parents' control. Obtaining emancipated minor status, which gives a minor the legal rights of an adult, is common with teens in the entertainment industry because it enables them to enter into legal agreements such as contracts on their own behalf, work longer hours, and gives them control to make financial decisions for themselves.

EP - Extended Play. Record containing at least 3 songs (2 songs per side is usual), but not as many songs as an LP.

EPK – Electronic Press Kit

Equity - Slang for Actors Equity, the union representing theater actors and stage managers.

Fair Use - A limitation and exception to the exclusive right granted by copyright law to the author of a creative work, is a doctrine in United States copyright law that allows limited use of copyrighted material without acquiring permission from the rights holders. Examples of fair use include commentary, criticism, news reporting, research, teaching, library archiving and scholarship. It provides for the legal, non-licensed citation or incorporation of copyrighted material in another author's work under a four-factor balancing test.

Fingerprinting - A way of recognizing digital files by patterns in their data. The fingerprint is a short code, which can be read by special software to reliably identify the title and other details of a particular track.

First Right – After completing a song, a songwriter has the right of FIRST USE. This is the period where they essentially hold a monopoly on the song. These means that songwriters own the monopoly to record the song first, or they may grant the first right to someone else to record the work. If a big name artist wants to use your song on their next CD, you can give them a temporary exclusive.

Fly - To suspend equipment (or people) above the stage via a system of trusses and cables. Riggers are the crew members in charge of doing this.

F.O.H. – Slang for Front of House.

Format - 1. Type of music or programming on a radio station (CHR, AOR, Talk Radio, etc.). 2. Less commonly, the type of playback media music is available on (CD, MP3, etc.)

Front of House - (F.O.H.) 1.The area around the main sound console, in the audience portion of the venue. 2.The audience area of the venue, nearest the stage. 3. Slang for the crew member who mixes sound for this part of the venue.

Four-Walling - Producing a show at a location that is rented out for a single evening, is called "four-walling," as it entails renting a venue and receiving no additional services or technical equipment other than the space itself.

Gig – a live performance

Gold Record – In the USA, units shipped of over 500,000 units. In Uruguay, a Gold Records indicates units shipped of over 2000 copies.

Harry Fox - The Harry Fox Agency (HFA) represents music publishers for their mechanical and digital licensing needs. They issue licenses and collect and distribute royalties for their affiliated publishers. This includes licensing for the recording and reproduction of CDs, ringtones, and Internet downloads. HFA does not issue synchronization (or synch) licenses for the use of music in advertising, movies, music videos, and television programs. HFA also conducts royalty examinations, investigates and negotiates new business opportunities, and pursues piracy claims.

Head Shot – a photograph of an artists face & head

Headliner – One or more artists who are the primary reason why a performance ticket is sold.

Hook – A hook in a song is a phrase of words or music that catches the listeners ear. If the listener remembers anything of the song, it's usually the hook.

House - The audience portion of a concert venue.

IFPI - The International Federation of the Phonographic Industry is the international trade body for major labels and large independents.

In-Ears - In-ear monitor system that makes it easier for musicians to hear each other onstage than with traditional wedges.

Independent - Independent normally means record labels that are not majors.

Indie - A broad term with many general meanings. It refers to independent record labels, several ways of doing business, various styles of music and a number of philosophies.

Intellectual property - A form of creative endeavor that can be protected through a copyright, trademark, patent, industrial design or integrated circuit topography.

ISRC - International Standard Recording Codes identify recordings (tracks).

ISWC - International Standard Musical Works Codes identify compositions.

J-Card - The front insert for a slim jewel case.

Jewel Case - A standard plastic CD case.

Kill Seats - (sometimes called "kills") Concert tickets held from sale until after stage set up for seats expected to be unusable ("killed") due to staging elements or the sound board being in the way. The number of kill seats is usually overestimated, and after the stage is set, any seats not eliminated are put on sale. (Those with "partially obstructed views" are marked as such). In the past, kill seats could often be bought at the venue box office close to show time, but the advent of more online ticket sellers have virtually eliminated their availability at the venue.

Label Code - The Label Code (LC) was introduced in 1977 by the IFPI (International Federation of Phonogram and Videogram Industries) in order to unmistakably identify the different record labels for rights purposes.

License – A License is simply the permission to use something. It is the right, granted by the copyright holder, for a given person or entity to broadcast, recreate, perform, or listen to a recorded copy of a copyrighted work. A License is the right, granted by the copyright holder, for a given person or entity to broadcast, recreate, or perform a recorded copy of a copyrighted work. Types of licensing contracts can include: 1) A flat fee for a defined period of usage, or 2) Royalty payments determined by the number of copies of the work sold or the total revenues acquired as a result of its distribution. Most music licensing agreements include some form of compensation of the copyright owner when the work in which it is included (i.e. movie, play) is financially successful.

Licensee - the person or entity to whom the work is licensed.

Licensing or Clearance Houses - To clear a piece of material is to obtain the legal rights necessary to use it. The agents for licensing for the film/ tv shows who obtain (by contracting in writing) (i.e. to obtain licenses) all the necessary legal rights in the show for all the music usages. Licensing houses may also sometimes supply music for productions.

Licensor - the owner of the licensed work and offers the Work under the terms of a License.

Line-Up - The bands that are supposed to play a particular show together make the "line-up." Also known as The Bill

List - If you're on "the list," your name is on the list of people who do not have to pay to get into the show. People who put names on "the list" include: someone who works at the venue, the artist, the record label, the concert promoter, or the publicist.

Literary work - Work consisting of text, which includes novels, poems, catalogues, reports tables and translations of such works. It also includes computer programs.

Live Nation – A concert promotion company which was spun off from Clear Channel Communications.

Load-In – A term used to describe the process of moving equipment into a venue.

Load-Out – A term used to describe the process of moving equipment out of a venue.

Long-box - An oversized cardboard package that CDs used to be sold in, a form of exterior cardboard packaging for CD's in widespread use in North America in the 1980s and early 1990s. When compact discs first began to appear in the retail stores, the long-box packaging served a transitional purpose, allowing shops to file new compact discs in the same bins originally used for vinyl records. Long-boxes are 12 inches tall by almost 6 inches wide, and capable of containing two separate discs when necessary. Most long-boxes were full color, with details about the compact disc on the back, and artwork that was frequently taken from the original square album cover art, reworked for the new shape and size.

Loop - A piece of music that is repeated in a song.

L.P. – Long Play – more than 4 songs on an album. Longer than an E.P.

Major - A major record label. The major record labels are the biggest members of record industry trade bodies (e.g. RIAA in America and BPI in the UK). There isn't a fixed definition—the majors are just the labels that sell most records.

Manager - Business Manager, Personal Manager, Tour Manager, Stage Manager

Market - 1. Audience which can be identified through demographic research and/or preference analysis. 2. Group of buyers or consumers. 3. Sometimes, slang for a market city.

Market City - Area of a state or country large enough to support an arena or stadium concert. Often the capitol. Some states and countries have several market cities.

Master Rights (Master Use Rights) - The right to use a Master Recording of a song. This means the Album, CD, DAT that the song is embodied on.

Master Use Licensing - the licensing of the recording of a musical work to be performed as a soundtrack, bumper, lead-in or background to a motion picture.

Master Use License - A master use license is a phonographic copyright license to pay recording owners for music used in film, video, or TV soundtracks. There is no fixed fee for master use licenses.

Mastering - The final engineering stage in audio production, normally for duplication. It is a skilled, genre-specific job. Mastering is completed after tracking, editing, and mixing.

Mechanical Rights - This is the right to record a song to sell it on a record, MP3, laser disc, mini disc, video, CD rom, etc. The " MECHANICALS " are the SALES MONIES from the sales of the record or above medium. Compulsory Mechanical Royalties are 9.1 cents per song per sale for songs up to 5 minutes. Mechanical Royalties get larger for longer songs for longer songs. The present statutory rate for songs between five minutes and six is 10.5 cents per copy made. It's 12.25 cents if the song is over six minutes long, and you get 14 cents a copy for songs longer than 7 minutes, and so on.

Mis-pressings: A mis-pressing is when a record or CD is pressed with different music to what is stated on the label. Mis-pressings are actually quite common, particularly on CD. If the labels are simply stuck on the wrong sides of a record it is not strictly a mis-pressing. I.e. the labels should denote a different release to the music that is actually on the record. Some vinyl records by famous artists sell for extra if mis-pressed but with CDs there is almost no added value.

Monitor - A speaker or in-ear system that lets musicians hear each other onstage. (See also, in-ears, wedges.)

MP3 - A popular music file format used for downloading and digital music players. File sizes are generally about a tenth of the original size. MP3 was invented in 1987 and available publicly from 1995. MP3 is an MPEG standard.

Music Sup – slang for Music Supervisor. One who make decisions on which songs are used in TV, film or commercials.

Neighboring Rights – The rights granted for the use of a song in a recorded format. A Circle P copyright is a neighboring right.

Non-Routed Date - A show that does not fall in the natural path of travel between two other shows that were previously booked. They are usually either private gigs on a night off or special "one night only" performances when the artist is on a break from touring.

One Sheet – A promotion item that provides a picture, bio and other information on one sheet of paper.

Opener – A term used to describe an artist who does not have the draw of a headliner and is used to prime the audience before the headliner's performance. An opening act.

Option - An option is normally an option to extend the term of a contract but it doesn't mean everybody has options. Sometimes only the label has the option and it may be automatic.

Original - (Original Songs) 1. A song not previously recorded by another artist. 2. Song written by the artist who performs it.

OSHA - Occupational Safety and Health Administration. US Government Agency that regulates job-related safety and health issues. OSHA's mission is "to prevent work-related injuries, illnesses, and deaths."

PA - 1. "Public address system". Delivers sound into the concert venue so that the audience can hear the band. 2. Slang for Production Assistant or Personal Assistant.

PA Copyright Form - This is the registration form from the Library Of Congress that you use to register a song. It protects the copyright in and to the words and music of the song.

Paper - Slang for tickets given away to fill seats and give the appearance of a full concert venue.

Papering the House - The act of giving tickets away to fill seats and give the appearance of a full concert venue.

Per Diem - Money allotted to the artist and each crew member for daily living expenses on the road.

Per Program License - A "per program" license is similar to the blanket license in that it authorizes a radio or television broadcaster to use all the works in the Performing Rights Organization's repertory. However, the license is designed to cover use of music in a specific radio or television programs, requiring that the user keep track of all music used. Also, the user must be certain to obtain rights for all the music used in programs not covered by the license.

Performance - the live performance of a musical piece, regardless of whether it's performed by the original artist or in the manner it is best known.

Performance Rider - (see also Technical Rider or Rider) Part of the artist's contract that details production requirements and staging for the artist's show. The rider also outlines details pertaining to the care and feeding of the artist and touring personnel.

Performing Rights Society - (AKA Performing Rights Organization) Organization that grants licenses for performances of a given songwriter or publisher's music. In the United States, there are three: ASCAP, BMI, and SESAC.

Personal Assistant - (AKA PA) Assists an artist or executive with day to day personal tasks such as scheduling, travel arrangements, correspondence, picking up dry cleaning, hiring domestic help, coordinating meetings, shopping for gifts or personal necessities, etc. Usually travels with the artist.

Personal Manager – A Manager who oversees the artist's career. He or she does big picture, long-range planning and acts on the artist's behalf.

Platinum Record - In the USA, units shipped of over 1,000,000 units.
In Uruguay, it is unit shipped of over 4,000 units.

Podcast - A podcast is a download through podcasting software such as iPodder. Podcasting software finds new downloads using RSS and adds them to playlist software for automatic transfer to a music player

Points - A point is a percentage point (one hundredth, or a penny in the pound). It normally applies to royalties. The total amount (100%) is not always what it appears to be.

PR - Technically means "press relations" but is also used in a slang way to refer to a person who works in press relations. PR is also known as "publicity." PR companies/PR people are usually hired to work on a campaign basis to promote a new album, single or tour. Some PR people only promote to print media, some only to websites, some only to TV and some to a combination of mediums. Some PR people also work in radio plugging, but often radio is treated as a separate entity.

Pre-Cleared Music - music that has been pre-negotiated for price, distribution and legal use, generally through licensing for film, video, television (commercials and programs), Internet, events, video games and multimedia productions.

Press Kit - A professional folio containing your resume and/or bio, photograph, CD, list of venues you have performed, press clippings, recommendations, posters and mementos from concerts (especially those with your name listed,) lyric samples, and other materials to support your professional viability.

Private Date - A show an artist plays that is not open to the public, such as a wedding, private party, invitation-only fundraiser, or corporate convention. Sometimes it is called a corporate date.

PRO - Performing Rights Organization is a general term for publishing rights societies like ASCAP, BMI, SESAC or PRS in the UK

Product - Label speak for CD's, cassettes, etc. Retail term for inventory.

Production – usually means sound and light equipment.

Production Manager - In charge of the technical equipment for the artist or venue. Rents the staging and equipment, keeps the mechanical stuff working.

Promo Package - (Promotional package, Promo Kit, Promo) A package of materials assembled to attract labels or talent buyers. Contents may vary depending on the purpose of the promo package but typically include a CD of the artist's music, a bio, a photo, and press clippings.

Promoter - Slang for concert promoter. Makes offer of employment through artist's agent.

Promotion Manager - Person at radio station in charge of the stations promotions.

Public Domain - Not copyright. This happens when copyright expires or the owner explicitly puts the material in the public domain.

Public Performance - A public performance is one that occurs "in a place open to the public or at any place where a substantial number of persons outside of a normal circle of a family and its social acquaintances is gathered." A public performance also occurs when the performance is transmitted by means of any device or process (for example, via broadcast, telephone wire, or other means) to the public. In order to perform a copyrighted work publicly, the user must obtain performance rights from the copyright owner or his representative.

Publish - Publishing used to refer to the availability of printed sheet music. Today it refers to the public availability of copyright material in any form.

Publisher - for the purposes of copyright, a publisher is the owner of the copyrighted work.

Publishers Share - (The following example given is @ 100% Publishing) If you divide 100% of The Song in Half -- the remaining 50% is the Publishers Share -It is then referred to as 100% Publishers Share .

Publishing Administration - is limited to royalty collection. The publisher will not get additional customers for the compositions. The rate for administration is normally about 10%.

Purchaser - Music industry contract language for the talent buyer or concert promoter. Purchasers make offers of employment to artists through the artist's agent.

Pyro - Slang for pyrotechnics. Fireworks or sparkler type effects used at a concert are considered pyro and requires a highly skilled licensed pyro technician.

Q - Rating Research product of the Long Island-based research company Marketing Evaluations, used to rate the "liability" and appeal of various celebrities on TV on a scale from 0-50. Good looking and personable celebrities typically get the highest Q ratings. www.qscores.com

Radio Plugger - Also sometimes simply known as a plugger, radio pluggers promote releases to radio. Pluggers usually work with specific singles and go around to radio station playlist meetings, playing the singles they are representing and trying to get them placed on a playlist. In some cases, pluggers may work with full albums, letting the stations themselves decide what the single is.

Record Label - A record label (or record company) makes, distributes and markets sound recordings (CD's, tapes, etc.) Record labels obtain from music publishers the right to record and distribute songs and in turn pay license fees for the recordings.
A record label was originally a company that made recordings (their company or imprint label was stuck on the centre). Today few if any record labels make records themselves. Now, record labels invest in artists, promote recordings and collect earnings from phonographic copyrights.

Recoupables - Expenses charged by a label against an artist's royalties. Recoupables are deducted before the artist sees any money, so a tight rein should be kept on the recording and promotional budgets. (See charge-backs.) Can also refer to expenses a manager covers for the artist which will be paid back at a later date.

Red Book - The technical rule book for standard audio CDs is known as the Red Book.

Reflux - Laryngitis Throat condition caused by acid reflux in which stomach acid rises to the throat area and causes hoarseness and other throat symptoms.

Region – Label or radio speak for a geographical section of the country or world.

Release - The release of physical (vinyl, cassette, CD) records to radio and retail was always coordinated and formal. The release of a big record was staged like the premiere of a major film. This still happens in the mainstream but the delivery of content on an independent artist's site is normally much less formal.

Retransmission - A transmission of a performance is one that is sent by any device or process (for example, radio, TV, cable, satellite, telephone) and received in a different place. A retransmission is a further transmission of that performance to yet another place.

Reversion is when a copyright assignment ends. Assignments are normally limited to a period of time or some other condition depending on the circumstances of the original rights owner.

RIAA - Recording Industry Association of America. Trade association that represents the labels and certifies albums "Gold," "Platinum," and "Diamond.," all of which are trademarks of the RIAA.

Rider - (see also Technical Rider or Performance Rider) Part of the artist's contract that details production requirements and staging for the artist's show. The rider also outlines details pertaining to the care and feeding of the artist and touring personnel.

Rigger - Tour or venue personnel who "fly" lights and other staging equipment above the stage.

Roadie - Dated term for a member of the road crew. In some circles, a derogatory term. When in doubt use "crew member" or "tech." (See Tech.)

Road Manager - See Tour Manager.

Rotation - Frequency of radio or video airplay in a 24-hour period. Heavy rotation is many plays per day, light rotation is few.

Routed Date - a show that falls in the natural path of travel between two other shows that were previously booked. It's often a private gig on a night off.

Routing - The route a tour takes across the country or around the world. Tours are usually routed by the artist's agent with input from the artist's management, usually 6-9 months in advance. Most major tours are routed to follow the sun as much as possible in order to avoid weather-related travel problems and ensure best attendance; warm climates in Winter, cooler climates in Summer.

Royalties - fees paid to rights owners (normally record labels, publishers, writers and performers) for the use of their work.

Runners - Local crew members who run errands during the time the artist is in town. May also shuttle the touring party to and from the airport, hotel, and venue.

Runs - Aguillera-esque vocal tricks in which the singer sends each note up and down like a multi-hilled rollercoaster. Runs have existed in R&B and gospel music for decades, but were made popular in the mainstream by such artists as Mariah Carey and Christina Aguillera.

Sampling - requires record label and publishing clearance. There is no fixed rate for clearance. Sampling may be allowed under the terms of a blanket MCPS assignment to pay the writer mechanical income. If the work is not assigned to MCPS the sample should also be cleared through the publisher.

Scalpers – Persons who buy tickets with the intent to sell them for a higher amount.

SCMS - The Serial Copy Management System stops controlled digital media from being copied on certain machines by setting a marker on new recordings. Recordings with the marker cannot be copied again in these machines. SCMS is part of the Sony/Philips Digital Interface (S/PDIF) format.

Secular Music - Non-religious music.

SESAC – One of three organizations that grants licenses for performances of a given songwriter or publisher's music.

Session Musicians – Musicians who are paid a one-off fee (which should not be less than the Musicians' Union rate) for playing at recording sessions.

Set - A group of songs performed by an Artist . An artist may perform more than one set with a break in between.

Settlement - The completion of paperwork, deduction of expenses, and payment of the artist after the show.

Silver Record - In the USA, units shipped of over 100,000 units.

Song Hold - The process in which an A&R Rep, Manager, or Producer claims "first dibs" on a song to prevent another artist from recording and releasing it. A typical hold is 90 days with first rights, but 30-day and 60-day holds are also common.

Song Plugger - Person at a publishing house who tried to get record labels or artists to record their songs. In the days before demo tapes, the songs were presented live by singers hired just for this purpose by the song plugger.

Song Shopping Agreements - This is a letter of intent from Writer to Publisher (or vice versa) spelling out the terms and conditions and time limit the publisher has to get the song placed. These agreements can be extremely specific with percentages of Publishing granted when the Publisher gets a cut (or placement) in the set time period specified. It will most likely contain further options.

Song Shopping Agreements - This is a letter of intent from Writer to Publisher (or vice versa) spelling out the terms and conditions and time limit the publisher has to get the song placed. These agreements can be extremely specific with percentages of Publishing granted when the Publisher gets a cut (or placement) in the set time period specified. It will most likely contain further options.

Sound Exchange – a non-profit performing rights organization that collects royalties on behalf of sound recording copyright owners and featured artists for non-interactive digital transmission, including satellite and internet radio.

Sound and Lights - Contract term pertaining to stage equipment for sound and lighting needed for a concert. Term also referred to as "production."

Sound Recording - A sound recording refers to the copyright in a recording as distinguished from the copyright in a song. The copyright in the song encompasses the words and music and is owned by the songwriter or music publisher. The sound recording is the result of recording music, words or other sounds onto a tape, record, CD, etc. The copyright encompasses what you hear: the artist singing, the musicians playing, the entire production). The sound recording copyright is owned by the record label. The copyright in the musical work itself is owned by the music publisher, which grants the record label a "mechanical" license to record and distribute the song as part of the record.

SoundScan - SoundScan is the official method of tracking sales of music and music video products throughout the United States and Canada

Spider - A small piece of plastic that holds CDs in a card case.

Soundman – A technician who operates the sound production at a performance.

Split Point – The point negotiated between Promoter and Agent where percentages of income are split. This point is usually determined after expenses and a reasonable return on investment.

SR Copyright Form - This is the registration form from The Library Of Congress that you use to register the sound recording only (that the song is embodied on) i.e-The master recording as its embodied on the Cassette, Record, CD that you enclose for deposit materials.

Stage Left - The side of the stage on the artist's left as he/she looks out at the audience from the stage. (Stage Left is the audience's right as they look up at the artist.)

Stage Plot - A map of where the artist's equipment goes onstage. Part of the technical rider.

Stage Right - The side of the stage on the artist's right as he/she looks out at the audience from the stage. (Stage Right is the audience's left as they look up at the artist.)

Standing Waves - An acoustic phenomenon in which a reflected signal intersects the original signal and there's a halving or doubling of frequencies in that area. You can hear this for yourself by going into a narrow hallway with hard surfaces on both sides and no thick floor coverings. Clap your hands. The sounds will seem to "collide" with each other.

Stanza – A stanza in a song is similar to a paragraph in a book. A stanza is a section of grouped lines. Usually a song will have multiple verses and a chorus. A verse is a stanza.

Sync Rights (Synchronization Rights) - A synchronization or "synch" right involves the use of a recording of musical work in audio-visual form: for example as part of a motion picture, television program, commercial announcement, music video or other videotape. Often, the music is "synchronized" or recorded in timed relation with the visual images. Synchronization rights are licensed by the music publisher to the producer of the movie or program.

Synchronization Licensing - the licensing of musical works to be synchronized with moving pictures as background in a motion picture, television program, video, DVD, etc.

Talent Buyer - (Purchaser, Concert Promoter, Promoter) Makes offers of employment to artist through the artist's agent.

Tech - (Technician) Member of the crew. Often specializes in one area of production, such as lights, pyro, drums, etc.. Formerly known as "roadies."

Tech Rider - (Technical Rider) Part of the artist's contract that details the technical aspects of the artist's production requirements, including equipment, its placement on the stage, and local personnel needed.

Technical Rider - (Tech rider) Part of the artist's contract that details the technical aspects of the artist's production requirements, including equipment, its placement on the stage, and local personnel needed.

Ticket Buys – a term used for the number of tickets a record label purchases for one of their artists shows. Usually ticket buys are used a giveaways on the radio.

Tip Sheet - Newsletter which lists various music opportunities and jobs for songwriters and composers.

Tour Manager - (Road Manager) The artist's representative on the road and works closely with the Personal Manager. A tour manager may have many functions, depending on the size of the tour. On very large tours, there may be both a Tour Manager, who oversees the entire tour, as well as a Road Manager, who represents the artist in day-to-day activities on the road on behalf of the Personal Manager.

Tour Support – Financial support provided by a record label to an artist to help the artist with their promotion while on a performance tour. This is done in coordination with the release of a current album.

Trademark - The legal protection of a trademark is about misuse of the business asset, passing off and confusing potential customers. It isn't an exclusive right to the trademarked name.

U -Card - The paper CD tray or back insert for a jewel case.

Upstage - The part of the stage farthest from the audience.

Upstream – When an Independent Record label encourages their artist to sign with a larger label.

Venue - Place where a concert is held.

Wedges - Wedge-shaped monitors.

Artist Development in the Music Business
Chapter 25 – Forms and Sample Agreements

Forms Sections
SAMPLE MANAGEMENT AGREEMENT
The following management agreement is a simplified letter from you the artist to the person who wants to manage you, to enable you to compare with contracts you may be offered. It is not a substitute for a formal agreement drafted and negotiated by a professional music business solicitor which is likely to be far more complex!

Before signing any form of management contract seek advice from a solicitor and establish who owns the company you are expected to sign to and whether the manager will actually be responsible for your day to day affairs.

DISCLAIMER
This article is offered as an educational and informational tool only, and should not be relied on as legal advice. Applicability of the legal principles discussed may differ substantially in individual situations. The sample contract is for illustrative purposes only, and has not been verified for compliance with the law of any particular state. If you have a specific legal problem or concern, you should consult an attorney.

Agreement for Personal Management
The signatories hereof warrant to each other that each has taken the professional advice of a solicitor specializing in such agreements before their signature hereof.

Artist Name:-
Stage Name:-
Address:-

Managers Name:-
Address:-

Agreement Date:-

Dear Sir/Madam:-

We confirm our Management Agreement whereby we appoint you to represent us as our sole and exclusive manager under the provisions of this agreement as follows:-

1. This agreement relates only to my professional activities and confers the right to represent me as a solo artist. (Bands/groups/duo's etc need to specify that only the band as a whole is represented and any solo activity requires separate consent).

2. Both you and I warrant by our respective signatures that there are no existing restrictions that prevent either party from entering into this agreement or performing any of our obligations.

3. This agreement relates solely to activities as a musical artist and in no way confers the right to represent or hold yourself as representing me in any other field of entertainment or area of work not connected with the music business without prior written consent.

4. During the Term of this agreement defined below you shall have the following obligations:

   a) To use your best endeavors to promote and develop my career as a musical artist and provide me with regular reports on your work.
   b) To ensure all monies due to me are promptly collected and remitted directly to me by the parties from which they are due.
   c) To refer all enquiries connected with our work in areas which you are not permitted to act directly to me.
   d) You shall not have the right to assign or transfer obligations to any other person or company without prior written consent, any such act shall immediately and retrospectively terminate your appointment and this agreement.

5. The following are the obligations I agree to:

   a) To be available and comply with your reasonable requests to undertake activities pertaining to my career at my sole discretion.
   b) Not to attempt to negotiate agreements with 3rd parties directly which relate to activities which you are responsible for and to refer all such third parties to you.
   c) To refer all Press enquiries to you.
   d) To notify you of any changes in address or contact numbers.

6. During the term of this agreement I shall reimburse any expenses directly relating to your activities as my manager upon request by you, with the exception of office expenses i.e., telephone, staff etc., which will be your sole responsibility.
Expenses in excess of $_____ for any single item must have been approved in writing prior to being incurred or will not be reimbursed.

7. If you are permitted to manage other artists then I require you to submit written details in respect of expenses that are related solely to your activities as my manager and not as manager of other artists.

8. During the Term of this agreement you shall not be entitled to manage other artists without my prior knowledge and/or consent and you shall ensure that management of said artists does not adversely affect your obligations set out within this agreement.

9. You shall be entitled to charge for your services a commission of 15% (maximum 20%) of the (gross or preferably net) income received by myself in respect of the activities the subject hereof during the Term and Commission Period (excepting that following termination of the Term the commission payable shall reduce to 10% of the (gross/net) income and will be subject to the limitations on the source of such income set out below). Commission shall be payable based on net income received by myself for live work during the Term and for the avoidance of doubt during the Commission Period you shall only be entitled to you commission in respect of income derived from recordings and compositions made in whole during the Term. You shall be solely responsible for meeting your own income tax, insurance, and business tax.

10. The Term of this agreement shall be 2 years from the Agreement Date with the provision that I shall be entitled at my sole discretion following the expiry of 6 months from the Agreement Date to terminate the Term in the event that you have not procured the signature of a publishing or recording agreement by such date. The Commission Period following the expiry or termination of the Term whereby you are still entitled to receive commission as set out in Clause 10 shall be 2 years from the date of termination, however in the event that I have exercised the right to terminate the term after 6 months you shall not be entitled to receive commission on future income derived from recordings or compositions made during the Term.

11. The Territory governed by this agreement shall mean the _____. (United States, World, whichever country you reside and/or any countries you designate)

12. You shall be entitled to appoint another person as my manager in certain countries or territories of the Territory provided I grant consent to such appointment and the identity of such person and provided that such appointment shall not discharge you from any of your managerial obligations as set out in this agreement.

13. Nothing within this agreement shall be deemed to create a partnership or joint venture between the signing parties.

14. This agreement shall be governed by the laws of _____.

Please indicate your acceptance of the terms hereof by signing and returning the attached copy to me.

Yours faithfully

Names and dated signatures of artist/s

WAIVER
ASCAP/BMI / SESAC INDEMNIFICATION LETTER

Venue requirements mandate that we ask you or a representative from your band sign this letter stating that your works are original or that non-original music be licensed for you or with your group for public performance with an appropriate licensing company.

Performing Rights Indemnification Letter

The following performers/groups whose signatures appear below agree to indemnify _____ Zoo from any action by or from any music licensing company for the upcoming event on _____ concert/event to take place _____ at the _____. I/We hereby attest that all the music played at the concert/event by myself or our band is original music or covered by ASCAP or BMI or SESAC licensing for today's event.

Please sign and return this letter no later than _____.

Date of performance:

Band or Performer:

Signature of band representative:

Printed name of band representative:

Today's date:

DISCLAIMER
This article is offered as an educational and informational tool only, and should not be relied on as legal advice. Applicability of the legal principles discussed may differ substantially in individual situations. The sample contract is for illustrative purposes only, and has not been verified for compliance with the law of any particular state. If you have a specific legal problem or concern, you should consult an attorney.

Band Member Agreement Sample
For _____(Insert band name)

AGREEMENT made this _____ day of _____, 201_, by and between the undersigned Artist and the undersigned Musician(s).
This Agreement is entered into in the City of _____ and County of _____, State of _____ and is guided by and governed by the laws of that state.

The undersigned parties hereby agree to the following responsibilities:

1. Show up for practice as agreed upon failure to do so can void contract and end any future agreements. UNLESS there is an emergency or other uncontrollable circumstances out of the Musician(s) control. (Example: Death of family member, illness, accident, act of God.) If there is a problem notify Artist within _____hours before rehearsals were to commence.

2. It is the Musician(s) responsibility to keep their equipment in good working condition, and upgrade appropriately when the revenue is available.

3. There should be no drinking/smoking on stage, always maintaining good showmanship/ quality as deemed by management and myself.
Musician(s) will follow the instructions of the Artist and management team.
Other Provisions

4. Under no circumstances is a band member (Musician(s)) allowed to talk to club owners, record labels, radio stations, etc in regards to setting up anything for the band, in which promises are made or money is mentioned, etc.. The band members (Musician(s)) should direct all inquires to myself and then I can pass it along to management, or hand out business cards with our managements contact info on it.

5. Any other outside performing with another band or engagement that interferes with the schedule of Artist will void the contract if necessary.

6. Understanding that the band members (Musician(s)) main job objective is bring to life songs that are in the Artist format and 100% attention, enthusiasm and dedication is needed to make things happen. Lack of any of the above can void contract if it is detrimental to our success.

7. The Artist makes no promises or guarantees about Rewards and compensation but every effort will be in achieving the goals and payment will be made to the Musician(s) when possible.

8. The following conditions are in effect only as long as the contract is valid.

9. Live performances, band member (Musician(s)) will receive 20% of the performance fee.

10. In regards to royalties from any independent release that a band member plays on (examples would be cd's, cassettes, EPK's, singles, etc., that has been financed by myself and/or management team. The band member (Musician(s)) will receive a percentage of 15% after the cost of manufacturing and distribution, production has been made back. Example - I spend 1500 to record and manufacture 2000 cd's, after the 1500 is made back from the sales of the item, royalty checks will go out in accordance to what was agreed upon. In the event of signing with a major or Indie label the royalty rates may be renegotiated at that time.

11. There will be specific pay days, and dates for all compensation. Band member should not expect payment right after a gig or a sale of a cd.
Merchandising

12. Merchandising (T-shirts, hats, etc), Musician(s) will receive a percentage after the cost is made back. The percentage will be in the 2-10% range, due to the fact that this money will be used to finance upcoming events for the band-tour support, recording, etc.

13. When and if the Artist is signed to a label or any other organization that handles booking, distribution, etc than what is in place presently, then contract will need to be renegotiated to exact out new figures.

14. This contract is an open agreement voided at such time the Artist or Musician(s) deems necessary.

Touring

Musician(s) should meet to discuss all touring and gigs before the actual date. A plan will be made then in the event of prolonged touring to ensure all Artists and Musician(s) are in essence in the right place at the right time. Equipment checklists will be made and followed as well as set lists for shows. Musician(s) are responsible for things such as personal leaves from day jobs for touring etc. Musician(s) will meet with the Artist on specific days and times to discuss issues pertaining to the tour work. Band members will not leave the tour group unless they have let other parties know where they are going. This is only a protection for the band as a whole should an accident or other uncontrollable circumstance arise.
Complaints

All complaints will be handled in an orderly manner. If Musician(s) feel they are being treated unfairly outside the realm of this agreement they may contact the management team and the complaint will be addressed and remedied in an efficient manner.
(Omit or replace with your management information) Management
You may also contact managers' assistants.

_____

Artist

_____

Musician(s)

DISCLAIMER

This article is offered as an educational and informational tool only, and should not be relied on as legal advice. Applicability of the legal principles discussed may differ substantially in individual situations. The sample contract is for illustrative purposes only, and has not been verified for compliance with the law of any particular state. If you have a specific legal problem or concern, you should consult an attorney.

Single Song Publishing Agreement Sample

AGREEMENT DATED __th day of _____, 201_ (Hereafter called "Agreement Date").

SINGLE SONG AGREEMENT: The Writer and _____ Music Publishing Company, hereafter called Publisher, do hereby agree to the terms of this Agreement under the following terms and conditions:

1. Publisher agrees that if the song by Writer now entitled _____ is not assigned a mechanical license to be recorded and released to the general public on phonorecords within 24 months of agreement date, the Writer may request, in writing, that the Publisher relinquish and return all rights and copyrights to the Writer.

2. If Publisher does not receive a written request for reversion of rights prior to the expiration date above, this agreement will self-renew for 12 months, and continue to do so every 12 months, indefinitely. A reversion request received at any time after the initial expiration date will be honored at the end of the current 12 month renewal period, or immediately, at Publisher's discretion.

3. The Writer shall not be held responsible for any payment to the Publisher regardless of the amount Publisher may have spent on the recording, development, promotion, or any other expense incurred by Publisher relating to this song.

4. In the event Publisher is responsible for the placement of said musical composition on phonorecords released to the public, Writer hereby agrees to affiliate with BMI, ASCAP, SESAC, or SOCAN, if not already so affiliated, and to sign a standard clearance form from such organization, listing Publisher as owning 100% of the publishing rights for said musical composition. This will be either submitted to Publisher for approval before filing, or may be supplied by Publisher.

5. Writer agrees that this agreement shall be in force and binding during the original specified period and during any self-renewal period, and will not assign the rights to the aforementioned song to any other until this Agreement has expired AND not been self-renewed, without the song being recorded on phonorecords for the public.

6. During the Agreement period, and any renewal periods, Publisher shall not be required to defend Writer against any legal action against Writer for copyright infringement, or any other proprietary right.

7. Writer grants permission for Publisher to play and freely copy all submitted demo material, for promotional purposes only, for the life of this agreement and any renewals thereof.

If any part of this agreement shall be held invalid or unenforceable, it shall not affect the validity of the balance of this Agreement.

We the undersigned do hereby acknowledge and agree to the terms of this Agreement.

Date: _____, _____. PAU Number: _____

BY_____   BY_____
PUBLISHER   WRITER

DISCLAIMER
This article is offered as an educational and informational tool only, and should not be relied on as legal advice. Applicability of the legal principles discussed may differ substantially in individual situations. The sample contract is for illustrative purposes only, and has not been verified for compliance with the law of any particular state. If you have a specific legal problem or concern, you should consult an attorney.

MANAGEMENT AGREEMENT SAMPLE

The following management agreement is a simplified letter from you the artist to the person who wants to manage you, to enable you to compare with contracts you may be offered. It is not a substitute for a formal agreement drafted and negotiated by a professional music business solicitor which is likely to be far more complex!

Before signing any form of management contract seek advice from a solicitor and establish who owns the company you are expected to sign to and whether the manager will actually be responsible for your day to day affairs.

Agreement for Personal Management
The signatories hereof warrant to each other that each has taken the professional advice of a solicitor specializing in such agreements before their signature hereof.

Artist Name:-
Stage Name:-
Address:-

Managers Name:-
Address:-

Agreement Date:-

Dear Sir/Madam

We confirm our Management Agreement whereby we appoint you to represent us as our sole and exclusive manager under the provisions of this agreement as follows:-

1. This agreement relates only to my professional activities and confers the right to represent me as a solo artist. (Bands/groups/duo's etc need to specify that only the band as a whole is represented and any solo activity requires separate consent).

2. Both you and I warrant by our respective signatures that there are no existing restrictions that prevent either party from entering into this agreement or performing any of our obligations.

3. This agreement relates solely to activities as a musical artist and in no way confers the right to represent or hold yourself as representing me in any other field of entertainment or area of work not connected with the music industry without prior written consent.

4. During the Term of this agreement defined below you shall have the following obligations:
(a) To use your best endeavors to promote and develop my career as a music artist and provide me with regular reports on your work.
(b) To ensure all monies due to me are promptly collected and remitted directly to me by the parties from which they are due.
(c) To refer all enquiries connected with our work in areas which you are not permitted to act directly to me.
(d) You shall not have the right to assign or transfer obligations to any other person or company without prior written consent, any such act shall immediately and retrospectively terminate your appointment and this agreement.

5. The following are the obligations I agree to:
    (a) To be available and comply with your reasonable requests to undertake activities pertaining to my career at my sole discretion.
    (b) Not to attempt to negotiate agreements with 3rd parties directly which relate to activities which you are responsible for and to refer all such third parties to you.
    (c) To refer all Press enquiries to you.
    (d) To notify you of any changes in address or contact numbers.

6. During the term of this agreement I shall reimburse any expenses directly relating to your activities as my manager upon request by you, with the exception of office expenses i.e., telephone, staff etc., which will be your sole responsibility. Expenses in excess of $_____ for any single item must have been approved in writing prior to being incurred or will not be reimbursed.

7. If you are permitted to manage other artists then I require you to submit written details in respect of expenses that are related solely to your activities as my manager and not as manager of other artists.

8. During the Term of this agreement you shall not be entitled to manage other artists without my prior knowledge and/or consent and you shall ensure that management of said artists does not adversely affect your obligations set out within this agreement.

9. You shall be entitled to charge for your services a commission of 15% (maximum 20%) of the (gross or preferably net) income received by myself in respect of the activities the subject hereof during the Term and Commission Period (excepting that following termination of the Term the commission payable shall reduce to 10% of the (gross/net) income and will be subject to the limitations on the source of such income

set out below). Commission shall be payable based on net income received by myself for live work during the Term and for the avoidance of doubt during the Commission Period you shall only be entitled to you commission in respect of income derived from recordings and compositions made in whole during the Term. You shall be solely responsible for meeting your own income tax, insurance, and business tax.

10. The Term of this agreement shall be 2 years from the Agreement Date with the provision that I shall be entitled at my sole discretion following the expiry of 6 months from the Agreement Date to terminate the Term in the event that you have not procured the signature of a publishing or recording agreement by such date. The Commission Period following the expiry or termination of the Term whereby you are still entitled to receive commission as set out in Clause 10 shall be 2 years from the date of termination, however in the event that I have exercised the right to terminate the term after 6 months you shall not be entitled to receive commission on future income derived from recordings or compositions made during the Term.

11. The Territory governed by this agreement shall mean the _____. (United States, World, whichever country you reside and/or any countries you designate)

12. You shall be entitled to appoint another person as my manager in certain countries or territories of the Territory provided I grant consent to such appointment and the identity of such person and provided that such appointment shall not discharge you from any of your managerial obligations as set out in this agreement.

13. Nothing within this agreement shall be deemed to create a partnership or joint venture between the signing parties.

14. This agreement shall be governed by the laws of _____.

Please indicate your acceptance of the terms hereof by signing and returning the attached copy to me.

Yours faithfully

Names and dated signatures of artist/s

Read and Agreed

Name and dated signature of the manager

Index

360 Deals 152
Active vs. Passive Income 158
Agent and Principals 139
Agreement Considerations 137
Agreement Types 146
Agreements 137
Agreements Overview 136
Alexander Technique 66
Arrangers 36
Artist Development Expectations 30
Artist Development Overview 1
Artist Development Tips 10
ASCAP 204
Attitude 85, 88
Attorney 215
Band Fund 158
Band Member Agreements 147
Band Names 132
BMI 204
Booking Agent 215
Brand 23, 124, 131, 232
Brand Identity 125
Branding 16, 121
Branding the Artist 130
Brass Instruments 209
Bridge 45
Building a Positive Team 216
Business 23, 106
Business Entity Comparison 111
Business Finance 169
Business Name Search 110
Business Names 109
Business Plan 107
Business Set-Up & Establishment 4
Business Types 111
Catalog 47
Chorus 45
Clearing House Libraries 167
Closing the Project 250
Coaching 63
Collaborator 228
Collaborator Agreements 148
Collaborators 24, 214, 217, 225
Company Summary 118
Compensation 79, 142
Competition Summary 119
Concert & Event Promoter Contracts . 149
Concert Promoter 216
Confidence 102
Confidentiality Agreements 148
Content 23
Content Acquisition 38
Content Creation 2, 33, 41
Content Creation Tips 48
Content Creators 35
Content Management 14
Content Protection 2, 50, 53
Content Users 34
Contract Clauses 142
Contract Establishment 138
Controlled Compositions 164
Copyright 52, 57
Copyright Infringement 55
Copyright Length 57
Copyright Notice 60
Copyright Ownership 54
Copyright Protection 56
Copyright Registration 53
Copyright Registrations 40
Copyright Symbols 59
Copyright Tips 61
Corporate Finance 169
Corporation 114
Cover Songs 40
Co-Writers 35
Creative Commons 40
Creative Commons Copyright 60
Creative Team 214
Creators 36
Customer Summary 118
Derivative Works 39
Design 14
Discography 14
Distribution 15
Education and Experience 65
Ego 85
Ego & Attitude, Passion & Grit 23
Ego, Attitude, Passion & Grit 3

Electronic Instruments	210
Endorsements	162, 208
Equipment	24, 207
Equipment List	207
Exclusivity	78
Executing the Project Plan	248
Executive Summary	118
Expectations	20
Expectations of Booking Agents	27
Expectations of Collaborators	25
Expectations of Co-Writers	26
Expectations of Managers	27
Expectations of Musicians	26
Expectations of Oneself	23
Expectations of Promoters	30
Expectations of Publishers	28
Expectations of Record Labels	29
Experience	82
Fair Use	58
Film & Video Production	14
Finance	24, 156
Finance & Funding	5
Finance Plan	120, 168
Finding Management	75
First Impressions	130
Foreign Royalties	196
Funding	156
Funding a Recording	268
Funds for Instruments	208
Gantt Charts	244
Gear	24, 207
Gear, Instruments & Equipment	6
General Partnership	112
Grand Rights Royalties	196
Grit	85, 102
Harry Fox Agency	166, 194
Holding Company	116
Image	23, 121, 124, 232
Image & Branding	4
Image and Branding Tips	130
Income	156
Income from Content Licensing	166
Income from Merchandise	168
Income from Other Sources	168
Income from Sound Recordings	167, 168
Income Sources	159
Instruments	24, 207
Intellectual Property	51, 119
Intellectual Property Attorneys	153
Investors	174
Jobs	21
John Latimer	5
Law of Attraction	99
Legal	23
Legal & Agreements	5
Legal Issues	135
Lessons	63
Lessons & Coaching	3, 23
License	252
Licenses	140
Limited Liability Company (LLC)	113
Limited Partnership	112
Logo Designs	186
Logos	124
Lyrics	44
Management	3, 23, 71
Management & Team	118
Management Contracts	77
Management Duties	73
Manager Collaborators	72
Manager Friends	75
Manager Types	73
Manufacturing	15
Marketing Plan	119
Mastering Recordings	14
Mechanical Royalties	194
Melody	44
Merchandising	17
Mission Statement	118
Monitoring the Project	249
Motivation	101
Music Business Conferences	68
Music Clearance	253
Music Genres	43
Music Notes	65
Music Schools	67
Music Supervision	252
Musical Instrument Care	210
Musical Instrument Types	208
Musicians	37, 214
Myths of Artist Management	82
Negative Attitudes	97

Niches	122
Packaging	15
Partners	217
Passion	85, 101
Payment Systems	156
Percussion Instruments	209
Performance Contracts	150
Performance Royalties	194
Performances	16
Performing Rights Affiliation	24
Performing Rights Organizations	6, 200
Positive Attitudes	92
Positive Thinking	93
Preparing for Product Development	7
Preparing Product Development	24
Preparing to License	7
Preparing to Merchandise	8
Preparing to Perform	8
Preparing to Record	8
Pre-Production	266
Pre-Promotion Preparation	9, 12, 24
Print Royalties	165, 196
Producer	267
Producing Recordings	13
Product Development	9, 12, 13, 232, 262
Product Development Agreements	149
Product Development Expectations	31
Product Development Tips	18, 234
Products & Services	118
Project Control	245
Project Definition	248
Project Finance	172
Project Funding Requests	174
Project Initiation	247
Project Management	8, 24, 242
Project Management Processes	247
Project Management Stages	247
Project Managers	246
Project Plan	245
Promises	138
Promo Kits	237
Promotion	15
Promotion Plan	119
Promotion Preparation	232
Proposal or Offer	137
Proprietary Rights	50
Protection	23
Public Domain	39
Public Performance Royalties	164
Publicist	216
Publicity	15
Publisher's Job	191
Publishers	40
Publishing	6, 24, 190
Publishing Royalties	193
Publishing Tips	198
Record Label	216
Record Label Contracts	151
Record Labels	14
Record Producers	36
Recording Audio	13
Recording Engineers	37
Recording Preparation	266
Recording Process	268
Recording Studio	267
Recording Tips	268
Relationships	120
Rhymes	45
Royalties	163
Sales	16
Sales Plan	119
Self Management	72
Self-Evaluation	22
Self-Publishing	149
SESAC	204
SOCAN	205
Song Review	46
Song Structure	44
Songwriter Career	48
Songwriter-Artist Agreements	149
Songwriters	35, 214
Songwriting Basics	44
SoundExchange	197, 205
Spending Strategy	170
String Instruments	209
Synchronization Royalties	165, 195
Talent Buyer	216
Talent Manager Agreements	148
Talent Managers	215
Team	24, 215
Team Building	75, 222
Teams	214

Teams & Collaborators 7	Trademark Categories 183
Technicians 38	Trademark Symbols 181
Technique vs. Groove 65	Trademark Types 180
Technology Summary 120	Trademarks 179
Term 78, 142	Verse 45
Territory 142	Video Directors 38
Tips about Talent Managers 84	Visuals 234
Tips for Artist Funding 176	Voidable Contracts 139
Tips for Brand Building 126	Web 17
Tips on Legal Issues 153	Wind Instruments 209
Trademark 5, 24	Work for Hire 56
Trademark - How To 184	Working the Product 17
Trademark Advantages 182	

To Do

Notes:

To Do

Notes: